Norman Geras

Thinking towards humanity

Manchester University Press

Thinking towards humanity

Themes from Norman Geras

Edited by Eve Garrard and Stephen de Wijze

Manchester University Press

Manchester and New York

Distributed in the United States exclusively
by Palgrave Macmillan

Published by Manchester University Press
Oxford Road, Manchester M13 9NR, UK
and Room 400, 175 Fifth Avenue, New York, NY 10010, USA
www.manchesteruniversitypress.co.uk

Distributed in the United States exclusively by
Palgrave Macmillan, 175 Fifth Avenue, New York,
NY 10010, USA

Distributed in Canada exclusively by
UBC Press, University of British Columbia, 2029 West Mall,
Vancouver, BC, Canada V6T 1Z2

British Library Cataloguing-in-Publication Data
A catalogue record for this book is available from the British Library

Library of Congress Cataloging-in-Publication Data applied for

ISBN   978 07190 80876 hardback
ISBN   978 07190 80883 paperback

First published 2012

The publisher has no responsibility for the persistence or accuracy of URLs for any external or third-party internet websites referred to in this book, and does not guarantee that any content on such websites is, or will remain, accurate or appropriate.

Typeset
by Action Publishing Technology, Gloucester
Printed in Great Britain
by CPI Antony Rowe Ltd, Chippenham, Wiltshire

Contents

List of contributors

David Aaronovitch is a regular columnist for *The Times*. He won the George Orwell prize for political journalism in 2001 and was the 'What the Papers Say Columnist of the Year' for 2003. He blogs at http://timesonline.typepad.com/david_aaronovitch.

Ophelia Benson is the editor of the website Butterflies and Wheels and associate editor of *The Philosophers' Magazine*. She is co-author (with Jeremy Stangroom) of *Why Truth Matters* (Continuum, 2006) and *Does God Hate Women?* (Continuum, 2009).

Gideon Calder is Reader in Ethics and Social Philosophy at University of Wales, Newport. Recent books include two on the philosophy of Richard Rorty, and the co-edited *Citizenship Acquisition and National Belonging* (Palgrave, 2009), *Diversity in Europe: Dilemmas of Differential Treatment in Theory and Practice* (Routledge, 2010), and *Climate Change and Liberal Priorities* (Routledge, 2011). Most of his writing has been in applied ethics, on topics including disability, sport, sexual consent, public transport, and organ donation. Co-editor of the journal *Res Publica*, he is currently writing a book about democracy.

Nick Cohen has written for the *Birmingham Post, Independent, Independent on Sunday, New Statesman,* and *London Evening Standard*. He currently writes for the *Observer*. His most recent book is *You Can't Read This Book: Censorship in an Age of Freedom*, published 2012. He blogs at www.nickcohen.net.

Damian Counsell has a BA in Physiology from Balliol College, Oxford University, and an MSc in Physics from Imperial College, London University. He has spent most of his working life in science, at Oxford University, the Institute of Cancer Research in London, and the Human Genome Mapping Project Resource Centre, Cambridge, UK. He writes a blog called PooterGeek (www.pootergeek.com) and is a co-author of the Euston Manifesto.

Eve Garrard is Honorary Research Fellow in the Department of Philosophy at the University of Manchester. Her main research interests are in moral theory and bioethics, and also in philosophical issues related to the Holocaust. Before becoming a research fellow at Manchester she lectured at Keele University and worked for several years for the Open University. She has a special interest in teaching philosophy to beginning students. She has published papers on the nature of evil and of forgiveness, and has jointly edited *Moral Philosophy and the Holocaust* (Ashgate, 2002). She has recently (with David McNaughton) published *Forgiveness* (Acumen, 2010).

Norman Geras is Professor Emeritus of Government at the University of Manchester. He is author of *The Legacy of Rosa Luxemburg* (1976), *Marx and Human Nature: Refutation of a Legend* (1983), *Literature of Revolution: Essays on Marxism* (1986), *Discourses of Extremity: Radical Ethics and Post-Marxist Extravagances* (1990), *Solidarity in the Conversation of Humankind: The Ungroundable Liberalism of Richard Rorty* (1995), and *The Contract of Mutual Indifference: Political Philosophy after the Holocaust* (1998).

Ian Holliday is Professor of Political Science, and former Dean of Social Sciences, at The University of Hong Kong. Previously, he served as Dean of Humanities and Social Sciences at City University of Hong Kong, and taught at the University of Manchester and New York University. Ian was educated at the University of Oxford (DPhil, MPhil) and the University of Cambridge (MA, BA). His current research interests focus on Myanmar, and embrace problems of political reform inside the country, and human security challenges facing migrants outside the country. His most recent book is *Burma Redux: Global Justice and the Quest for Political Reform in Myanmar* (Columbia University Press, 2012).

Alan Johnson is a member of the *Dissent* editorial board and a senior research fellow at the Foreign Policy Centre. A professor of democratic theory and practice at Edge Hill University, he was the founder and editor of *Democratiya*, a free online journal of international politics that merged with *Dissent* in 2009. His book, *Global Politics After 9/11: The Democratiya Interviews*, was published by The Foreign Policy Centre in 2007.

Shalom Lappin is Professor of Computational Linguistics at King's College London. He has taught at Ben Gurion University, University of Ottawa, University of Haifa, Tel-Aviv University, and the School of Oriental and African Studies and King's College at the University of London. His areas of research and teaching are formal and computational semantics, formal grammar, natural language processing, and logic. His current research activities include the formal foundations of semantics, type theory, machine learning, and the cognitive basis of natural language.

David McLellan is Fellow of Goldsmith's College, University of London. He is currently completing a revised edition of his biography of Simone Weil.

Shane O'Neill is Professor of Political Theory and Dean of the Faculty of Arts, Humanities and Social Sciences at Queen's University, Belfast. His most recent books include *Recognition, Equality and Democracy* (Routledge, 2008), co-edited with Jurgen de Wispelaere and Cillian McBride, and *After the Nation?* (Palgrave Macmillan, 2010), co-edited with Keith Breen.

Jon Pike is a Senior Lecturer in the Philosophy Department at the Open University. He is the author of *From Aristotle to Marx*, and author or co-author of three textbooks in political philosophy. He is currently working on problems of political obligation and democratic political action.

Philip Spencer is Professor of Holocaust and Genocide Studies at Kingston University, where he is also the Director of the Helen Bamber Centre for the Study of Rights, Conflict and Mass Violence. He is the author (with Howard Wollman) of *Nationalism: A Critical Introduction* (Sage, 2002), and *Nations and Nationalism* (Edinburgh University Press, 2005). He is currently writing a book on genocide since 1945.

Hillel Steiner is Emeritus Professor of Political Philosophy in the University of Manchester and a Fellow of the British Academy. He is the author of *An Essay on Rights* (Blackwell, 1994) and co-author, with Matthew Kramer and Nigel Simmonds, of *A Debate Over Rights: Philosophical Enquiries* (Oxford University Press, 1998). His current research projects include ones on the concept of 'the just price' and the application of libertarian principles to global, and to genetic, inequalities.

Laurence Thomas is Professor of Philosophy and Professor of Political Science in the Maxwell School, Member of the Judaic Studies Program and the Religion and Society Program, and member of the Center for European Studies in the Maxwell School. In France, he is an advisor for the group *L'Amitié Judéo-Noire*. His most recent book is *The Family and the Political Self* (Cambridge University Press, 2006). He has written more than 70 articles.

Michael Walzer is Professor Emeritus of Social Science, Institute for Advanced Study, Princeton, NJ. As a professor, author, editor, and lecturer, Michael Walzer has addressed a wide variety of topics in political theory and moral philosophy: political obligation, just and unjust war, nationalism and ethnicity, economic justice, and the welfare state. His books (among them *Spheres of Justice* (Basic Books, 1984), *Thick and Thin: Moral Argument at Home and Abroad* (University of Notre Dame Press, 1996), *On Toleration* (Yale University Press, 1997), *The Company of Critics* (Basic Books, 2002), and *Just and Unjust Wars* (Basic Books, 2006)) and essays have played a part in the revival of practical, issue-focused ethics and in the development of a pluralist approach to political and moral life. Walzer is a contributing editor for *The New Republic*, and co-editor of *Dissent*. His articles and interviews frequently appear in the world's foremost newspapers and journals. He is currently working on the toleration and accommodation of 'difference' in all its forms, and also on the third volume of *The Jewish Political Tradition*, a comprehensive collaborative project focused on the history of Jewish political thought.

Stephen de Wijze is Senior Lecturer in Political Theory at the University of Manchester. Among his recent publications are 'Defining Evil: Insights from the Problem of "Dirty hands"' in *The Monist* (2002), 'The Political Limits of Reasonableness' in *Imprints* (2002), 'Tragic-remorse: The Anguish of Dirty Hands' in *Ethical Theory and Moral Practice* (2004), and 'Recalibrating Steiner on Evil' in *Hillel Steiner and the Anatomy of Justice* (Routledge, 2009). He is co-editor of *Representation: The Journal of Representative Democracy*.

Preface

The idea for this book arose out of a Manchester Political Theory (MANCEPT) conference at the University of Manchester in March 2004 entitled 'Thinking toward Humanity', in honour of Norman Geras on his retirement after 36 years of service. The enthusiastic response we were given when approaching possible contributors, and the range of interesting and challenging contributions we have received, has made the editing of this book a great pleasure. Given space constraints, we were unable to request chapters from the very many people who would have wished to contribute to this festschrift. We apologise to them and hope nonetheless that the chapters in this book on Geras's work give our readers some sense of the breadth, depth and importance of his scholarship, and also of his recent blog-related writings.

The chapters in this collection critically discuss and develop many of the ideas central to Geras's work since the 1980s. We have also taken the unusual step of including five 'blogging interludes' which refer to and highlight the enormous impact which Geras's weblog – entitled normblog (http://normblog.typepad.com/normblog) – has had since it began in July 2003. It is internationally known and considered to be among the best political blogs both in the UK and further afield.

We would like to thank the contributors to this volume for submitting their chapters on time (most of them anyway), and putting up with our many requests for administrative and other information. We especially want to thank Norm for his extensive and insightful response to the contributions in the book, and for helping us in a myriad other ways with patience and good humour in the production of this festschrift. We are also very grateful to the editorial team at Manchester University Press for their help and support during the creation of the book, and especially to Tony Mason for his enthusiasm and assistance, from the early stages of the book's inception right through to the finishing line.

Stephen de Wijze
Eve Garrard
December 2010

List of figures

Introduction

Norman Geras – Marxist, philosopher, and blogger – is an unusual and in some ways paradoxical figure in British intellectual life. He is a life-long socialist who also defends liberal values and procedures; an outstanding Marxian academic who supports British and American intervention in some of the world's greatest trouble spots; and a political philosopher who writes with deep love and enthusiasm about cricket. A social radical who is committed to Enlightenment values, he maintains a blog in which politics and philosophy rub shoulders with jazz, country and western music, and the triumphs of Manchester United football team. Some of his interests are reflected in this volume of essays; to capture them all, however, the book would have had to be much longer than it already is.

Geras was born and grew up in what was then Southern Rhodesia (now Zimbabwe). He left that country in 1962, came to England, and read for a Philosophy, Politics and Economics degree at Pembroke College Oxford. The United Kingdom has been his home ever since. He graduated in 1965, and after a brief stint as a research student at Nuffield College Oxford (1965–67) was appointed to the staff of the Government Department (now Politics) at the University of Manchester. This is where he spent his entire academic life, becoming a central figure in the life of the Department. In 1997 he became Head of Department for four years, and he retired in 2003 after thirty-six years of service. Geras was undoubtedly a key figure in enhancing the reputation of the Government Department, and the Manchester Centre for Political Theory (MANCEPT), the name of which was his suggestion; he was a leading member of a large team of well-known and respected political theorists. This group rightly gave the Government Department international recognition as one of the best centres for political theory in Britain and further afield, with a reputation based on the work done by Geras and others at the cutting edge of political theory. Geras's work on Marxism – notably his books *The Legacy of Rosa Luxemburg* (1976) and *Marx and Human Nature: Refutation of a Legend* (1983), and also his essays on Marx and justice (1992, 1985) – is widely respected and internationally influential. He is also rightly credited with ground-breaking work in engaging political theory with the catastrophe of the Holocaust through his book *The Contract of Mutual Indifference: Political Philosophy after the Holocaust* (1998). His works are seen as important contributions to political theory and stand today as required reading for anyone seeking to understand and contribute to scholarship in these areas.

Until fairly recently, Geras's views have been disseminated almost entirely through academic journals and books. However, since July 2003 he has also maintained a weblog – *normblog* – which he began primarily as a way to engage in the vigorous and often heated arguments, particularly within the liberal/left, for and against the Iraq war, and more generally in response to the atrocities of 9/11 and the following fight against al-Qaeda-sponsored terrorism. Geras was appalled by the responses to that terrorism from a section of the liberal/left, in Britain and elsewhere, that seemed to be gaining momentum as the wars in Afghanistan and later Iraq progressed. In one of his first posts on *normblog*, dated 29 July 2003 and entitled the 'The War in Iraq', Geras makes clear the reasons why he is so dismayed by comments and views that amount to an apologia and an excuse for terrorism.

> On September 11 2001 there was, in New York, a massacre of innocents. There's no other acceptable way of putting this: some 3000 people (and, as anyone can figure, it could have been many more) struck down by an act of mass murder without any possible justification, an act of gross moral criminality. What was the left's response? In fact, this goes well beyond the left if what is meant by that is people and organizations of **socialist** persuasion. It included a wide sector of liberal opinion as well. Still, I shall just speak here, for short, of the left. The response on the part of much of it was excuse and apologia.

> At best you might get some lip service paid to the events of September 11 having been, well, you know, unfortunate – the preliminary 'yes' before the soon-to-follow 'but' (or, as Christopher Hitchens has called it, 'throat-clearing'). And then you'd get all the stuff about root causes,

deep grievances, the role of US foreign policy in creating these; and a subtext, or indeed text, whose meaning was America's comeuppance. This was not a discourse worthy of a democratically-committed or principled left, and the would-be defence of it by its proponents, that they were merely trying to explain and not to excuse what happened, was itself a pathetic excuse. If any of the root-cause and grievance themes truly had been able to account for what happened on September 11, you'd have a hard time understanding why, say, the Chileans after that earlier September 11 (I mean of 1973), or other movements fighting against oppression and injustice, have not resorted to the random mass murder of civilians.

Why this miserable response? In a nutshell, it was a displacement of the left's most fundamental values by a misguided strategic choice, namely, opposition to the US, come what may. This dictated the apologetic mumbling about the mass murder of US citizens, and it dictated that the US must be opposed in what it was about to do in hitting back at al-Qaida and its Taliban hosts in Afghanistan.[1]

This is vintage Geras – incisive, analytic, and unafraid to wade into controversial discussions in the pursuit of truth and in the defence of values he holds dear. It is precisely this combination of careful analysis and forceful yet measured attack which makes Geras's work so interesting, informative and widely read. He is unswayed by academic fashions, and even less by political ones; above all, he abjures both the obfuscation and the hackneyed invective which so disfigure some current academic and political writing. The careful, clear, and humane argumentation which he provides in defence of his views is supplemented by a powerful rhetoric which displays the strength of his positions on some of the most heated and controversial topics of our times.

Geras holds, as he puts it, a liberal socialist set of values, and does so unapologetically. This is a position that seeks to combine the individual rights and freedoms which are the hallmark of liberalism with the political and socio-economic insights derived from a Marxist critique of capitalism. When asked if he was still a Marxist in an interview in the journal *Imprints*, Geras's response was an unequivocal yes:

I am still a Marxist. There are different ways of explaining why. Karl Marx was, and he remains, the greatest single thinker of modern times. His writings (of all sorts: from the Economic and Philosophical Manuscripts and the Grundrisse to *Capital*; from the Communist

Manifesto to the Critique of the Gotha Programme) constitute a life's work of towering genius. They weld the aspiration for equality and social justice to a powerful analysis and critique of the capitalist order, highlighting at once – through the notions of alienation and commodity fetishism – its opaque and brutal inner logic, the exploitative relations integral to it and the close lines of influence between economic and political power that constrain and impel every state.

A little later in the interview, Geras adds:

> I have occasionally found myself identified with analytical Marxism, and I do recognize a loose relationship to it, but it is no more than that. I have benefited from reading the work of some of the leading figures of analytical Marxism, in particular Jerry Cohen's, and I share a general attachment to the 'analytical' standards that members of this intellectual current have aspired to: standards of clarity, precision, consistency and so forth. I share with them, too, an interest in the appropriate normative foundations of a left-wing critique of capitalist societies, a belief in universalist values and an openness to the intellectual resources of liberal political thought. On the other hand, I do not myself have the same interest in, much less attachment to, rational choice or methodological individualist models of social explanation as some of the analytical Marxists have had, and the questions which have most preoccupied me over the last decade are different from the principal questions associated with analytical Marxism.

Geras's core values are in evidence in all his political writing, and they are combined with an integrity which prevents his work (both in academic journals and on his blog) from descending into *ad hominem* arguments or 'cheap shots' at opponents. As Ophelia Benson's piece in this volume 'What is it like to be a blogger?' points out, Geras has a conspicuously liberal blog:

> It is liberal in the obvious sense in that it is very often focused on issues to do with human rights, interventionism, tyranny and what to do about it, international law and justice, war crimes, universalism, and the like. But it is also liberal in the way it approaches such issues: via measured argument as opposed to vituperation and misrepresentation, and via open unfettered inquiry rather than by peremptory demands for conformity or silence. And in the broadest and most basic sense it is liberal in the breadth of its interests. Along with discussing liberal politics it also converses about the liberal arts – literature, jazz, cricket, films, popular music. (Benson, this volume p. 68)

Geras's blog is read and respected across the political spectrum.[2]

Damian Counsell, in his short chapter 'A Fine Site' in this volume, points out that although he has a deep antipathy to Marxism, and although he knows that Geras is a Marxist, nevertheless he reads *normblog* daily for its political discussions and much else. He does this because it is a blog that dissects the arguments, is rigorous and honest, and always retains its civility. *Normblog* has the hallmark common to all excellent weblogs: it is a place to go, as Counsell puts it, 'in the hope that my mind will be changed'. (Counsell, this volume p. 132)

Geras's stringently honest account of his views has at times brought him considerable obloquy from many of his former colleagues and friends on the left. Geras is quintessentially of the liberal/left, and his concern for its condition is never far away.[3] When he believes that others on the left are betraying their core values he says so lucidly and forcefully. Nick Cohen, in his piece 'Professor Geras and Blogger Norm', emphasizes this aspect of his work, pointing out that Geras has done the liberal/left a great service by challenging the conformism within its thinking since 9/11. As Cohen puts it:

> The great service *normblog* and its comrades on the Net provided was to break down the gates and allow fresh arguments in new intellectual spaces. New alliances brought contrary opinions and new sources of information to the reader. For someone writing from a similar position at the time *normblog* began, I cannot over-emphasize how important it was to realize that I had comrades out there. (Cohen, this volume p. 46)

Aaronovitch is one of the comrades to whom Cohen refers, and he too feels a deep disquiet over the abandonment of liberal/left values by some on the left since the events of 9/11. In his piece in this volume, Aaronovitch forcefully argues that 'progressives should always find themselves on the side of democracy first' (Aaronovitch, this volume p. 180). He takes to task those on the liberal/left who support anti-democratic regimes and religious groups holding views about women, gays, free speech (to mention just three issues) that are deeply antithetical to their own core values – views which the liberal/left would never allow to be imposed on their own lives. By endorsing such regimes they are engaging in the same appalling behaviour for which they criticized Western politicians who tolerated or supported unjust and tyrannical regimes such as those of Franco,

Pinochet, and the Somozas. A decent left must support democracy; it is necessary for social justice, individual freedoms, and the free exchange of ideas. Democracy may not be sufficient to produce a functional and well-ordered society. But it is certainly necessary: without it, Aaronovitch argues, everything else that progressives are committed to is likely to fail.

The purpose of the collection of chapters and shorter blog pieces in this volume is to pay tribute both to Geras's scholarship and to his political engagement, and to bring together a collection of articles by well-known scholars and others on major themes that Geras has developed since the early 1970s. He has published six books and over fifty articles (translated into many languages), and has recently completed a manuscript on crimes against humanity (Manchester University Press, 2011). His work on Marx, the Holocaust, and other topics is consulted worldwide as indispensable for those seeking to further their education in these areas of scholarship. Although Geras's subject matter is wide-ranging and diverse, it is united by humanitarian concerns that are particularly relevant to major aspects of twentieth- and twenty-first-century political theory. Bertrand Russell famously summed up the motivations in his life as based on three passions: 'the longing for love, the search for knowledge, and unbearable pity for the suffering of mankind' (Russell, 1967: 3–4). If we were to summarize the key motivations behind Geras's work in academia and when writing on political issues on *normblog*, they would be the search for social justice, the drive to establish the truth, and the desire to use that truth for the betterment of people's lives everywhere. Tyranny and abuse must be identified and confronted wherever they are found, whether they take the form of the terrible violence and mass murder of jihad-driven terrorists, the oppression and brutalization by tyrannical governments of their own or other populations, or the more subtle structural inequalities of capitalism that cause misery and suffering for the poor. The lives of everyone irrespective of their geographical location, their race or religion or creed, must be made tolerable – free of the perennial great evils of physical suffering, enslavement, starvation, and humiliation. For Geras, theory and practice cannot come too far apart, and one of the main tasks of a political theorist of the liberal/left is to raise his or her voice in defence and support of the many who are unable to do this for themselves.

This introduction does not intend to present the carefully argued comments of each of the authors in the volume – we think it best to leave that task to the authors themselves. However, it is useful to provide a brief account of the key focus of each chapter and why it is pertinent to Geras's work. The volume has six parts, five of which focus on and develop ideas and arguments that have been central to Geras's intellectual and other interests since the early 1970s. The sixth part is given over to Geras's responses to the other chapters in the book.

Part 1 of the book examines themes within Marxist and socialist thought, picking up on aspects of Geras's contribution and issues which relate to it. In the first chapter, Michael Walzer explores the manner in which left international politics has recently morphed into a form of anti-Americanism which supports some of the most vile regimes and dictators to be found anywhere. Walzer offers an account of left internationalism that does not require the surrender of left-oriented values, but rather becomes a politics of rescue and relief, solidarity, and democratic agitation to improve the lives of the poor and oppressed all over the world. The second chapter, by David McLellan, explores the trajectory of Geras's work on Marxist thought over the years, pointing out that unlike many thinkers on the left he demonstrates a remarkable consistency of thought and values. McLellan, himself a highly respected and well-known commentator on Marx and Marxism, argues that the key to understanding Geras's core ideas on Marx is to be found in his influential book *Marx and Human Nature: Refutation of a Legend* (1983). Here we find that the concept of human nature which is so central to Geras's work is 'an empirical construction', whereas justice is a trans-historical concept which contains, at least as a starting point, core liberal principles which are all but absolute. Understanding this, McLellan argues, resolves what may seem like an inexplicable tension between Geras's enthusiasm for the work of Luxemburg and Trotsky, and the fact that in 2003 he supported the invasion of Iraq by a right-wing US administration.

In 1998, Geras published *The Contract of Mutual Indifference: Political Philosophy after the Holocaust.* This book sought to make good what has been a significant lacuna in political thinking since the defeat of the Nazis in 1945. Political philosophers often regard the Holocaust as the quintessential example of organized political evil in the twentieth century, and the National Socialist regime in Germany as a political system 'primarily aimed at injustice and world-wide domination' (Hampshire, 1989: 67). Its ideology, as Stuart Hampshire points out, 'is an instructive case for moral philosophy, as a historical embodiment of pure evil both in aspiration and achievement' (1989: 67). Yet, unlike other academic disciplines, Anglo-American normative political philosophy has remained largely and surprisingly indifferent to the lessons arising from the catastrophe that overtook Europe in the middle of the twentieth century. Geras's book, more than any preceding work on the Holocaust in political theory, fills this gap by focusing on the implications of the Holocaust for our understanding of justice and of our duties towards others. Philip Spencer's chapter is a further contribution to this debate. He poses the question of why almost nothing has been written by historical materialists concerning this transformative event in history. Drawing on the work of Luxemburg, and especially her depiction of barbarism, Spencer begins to examine how socialists ought to think and act in situations where the internal possibilities for resistance to tyranny are virtually non-existent, and where the rescue of those under threat of annihilation can only be effected by using forces which are often opposed to socialism itself. As Spencer points out, these are hard questions for Marxists to contemplate, but they are as important today as they were at the end of the Second World War. If they are to meet the terrible challenges which the future may bring, Marxists must seek to incorporate one of the transformative events of recent times into their thinking about social revolution. In Spencer's view the distinction between liberation and emancipation must be maintained, along with the recognition that the former doesn't amount to the latter; but it must also be acknowledged that in extreme circumstances the former may take priority, and socialists should in such circumstances support external efforts to liberate those who labour under severe oppression.

The second part of the volume focuses on issues relating to the Holocaust and evil. Alan Johnson examines, through the work of Primo Levi, the warning to all of us provided by the very fact that the Holocaust occurred, and the chilling implication that it could happen again. Indeed, since the defeat of the Nazis there have been several further cases of genocide. Perhaps the most well known is that of the Rwanda massacres in the spring of 1994: in this catastrophe 800,000 Tutsis were slaughtered by their Hutu neighbours in the space of a few months. The world looked on, and did nothing to stop it. However, Johnson also argues for a politics of hope. In addition to

Levi's insights, Johnson draws on Geras's essay 'Socialist Hope in the Shadow of Catastrophe' (1996) to argue that in response to the catastrophe of the Holocaust we can acquire what Levi calls a 'truly solid moral armature' (1988: 49) by developing a set of cultural and institutional practices that involve 'witnessing, reasoning, judging, resisting, and advancing liberal democracy' (Johnson, this volume p. 69). The discussion of Holocaust-related issues continues with the chapter by Laurence Thomas, in which he examines the role our social networks play in facilitating or preventing evil. Thomas argues that our psychological happiness and well-being are more firmly tied to being socially affirmed than they are to being autonomous, and consequently the social contexts within which we find that affirmation should focus less on the creation and support of autonomy, and more on the deep inculcation within us of the values of equality and tolerance.

The final chapter in this second part explores the issue of forgiveness in the face of the horrific events of the Holocaust. Eve Garrard asks a troubling but obvious question in the face of such moral atrocities – how ought we to respond to the perpetrators of such crimes? Is there a role for forgiveness here, or ought we to banish them forever from our moral community? Garrard argues that we have reasons to forgive such perpetrators even if, controversially, they do not repent of their crimes. However, this forgiveness is supererogatory, and no stigma or blameworthiness results from choosing to withhold it. Furthermore, Garrard's conception of forgiveness addresses many of the key concerns of those who oppose her position, since on her account forgiveness remains compatible with feelings of strong indignation about the offence, and calls for punishment of the offender and a refusal in some cases to restore the *status quo ante* relationship that existed before the offence was committed.

Part 3 considers another area of scholarship to which Geras has made a valuable contribution. This is the topic of revolutionary ethics: the moral constraints on our behaviour in the context of revolutionary activity and resistance to tyranny and oppression. In his chapter 'Our Morals' (1990), Geras offers a carefully argued, clear and persuasive account of why revolutionary violence must be constrained by moral prohibitions. He examines what he calls 'the ethics of revolution' from a socialist perspective, and argues that there can be no excuse for the wanton disregard of individual rights or the commission of unusual and cruel actions. Many Marxists have believed that because revolutionaries are fighting in the service of the oppressed for a just society, the end will justify whatever means are used to bring it about. In Geras's view this essentially consequential-ist picture of socialist ethics is profoundly mistaken, and drawing on the resources of just war theory he offers a number of normative restrictions on how political violence may be permissibly used to bring about changes.

Both Pike and de Wijze seek to advance this discussion about the means/ends problem in politics, with Pike claiming that the means ought to prefigure the ends sought. The relation of prefiguring between means and ends is different from and independent of other possible means–ends relations such as being effective or being rights-respecting, and Pike argues that prefiguration is a distinct moral constraint on what means we may use to reach morally desirable ends. Where the aimed-at end has moral value, then the means which prefigure that end will exhibit the same morally relevant properties, and hence will have value too. The prefigurative constraint on political action is particularly important, so Pike argues, in the light of previous unsuccessful attempts to bring about socialism using non-prefigurative and counter-prefigurative means – attempts which have led to terrible harms, and which warn us of the necessity to use both rights-respecting and prefigurative means for any further efforts of this kind.

De Wijze examines another aspect of the need for restraints on political violence. He accepts that inevitably there will be situations where political actors seeking to bring about a just and fair society will need to get dirty hands – that is, they will have to decide how to act in situations where every choice involves some serious breach of moral constraints. As Geras points out in 'Our Morals', even though individuals have an inalienable right to life, this right can be violated in certain tragic circumstances; for example, in cases where not killing one individual leads to the deaths of very many other individ-uals. When this happens we properly violate our cherished moral constraints on political violence, but we do so knowing that we have done wrong in order to do right. In his chapter, de Wijze asks the question of whether even in such circumstances there are still normative constraints on what we may justifiably do to others. His chapter argues that there are such limits, and he proposes a number of constraints that continue to apply even when we legitimately do wrong in order to do right. Fully responsible agents, de Wijze argues, even when justifiably engaged in actions that violate moral principles, need to remain cognizant of the need for normative constraints on their behaviour towards others.

In part 4 there are two chapters which explore an important theme in Geras's work: his claims about the place of a philosophical account of human nature in relation to normative or critical theory. Geras argues that we can and must ground our normative values and political theory on rational philosophical foundations that are universal and morally substantive. This bedrock view lies behind his criticism of anti-foundationalists, relativists, and Marxists who reject a universal account of human nature. Geras's most extensive argument against anti-foundationalist positions is found in his book *Solidarity in the Conversation of Humankind* (1995), where he sets out to show that Richard Rorty's claim that we should abandon universal foundationalist claims in political theory is seriously flawed. Gideon Calder and Shane O'Neill both take on this argument and in different ways offer criticisms of Geras's claims. Calder supports a pluralist ethical naturalism where values are in part 'claims about well-being', which is a complex mixture of human and natural aspects. He distinguishes this view from any commitment to the 'thick' foundationalist claims about a universal human propensity to evil which he finds in some aspects of Geras's work. Calder goes on to argue that other aspects of Geras's thought, if understood correctly, in fact support the pluralist ethical naturalism which Calder himself endorses, and hence that Geras has no need to appeal to the controversial foundationalist claims that, in Calder's view, 'create problematic ambiguities in his [Geras's] explanatory and normative agenda' (Calder, this volume p. 184).

O'Neill also adopts a critical view of Geras's claims about human nature, and distinguishes three contrasting positions: Rorty's post-philosophical version of pragmatism, Geras's substantive philosophical humanism, and Habermas's procedural form of universalism. O'Neill favours the Habermasian approach, but suggests two moves to narrow the gap between Geras's position and Habermasian discourse ethics. He argues that Geras's position can be understood as fallibilist rather than foundationalist, and, on this construal, Geras's substantive view moves closer to O'Neill's own favoured Habermasian proceduralism. What is more, if this is correct, the coming together of these positions would offer what O'Neill takes to be the best universalist response to Rorty's work.

Part 5 offers two chapters that engage less directly with the principal themes in Geras's academic writing. Nevertheless, he has a keen interest in the issues addressed in these chapters and has often commented on them in his blog posts. Hillel Steiner, writing on the subject of political freedom, remarks that he has intermittently discussed this philosophical problem with Geras for over forty years (a discussion which led to a 2004 paper by Geras on the topic). Here Steiner explores a particular technical argument against his claim that there is a *Law of Conservation of Liberty (LCL)*, a view of political freedom that underlies Steiner's left-libertarian conception of justice. This view claims that (negative) liberty cannot in aggregate be increased or diminished, but only distributed in differing ways. Measures to increase the liberty of those who have little of it will not lead to an overall increase in the amount of liberty; rather, an increase in liberty for some people will necessarily mean a decrease for others. The (putative) LCL faces a number of strong criticisms, and Steiner's chapter focuses on responding to and rejecting one in particular, the 'Value Integration Claim' – the view that in assessing the extent of a person's freedom we must take into account the value of that freedom.

One of the recurring themes on *normblog* is the way in which, within the discourse in liberal/left circles and publications, there has been a revival of anti-Jewish sentiment that would have been unthinkable a few decades ago. Shalom Lappin's piece in this volume focuses on that issue. Unlike the other chapters here, it does not engage in political theory but rather offers a historical account of the relationship between the British state and its Jewish population over the last 350 years, since Cromwell's readmission of Jews to England in 1656. Lappin argues that the current view, propagated by British Jews and non-Jews alike, that Britain is a society tolerant of Jews, misrepresents the historical facts. The recent demonization of Israel, coupled with the frequent use of language and imagery associated with the long and shameful persecution of Jews throughout the ages, is not a new phenomenon in Britain. The theme of collective Jewish malevolence that drives an international conspiracy involving control of the press, economy, and foreign affairs revives classical anti-Jewish mythology prevalent in this country for many centuries. Lappin concludes that the current hostility to Jews in the UK, although packaged as 'progressive political comment' that is anti-Israel rather than anti-Semitic, has its origins in a hostility towards Jews that has been integral to Britain's history for centuries.

The final blogging piece in this volume focuses on one of Geras's deep passions: his love for the game of cricket. One of the ways in which this is exemplified on *normblog* is in its series on 'Memories of cricket', where Geras recounts his considerable experience watching cricket matches – accounts infused with his extensive knowledge of past and current players, Test match results, and many other aspects of the game.[4] In addition to his long list of academic publications, Geras has also found the time to publish two books on cricket, one of them written jointly with Ian Holliday in 1997 (*Ashes '97: Two Views from the Boundary*). Holliday's blogging piece in this volume celebrates Geras's love of the game of cricket, and his sturdy defence of its place, and the place of all competitive sport, in human affairs. However, as Holliday points out, even here Geras's political values are evident: sport, like any other aspect of human endeavour, cannot be entirely bracketed off from the moral and political challenges facing us. Hence Geras argued against a scheduled England tour of Zimbabwe in 2004, given the Mugabe regime's appalling violations of fundamental human rights. As Holliday puts it, 'Here the concern for humanity that animates most of Geras's work is explicit, and the extent to which cricket actually does matter is clearly stated' (Holliday, this volume p. 254).

The final part of this volume is given over to Geras's responses to the academic essays and blogging pieces in the volume. These replies reflect the fact that the core of his work has always lain in a deep commitment to justice, and to the use of human reason, flawed and fallible as it is, to help produce the conditions which will make for emancipation and for a tolerable life for all those who are now oppressed. In this project, Geras's formidable intellect and moral gravitas have made him a politically engaged theorist of great distinction. It is our hope that his responses here, and indeed all of his work, will spur others to continue these debates into the future, and to take up the project to which Geras has committed the whole of his working life.

Notes

1 See full post at www.normangeras.blogspot.com/2003_07_27_archive.html#105948316257163866.

2 In the seven years since *normblog* (http://normblog.typepad.com/normblog) was launched in July 2003 it has become one of the best

known single-authored political weblogs, and acquired an international readership. It has had several million visitors over that period. Geras uses his blog to discuss topical issues of the day, political theory, literature, music, sport, and other matters. *Normblog* won the best UK blog award for 2005 in a poll conducted by a US blog. Though there are now thought to be nearly 200 million blogs worldwide, in February 2009 the *Sunday Times*, in 'A Guide to the 100 Best Blogs', mentioned *normblog*, saying: 'Based in Britain, Norman Geras offers an indispensable window on the world, culling items from newspapers and blogs from around the globe so you get a regular focus on what's caught his eye, as well as his intellectual, humane comments on what he's found.' See http://technology.timesonline.co.uk/tol/news/tech_and_web/the_web/article5725644.ece?token=null&offset=12&page=2.

3 Geras's political engagement outside the academic world is expressed in his weblog, comment pieces to newspapers such as the *Times*, the *Guardian*, and the *Wall Street Journal*, and interviews on BBC Radio 4 and elsewhere. Geras was also the principal author of The Euston Manifesto and one of the founders of the group that took its name – a group of left/liberal academics, journalists and activists, who sought to define a framework for the liberal/left in the aftermath of 9/11 and the invasion of Iraq. For more information on the Euston Manifesto see http://eustonmanifesto.org and http://en.wikipedia.org/wiki/Euston_Manifesto.

4 For example, see this post on *normblog* at http://normblog.typepad.com/normblog/2007/06/memories_of_cri.html.

1

What is left internationalism?

Michael Walzer

I

We all know what left internationalism used to mean: the solidarity of the working class across national boundaries – the unity of the 'Workers of the World'. If we assume, as Marx did, that workers have no country, then internationalism is easy: the working class is already internationalist simply because it is the working class, exploited within a global capitalist system. And if it isn't internationalist, the problem must be 'false consciousness' – the distortions produced by religious indoctrination, state education, and the capitalist media. Whenever the working class has its own agencies of cultural production, it will produce and reproduce proletarian internationalism. On this view, internationalism is, as we used to say, 'the correct ideological position'. It requires no political or moral defence, and, since it reflects the actual interests of the world's workers, it is sure to be socialist in content.

But reality failed us here; the world turned out to be different from the way it was supposed to be. Workers did (and do) have countries, and they have very strong local loyalties, which aren't plausibly described as 'false'. Marxists predicted that these loyalties would always make for a reactionary politics, and sometimes, certainly, they did, and sometimes they do. But at other times they have proved invaluable to the left. Membership in a particular nation and the sense of solidarity with fellow members were key factors in the struggle for social democracy and the welfare state. There is, however, no automatic extension of loyalty beyond the nation-state, no group of people in the larger world to whom workers, or anyone else, have a pre-determined and necessary connection.

In the last four decades of the twentieth century, left internationalism was given another meaning: support for the victims of imperi-alism, the oppressed nations of the Third World. It didn't seem likely that these nations would automatically produce a socialist politics, but the leaders of their national liberation movements often called themselves socialists, and they worked out ideologies that were imitative of Marxism even as they were also adapted to harsh local circumstances: undeveloped economies, under-educated popula-tions, unreformed religions, and longstanding ethnic divisions. Inevitably, perhaps, the adaptations went awry, and it soon became difficult to recognize any leftist content in 'Third Worldism'. The new states produced by national liberation were – not all of them, but many of them – tyrannical, brutal, and corrupt. Some Western leftists worked very hard to love these states, but this was futile and ultimately dishonourable work. They weren't lovely. And still today, from Cuba, to North Korea, to Zimbabwe, they aren't lovely.

So a new shorthand politics is currently on offer: anti-Americanism. All we have to do to be good internationalists is to support the opponents of American hegemony. Among European leftists, an old maxim has been given new life: the enemy of my enemy is my friend. Since the recent enemies of America include Serbian and Iraqi dictators and the current enemies include radical Muslim jihadists, this is internationalism with gritted teeth and, happily, many leftists don't have the necessary grit. But anti-Americanism is nonetheless a popular politics in many parts of Europe, and if it doesn't reach to full support for every enemy of the Americans, it still reaches pretty far. It takes the form of apology and excuse or, more simply, it leads to a refusal to oppose America's opponents, however awful their politics is. And in the case of America's ally, Israel, it goes much further. English leftists marching in London in 2006 with banners saying 'We are all Hezbollah' certainly thought that they were practising a left internationalist politics. That Hezbollah was in no sense a leftist movement, that its militants were also religious zealots, made no difference so long as it was hostile to Israel and America.

But the truth about Hezbollah should have made a difference. For internationalism is not in fact the automatic support of the world's workers, or of every colonized people, or of every opponent of the United States. It requires a more nuanced politics and a more open-ended search for allies. My aim in this chapter is to provide what might best be called a practical account of this search. Perhaps we need a new theory of internationalism, but what we need first, it seems to me, is a close look at the actual circumstances in which we undertake 'the choice of comrades' (the phrase comes from Ignazio Silone) – and at the political and, what is even more important, the moral judgements that this choice requires.

Our comrades are not given to us by the laws of history; they are not people that we can identify mechanically by their place in the class structure. At home, the necessary choices are relatively easy: most of the time, we find ourselves in ideological agreement with men and women who are already familiar to us, with whom we share a wide range of commitments. We come together (though we may not stay together) without great difficulty. In the larger world, familiarity lapses – and none of the shorthand substitutes are much help: workers and peasants, oppressed nations, the victims of (American) imperialism. These are not men and women with whom we are familiar, and we don't naturally come together with them. Many of them are passive and politically invisible – passivity and invisibility are, after all, the standard effects of oppression. And when they are organized for political action, we see them only on our television screens, marching in demonstrations, shouting angry slogans about divine revenge or political destruction, invisible again in the crowd. How did they arrive at *those* slogans?

The people we actually encounter are militants who claim to act in the name of the oppressed, on their behalf. It is the militants whose arguments we come to know. And they argue with one another as much as with anyone else. They hold different beliefs, make different commitments. They adopt a wide range of ideologies and strategies, which are obviously not determined by the global economy or the politics of imperial power – else there would be no differences among them. In fact, the militants disagree in ways that are deep and often unbridgeable. Our comrades are the ones with whom we share a politics and a morality.

But isn't left internationalism driven by a commitment to oppressed people everywhere in the world – more than that, to people in trouble, whether or not the trouble is caused by recognizable forms of oppression? Yes, it is; the truth about left internationalism is that it breaks with what Norman Geras calls 'the contract of mutual indifference'. We are never indifferent to the suffering of people in near or faraway countries. But when internationalists today reject indifference, it is not because we share material interests with the people we want to help or because we are acting out, with them, a world-historical script. As Geras argues in his meditation on the Holocaust, the only possible basis of 'the duty to bring aid' is moral in character. 'On its own, self-interest, even if this is the interest of a group, offers an improbable route towards a state of things in which sympathetic care and support for others will have come to occupy a … prominent place' (Geras, 1998: 75). This is a profound revision of leftist doctrine. If we are not moved morally, emotionally, by the suffering of others, we won't be moved to do what most needs doing. 'An ethic of mutual concern … has to inform any worthwhile politics of justice, or equality, or socialism' (1998: 75–6). Yes; but the practical consequences of this ethic are not always easy to figure out. About whom should we be concerned? To whom, exactly, should we bring aid? Who will distribute the aid we bring to the people in greatest need? When is it right (or necessary) to use military force on behalf of people in desperate trouble? What political organizations should we support – and what forms of popular mobilization?

Unhappily, trouble and oppression are no guarantee of political goodness or even of decency. They can breed their own pathologies, producing a politics of resentment and rage. And they can be, they often are, exploited by people who have no leftist commitments at all. The militants who act in the name of the oppressed are sometimes the agents of a new oppression. Totalitarian movements, terrorist organizations, and parties with Maximal Leaders all claim to serve the interests of oppressed men and women, and all of them should be met with scepticism and hostility – scepticism because they almost certainly don't serve those interests, and hostility because they are, however they describe themselves, the enemies of freedom, democracy, and equality. Our comrades, by contrast, are the men and women who resist oppression and struggle to cope with their troubles in the name of socialist or social-democratic values. Left internationalism reflects a wide-ranging sympathy, but it is, it should be, a solidarity of leftists.

I don't mean to describe a sectarian politics. We can make alliances with all sorts of people, including centrist liberals and freedom-loving conservatives. And we can – we had better! – live with the political disagreements endemic to the left. But there is a line that we draw and defend, a moral line, which separates us from all the versions of a totalizing, hierarchical, authoritarian, or terrorist politics.

It is worth looking more closely at the terrorists, for terrorism, we are often told, is the inevitable choice of oppressed men and women (or of their militants); it is the 'politics of the weak'. But this is not a left politics – for three reasons. The first merely restates the old Marxist argument against terror: that it is the work of the few, an elitist strategy that seeks victory without mass mobilization and therefore without a democratic prospect. Terrorists, Trotsky wrote, 'want to make the masses happy without asking their participation' (Trotsky, 1974 [1935]: 124). The second reason for opposing terrorism is that the decision deliberately to kill innocent people here and now strongly suggests a disposition to rule violently in the future. And the third reason is that the decision to kill the 'others' – Europeans in Algeria, Jews in Israel, infidels in New York, Sunni or Shi'ite Muslims in Iraq – without discrimination, randomly, and in large numbers, signals a desire to destroy or subjugate the target population. In all these ways, terrorism reproduces oppression even as the terrorists pretend to be liberators. It might be possible to use terror and then get rid of the terrorists. I am told that within one year of Algerian independence, all the FLN militants who had been involved in the battle of Algiers were in prison, or in exile, or dead. Still, the initial choice of terror and perhaps also this method of dealing with its agents are reliable indicators of the authoritarian and brutal politics that was soon to follow in Algeria.

Left internationalists should never be defenders of authoritarianism and brutality. And yet some of us often are – why is that? George Orwell provides the most likely answer: 'I had reduced everything to the simple theory that the oppressed are always right and the oppressors are always wrong: a mistaken theory, but the natural result of being one of the oppressors yourself' (Orwell, 1937: ch. 9). Orwell had actually served in the colonial civil service; most of us are not oppressors in that sense, but we are citizens of states that are engaged or complicit in one or another form of oppression – or have been engaged or complicit in the not-so-distant past. And so our internationalism is often reduced to Orwell's simple theory. And the maxim that the oppressed are always right readily translates into the maxim that militants claiming to act for the oppressed are always right. That is not only a mistaken theory; it is often a kind of complicity in new oppressions.

There is another reason why left internationalism sometimes leads to a betrayal of the oppressed, and that is the belief of (some) leftist militants that our values have to be surrendered for the sake of historical advance. Freedom, equality, and democracy, they argue, are not suited to the brutal world of class struggle or national liberation; they don't make for victory; they have to be sacrificed. Tender-hearted bourgeois liberals will never usher in the bright tomorrow. 'We who wished to lay the foundations of kindness', Bertold Brecht wrote, 'could not ourselves be kind' (Brecht, 1976, 'To Those Born Later', part iii). But the surrender of leftist values is a bad idea, and its victims are not only squeamish liberals but ordinary men and women caught up against their will in brutal struggles. A bright tomorrow in which we can't participate – as we are, as democrats and socialists – is not likely to be bright for anyone. 'No future without us!' is a better internationalist slogan. On this point, Shakespeare's platitudinous Polonius was right: if we can't be faithful to ourselves, we will never keep faith with anyone else.

II

So left internationalists will have enemies on the left. This late in the day, that can't be a surprise. And it wouldn't be worth writing about if we could take it for granted that most leftists were critical of Third World tyrants and terrorists pretending to be liberators. Unhappily, that isn't so; it is still necessary to argue that left internationalism must always have a democratic and egalitarian content. The maxim, 'No enemies to the left!' is all too often an expression of indifference to cruelty and domination.

But once we affirm the democratic and egalitarian content of our politics, our major enemies are on the right. And they still have the old names: capitalism and imperialism. We oppose these two in our own country and in every other country – though the opposition is more complicated than it used to be, or better than we used to think it was.

Historically, the first enemy of left internationalism is that other internationalism of capitalist wealth and power, unregulated or regulated only in the interests of the wealthy and powerful. As Geras writes, the political economy of capitalism and the everyday practices that go with it work to 'underwrite' the contract of mutual indifference (1998: 59). Just as it encourages individuals to think only of their own 'bottom line', so it encourages countries to aim only at their own competitive advantage. But if capitalism is morally corrosive, it is also an immensely productive force, which has had (and continues to have) the liberating effects that Marx first described in the *Manifesto* and which helped to create the modern world that we defend – but also need to transform. Capitalist corporations and their governmental servants will never by themselves address avoidable hunger and disease, or work towards the elimination of global poverty; or defend the environment; or accede to the empowerment of their workers. They must be challenged by social movements and subjected to the political control of a mobilized *demos*.

Left opposition to global capitalism is itself a modernizing force, which seeks to turn the success of capitalist production to the benefit of ordinary people, who are commonly, in most of the Third World, people in trouble. As domestic capitalism was engaged and reformed by domestic social democracy, so now we need a global social democracy to deal with global capitalism. We haven't yet found the political space for global organization, but we know our organizing goals: worker empowerment, democratic regulation, redistributive taxation, and welfare guarantees. Our comrades, then, are the men and women, anywhere in the world, who share those goals, who work for socialism or social democracy in their own countries and look, with us, for whatever space exists for international agitation and mobilization.

The socialist/social democratic project also brings us into opposition to imperialism. I mean by this term nothing more than the standard effort by a powerful state to shape the political or economic policies of other countries in its own interest, without regard for the well-being of the inhabitants. No one is building empires in the old sense of that word, but the subordination and exploitation of the weak is as common as it ever was. US engagement in Central America, the French in francophone Africa, the Russians in eastern Europe, the Chinese in Tibet all provide useful recent examples. But sometimes the troubles of the other countries have deep-rooted local causes – it isn't true that all politics is local, but some politics certainly is. And sometimes the engagement of imperial powers is actually beneficial to the other countries. We are not root and branch opponents of American or European (or Chinese or Russian) engagement abroad. The US Marshall Plan of the late 1940s is an example of *liberal* internationalism (see my coda below), which leftists should have supported, though many didn't; and NATO's intervention in Kosovo is an even more interesting example of the use of 'imperial' power by centre-left parties for good internationalist reasons. Global interactions are immensely complicated, and so anti-imperialism can never be a knee-jerk politics. Still, leftists should be fighting to change much of what the great powers and their economic agents do in the larger world, and we should be supporting great power opponents like the East European dissidents before 1989 or Central American or Middle Eastern or Chinese or Burmese democrats today.

What American (and European) policies and practices need to be changed?

- political and military support for tyrannical, predatory, and corrupt regimes
- the refusal of trans-national corporations, based here at home, to respect environmental and safety laws and to recognize independent unions when they operate abroad
- the use of force to secure natural resources or strategic bases and the failure to use force to save human lives
- the gross inadequacy of resource transfers from rich to poor states and the unwillingness of the rich states, the US first among them, to organize a global campaign to end poverty and control pandemic disease.

That is a short agenda for left internationalists; I haven't said anything about the refugee crisis in Africa, or about immigration policy in Europe and the US, or about global warming, or about a war against terror in which we have enlisted the support of terrorist regimes – as we also did, remember, in the fight against Nazis and Stalinists. These aren't easy issues, and it is a great mistake to pretend that they are. In making international political alliances, for example, the question, 'Which odd bedfellows are too odd or too awful to take to bed?' has no general answer. We have to look at cases – and then we see many American bedfellows that are definitely too awful (and some, given the alternatives, that are not). Or consider the conflict imposed by global warming: between our obligations to future generations (which require us to slow down economic development) and our obligations to the poorest of the contemporary poor (for whose well-being development is probably necessary). I suppose that internationalists must also be inter-generationalists.

Our commitment is to people in trouble right now – and also to those who will be in trouble in times to come. But how do we strike the balance between these two groups? We have a lot of hard arguments to work through, and no help from the slogans of the old or new left. Future generations will no doubt include the workers of the world and the victims of imperialism, but that isn't necessarily the most useful way of thinking about them. They are also everybody's great-grandchildren – a new category in leftist discourse.

Faced with the scale of human misery in the world today, left internationalism is first of all a politics of rescue and relief. Faced with the dangers of environmental degradation, it is a preventive politics. Faced with the organizing struggles of factory workers in the Third World, it is an old-fashioned politics of solidarity. Faced with tyranny and repression, it is a politics of democratic agitation. It isn't, not now and not in the foreseeable future, a revolutionary politics. Except for a few sectarian Marxists, no one on the left expects a grand global transformation after which we will have no more troubles. But there is a sense in which left internationalism is and should be transformative. For it isn't our purpose to address the crises of poverty, homelessness, predatory rule, ethnic cleansing, and massacre in ways that relieve human suffering right now but guarantee that we will have to address the same crises again … and again. Our purpose is not only relief but also reconstruction; we want oppressed men and women to become political agents, who control their own lives. That's why we support leftist parties and movements in other countries and defend the right to organize unions. Left internationalists help people so that they can help themselves. Recall Trotsky's line about terrorists who want to make people happy without their participation. We want to make them participants. They will have to make themselves happy.

An internationalism of agency: that is what the commitment to freedom, democracy, and equality means in practice. And, in the world as we know it, the crucial agency of self-help is the state – I mean, a decent state, in the hands of its own people. There isn't any other political agent that can collect and distribute resources, provide welfare and education, regulate entrepreneurial activity, protect union organizers, enforce safety and environmental laws, and so on – the list is long. We still need global regulation by social demo-cratic versions of the IMF and the WTO; we still need resource transfers to the poorest states (like those now taking place within the European Union). But the benefits of a redistributive internationalism will themselves have to be distributed by the recipient states, and if these states are not democratic and free, their citizens will never get a fair share.

Left internationalists once imagined that their politics would lead them 'beyond the nation-state'. Maybe one day it will. But right now it leads us only beyond our own nation-state to a concern with people from other nations, who are not protected by a decent state, who have no means of self-help, who are the victims, endlessly, of natural disaster and human depredation. We are internationalists on their behalf; our comrades are those among them who aim to liberate themselves and one another. They may be workers, or farmers, or professional men and women, or bourgeois intellectuals, or civil servants and bureaucrats. There are no class limits, but there are moral limits: our comrades are not Maximal Leaders, or terrorists, or oligarchs. They must practise a politics of democratic solidarity with their own people before we can join them in a solidarity of left internationalists.

Coda: what is liberal internationalism?

There are interesting and important differences here, which needn't bar cooperation between leftists and liberals, but are worth noticing. The left version of internationalism is (or should be) focused on people in trouble – oppressed nations, exploited workers, persecuted minorities, imprisoned and tortured dissidents – and then on the social movements and political parties through which these men and women struggle to transform their political and economic condition. The liberal version has to do chiefly with cooperation among states: collective security, multilateralism, human rights conventions, environmental treaties, rules for fair trade – and then with international organizations like the United Nations, the ICC, the IMF, the WTO, where this cooperation is institutionalized and regulated. Left internationalists dream of cross-border political action by men and women who, despite ethnic or religious differences, recognize that freedom and democracy are common values. Liberal internationalists dream of a global rule of law worked out among state officials willing to sacrifice (some degree of) sovereignty for the sake of security and peace.

The two internationalisms overlap – most clearly, perhaps, in the case of humanitarian intervention, which we might think of as a material expression of the duty to bring aid. When massacre, ethnic cleansing, or religious persecution is stopped by a coalition of states (like NATO in Kosovo), leftist parties should support the coalition. When the UN Security Council authorizes the use of force to stop a campaign of terror (as in East Timor), leftist parties should support the UN. But the two internationalisms can also come into conflict. When multilateral politics fails, as it did in Rwanda, for example, left internationalists should still argue for military intervention, even if intervention challenges the rule of law. Solidarity trumps multilateralism. The Spanish Civil War offers an inexact but useful analogy: France, Britain, and the US decided, multilaterally, on a policy of non-intervention, but leftists insisted on going in anyway. The International Brigade has inspired some contemporary left writers to argue for a similar volunteer force in Darfur, where liberal internationalists seem to be stymied.

So, liberal multilateralism and leftist solidarity sometimes go together, and sometimes they don't. International law and international morality sometimes go together, and sometimes they don't. The case is the same in global as in domestic society: the liberal rule of law, for all its immense value, sometimes fails men and women in desperate trouble, who can only be rescued by illegal political action (including, sometimes, the use of force).

Civil society is the place where liberals and leftists co-exist most happily. Organizations like Human Rights Watch and Amnesty International serve both to monitor the rule of law and to sound the alarm when individuals or groups are in trouble. Still, these are characteristically liberal organizations that aim at state enforcement of treaties and conventions rather than at the political mobilization of persecuted or oppressed men and women. Their policies are shaped by professional staffs, not by members and volunteers. Leftists will more typically organize unions and parties – which are, in principle at least, bottom-up rather than top-down organizations, run by elected representatives. But groups of these different kinds can and do cooperate; they are all NGOs working in their own ways for greater freedom and democracy. In many parts of the world, that means that they are working for regime change. In fact, we can say that it is a primary goal of both liberal and left activists in international civil society to change brutal and authoritarian regimes –

through politics rather than war and through the action of local people rather than outside forces (but we outsiders will help in every way we can).

Sometimes war is a necessary instrument for the achievement of internationalist goals, but that necessity always follows from a failure of liberal and left politics. And, though the record is discouraging, we needn't always fail. The rule of law in global society and the practice of solidarity across borders – liberal and left internationalism – are the best means we have to minimize or avoid the use of military force.

2

The Marxism of Norman Geras

David McLellan

This chapter has two aims: first, and mainly, to give the reader an account of the content and trajectory of Norman Geras's writings on Marx and Marxism. Geras is an essayist: his work is contained mainly in lengthy journal articles, of which he has issued several collections (see bibliography on p. 280) with his short book on human nature being, as I shall argue, *the* key text for an understanding of his approach. These essays are somewhat scattered in different collections, so I believe that the overview I am now offering may prove useful. Second, I want to suggest that the approach of Geras to Marx and Marxism has – unlike many thinkers on the left – a remarkable consistency. It may seem surprising that a thinker who was so enthusiastic in his earlier work for Luxemburg and Trotsky should have been a supporter of the United States invasion of Iraq in 2003. But, as I shall eventually argue, this is not the only too familiar abandonment of youthful ideals by those who claim that (conservative) wisdom comes with age and experience; there is an underlying intellectual thread which links both the young and the (relatively) old Geras. It is not that Geras is immune to changing his mind on some points (see, for example, his brief autobiographical comments in *Literature of Revolution* (1986: xiii ff.)), but the fundamental components of his thought have not changed.

My task is made easier by the clarity of Geras's writing. Given the cloudiness, jargon-ridden, and sometimes virtual impenetrability of much work on Marx and Marxism, it is a real pleasure to read Geras. He has a precision of expression which means that you know exactly what he is saying. In fact, occasionally he may be, as we shall see, a little too clear. And this clarity is combined with an exemplary scholarship with detailed and careful referencing for his claims. For this any reader – including myself – can only be extremely grateful.

I begin with the early 1970s when Geras published a series of substantial articles on approaches to Marx. Three stand out – all written, in part at least, as responses to the work of Althusser who was, at the time, a (if not *the*) dominant influence on Marxist theory.

In the first, entitled 'Essence and Appearance: Aspects of Fetishism in Marx's *Capital*' (Geras, 1971), Geras aims to analyse the doctrine of fetishism as the key to Marx's claim that any and every science (including his own) involves a distinction between essence and appearance. Describing his approach, Geras writes

> it seems necessary, therefore, to adopt an analytic procedure, in an attempt to isolate different aspects of the concept and to examine them separately, even if such a procedure runs the risk of fragmenting what Marx conceived to be a unified phenomenon. (Geras, 1986: 66)

He begins his analysis by contrasting the different concepts of alienation in the *Economic and Philosophical Manuscripts* (Marx, 1988) and in *Capital* (1976): in the latter 'in place of a concept of alienation founded on an essentialist anthropology, we have one tied to the historical specificity of forms of domination' (Geras, 1986: 68). Here he takes issue with Althusser's approach, which separates fetishism from the (pre-Marxist) concept of alienation and treats the former as mystification rather than the actual domination of human beings by their own products. Geras stresses that 'for Marx, neither values nor value relations are imaginary. They are not illusionary appearances, but *realities*' (Geras, 1986: 71). In other words, if capitalist society is experienced as something other than what it really is, this is fundamentally because capitalist society in fact presents itself as something other than what it really is. Geras goes on to discuss the wage-form as the prime example of mere appearance, concealing as it does the fundamental characteristic of capitalist society – exploitation. As an excursus, Geras dissects the false disjunction between the theory of the theoreticians and the political action of the masses. In particular, he rejects Althusser's idea that ideology will persist in communist society – in contrast to Rosa Luxemburg's insistence on the demystifying effect of class struggle.

The critique of Althusser is taken up in the second article, which offers a general account and assessment of Althusser's Marxism. In the first part, Geras gives us an admirably clear exposition (not easy!) of Althusser's theoretical positions in *For Marx* (Althusser, 1969) and *Reading Capital* (Althusser and Balibar, 1970). In the second half, Geras proceeds to an assessment. While granting Althusser's achievements in reacting both against the reductionist economism of the Second International and against the excessive Hegelian humanism of Lukacs and Korsch, and in elaborating his concept of the problematic, Geras mounts a broad critique of Althusser's whole concept of science. For Althusser, Marxist science is something produced outside the working-class context. But

> to reduce the whole process by which Marxist theory was produced to a theoretical activity *autonomous* of the political practice of the working class, *autonomous* of the class and political conditions which were *its* indispensable, if not sufficient, conditions of production, is to perpetrate a reduction as grave as any of those castigated by Althusser himself. (Geras, 1986: 127)

In particular – and prefiguring a theme of much of his later work – Geras contests Althusser's view that *Capital* is value-free and claims that Marx's concept of exploitation, for example, has critical as well as cognitive functions. To think otherwise would be to follow Hilferding who, Geras tells us in too generous an assessment, 'with a logic that was flawless and a historical understanding that was limited, believed one could accept the whole of Marxist science without the least commitment to socialism' (Geras, 1986: 130). His assessment of Althusser a decade later was no less negative (Geras, 1986: 85 ff.).

The final (and much shorter) article mentioned above echoes these themes. Here Geras insists again that 'the political struggles of the proletariat which aim at the destruction of capitalist society are the condition of possibility of the science of Marxism which comprehends and explains capitalist society as one social formation amongst others, having a historical origin and a historical term' (Geras, 1986: 140). This, he tells us, is no endorsement of relativism in that there is a 'necessary logical distinction between the sociological question of the genesis of a thought and the epistemological question of its truth' (Geras, 1986: 140). Exposition of this distinction in the case of Marx, together with discussion of its validity, will occupy much of Geras's later work.

The 'sociological question of the genesis of a thought' alluded to above is pursued in Geras's study of Rosa Luxemburg. His 1976 *The Legacy of Rosa Luxemburg* is a collection of articles (or essays) each of which deals with a specific aspect of Luxemburg's thought. The first examines the relationship between her economic ideas on capitalist breakdown and her 'spontaneist' conception of class struggle. Here Geras claims – against a perhaps more common interpretation – that, for Luxemburg, the former was not the basis for the latter. He writes:

> if it is true that she subscribed to a theory of capitalist breakdown based ultimately on the postulation of purely economic disequilibria, and in *that* sense economist, it is also true that this did not serve as the springboard toward what is more usually understood by 'economism': the denigration or underestimation of theory and ideological combat, of political organisation and leadership, uncritical faith in the power of 'spontaneity', etc. It did not because it could not, the collapse of capitalism and the creation of socialism not being identified in Luxemburg's mind. (Geras, 1976: 35)

In offering a more nuanced account of Luxemburg's economic and political ideas, Geras takes issue with what he regards as the sometimes one-sided accounts by such writers as Stedman Jones, Magri, Nettl et al. He is particularly illuminating on two interconnected points. First on whether – and, if so, with what implications – Luxemburg thought socialism to be inevitable. As against Nettl and Lowy, Geras shows convincingly that Luxemburg's view of the inevitable breakdown of capitalism in her *The Accumulation of Capital* (Luxemburg, 1968) is indeed compatible with her advocacy of class struggle and the mass strike. Second, and more specifically, he is helpful in understanding Luxemburg's slogan 'Socialism or barbarism'. He shows that, for Luxemburg, the inevitable collapse of capitalism and the idea of socialism – or, barbarism – far from being contradictory, are 'one and the same idea' (Geras, 1976: 31). Barbarism signified the collapse of capitalism and only conscious political intervention could prevent the slide into catastrophic anarchy.

In his second essay, Geras examines Luxemburg's contributions to the debate after 1905 of the nature of the Russian revolution. Here again he takes issue with the many commentators who claim that before 1917 Luxemburg shared Trotsky's theory of permanent revolution – in other words, that the vanguard role of the proletariat would 'destroy the barriers between the minimum and maximum programme of social democracy' (Trotsky in Geras, 1976: 47) and move directly from bourgeois-democratic aims to socialist ones. Geras shows in detail that Luxemburg, in the decade following the

1905 revolution, does not speak of the next revolution as going beyond bourgeois democratic objectives. 'After the fall of Tsarism', she wrote in 1906,

> power will pass into the hands of the most revolutionary section of society, the proletariat; for the proletariat will seize all the positions and stand guard so long as power is not in the hands legally entitled to hold it, in the hands of the new government which the Constituent Assembly, as the legislative organ elected by the whole population, is alone able to determine. Now it is self-evident that it is not the proletariat but the petty-bourgeoisie and the peasantry that constitute the majority in society, and that, consequently, in the Constituent Assembly it will not be the Social-Democrats who form the majority but the peasant and petty-bourgeois democrats. We might deplore this but we can in no way change it. (Geras, 1976: 102)

Thus her approach was much nearer to that of Lenin than to Trotsky. It was only in 1917 that she, like Lenin, came to agree with Trotsky.

The theme of the coherence and consistency of Luxemburg's thought is continued in Geras's third essay, which deals with Luxemburg's idea of the mass strike. Here he contests 'the widespread tendency to locate the source of Luxemburg's attitude to the masses somewhere beyond or beneath the realm of rational discourse' (Geras, 1976: 111). Building on his discussion in the first essay, where he tried to show that the charges frequently levelled at Luxemburg of spontaneism and economism could find no vindication in her theory of capitalist breakdown, Geras here claims that the same applies to her thinking on the mass strike, where, 'correctly understood, the political and tactical conceptions at the heart of it lead away from spontaneism and economism' (Geras, 1976: 126) in that

> a tendency exists for each serious mass action to overflow its original objectives and to generate or merge with other demands and other struggles. By virtue of this tendency, the boundary placed by bourgeois society between the economic or trade-union struggle on the one hand, and politics on the other, begins to dissolve. The strike becomes a political weapon. Political and economic demands run into one another. Partial conflicts are more frequently and more easily generalised. A dynamic takes shape which contains the *potentiality* that partial demands, immediate concerns, urgent needs, can be linked up into a global revolutionary challenge to the existing order. (Geras, 1976: 121)

Thus, in Geras's view, it is precisely Luxemburg's espousal of the mass strike that was central to her theoretical and practical achievements: before the First World War, he claims,

> Luxemburg was the very *first* to draw the lessons of 1905 for the advanced capitalist countries and to begin to pose the question of power there in a serious, and no longer purely propagandist way. She was the first to challenge the facile optimism of peaceful linear growth implicit in the tactics of German Social Democracy, the first to counterpose to them a Marxist strategy recognising that the power of the bourgeoisie can only be destroyed by the widest and deepest mobilisation of the masses. (Geras, 1976: 124)

And it is the achievement of Geras here to have rescued Luxemburg from some of the rather patronising characterizations of her as entertaining an irrational faith in mass spontaneity.

In his final essay, Geras elaborates on Luxemburg's treatment of the difference between bourgeois and socialist democracy, a difference that had been sketched out in her discussions of the mass strike. He takes up this question directly in connection with Luxemburg's criticism of the Bolsheviks in 1918 and the ways in which attempts have been made to contrast her allegedly libertarian approach with that of revolutionary Marxism and to oppose her belief in 'democracy' to the necessity of proletarian revolution. Geras makes a good case for rejecting this opposition. At the same time, he has an interesting excursus on the relation of means to ends in revolutionary thought. He makes short shrift of those who have wished to recruit Luxemburg to their cause by their insistence that the end of any political action must be expressed in the means of achieving it as some kind of immanent presence there. More interestingly, he takes issue with anarchists such as Murray Bookchin, who has claimed that 'a libertarian society can only be achieved by a libertarian revolution' (Geras, 1976: 142). Geras denies that means must, in this strong sense, 'prefigure' ends, in that this view

> abstracts from the objective reality which is the irreducibly given, if changing, point of origin and focuses exclusively on the nature of the projected end. On this basis, and only on this basis, which transforms the end itself into the origin – first principle and source of all others – is it possible to insist that the means must express the end. For an end abstracted from material reality is a project without objective preconditions or limits, a project whose every aspect must express its purpose

since it is governed only by that purpose, indeed *is* that purpose. (Geras, 1976: 150)

Applying this to Luxemburg, Geras defends her post-1917 writings against attempts both by libertarians and ultra-Leninists such as Lukacs to appropriate her for their cause. In Geras's view, Luxemburg's 'concern about freedom is manifestly over its scope within the dictatorship of the proletariat rather than over a principle above the dictatorship of the proletariat. It is a concern for the most extensive, thoroughgoing, "unlimited", democratic rights and liberties compatible with proletarian rule' (Geras, 1976: 178).

Although Geras can be critical of Luxemburg – for example, her economic theory in *The Accumulation of Capital* (see Geras, 1976: 38 ff.) – the four essays briefly described above provide the best short account and defence of Luxemburg and her legacy. They serve as a strong corrective to most previous commentators. Indeed, it is striking how Geras almost always introduces his own interpretation by a strong critique of his predecessors. As a writer who prizes evidence and logic, he tends sometimes to make Luxemburg a little *too* coherent. His declared aim is to 'emphasise the actuality of her thought, and to try to appropriate to the present the most valuable aspects of it' (Geras, 1976: 10). And the influence of her thought on his own later writings is encouragingly apparent.

Here we come to the linchpin of Geras's account of Marxism as contained in his book *Marx and Human Nature: Refutation of a Legend* (Geras, 1983) in which the above-mentioned sociology/epistemology distinction is elaborated. In an original treatment of an old topic, Geras finds himself facing in two diametrically opposite directions: within the Marxist tradition, there are those who wish to deny legitimate room for any concept of human nature; and there are others who, so far from wishing to deny the attribution of common characteristics to human beings, think such statements about human nature to be merely self-evident, banal and therefore no integral part of a Marxist perspective. In spite of having to direct his attention to both these groups at once, Geras has avoided developing an intellectual squint by producing a precise and sharply focused discussion. As might be expected from the no-nonsense analytical style and the largely exegetical approach, he is more successful in the narrower task of disposing of the opponents of human nature than in dealing with those who insist on its irrelevance to Marxism.

Geras bases his approach on a refreshingly commonsense materialism, and argues that the more mundane material facts of human existence are neglected by Marxists at their peril. It is a commonplace that Western Marxism, for historical reasons, has had a tendency towards idealism, a purer and purer theory replacing the apparently declining opportunities for successful practice. Indeed, the long quarrel between those favouring structure as opposed to subject or subject as opposed to structure – a quarrel so central to much of Western Marxism – often has very idealist overtones on both sides. For both the Althusserian and the Lukacsian traditions have little regard for empirical material. Thus work which manages to combine both philosophical rigour and respect for the self-evident realities of material life is extremely welcome.

This short book (it is barely over a hundred pages) aims to do two things: to show that Marx did not reject the idea of a human nature and also to show that he was in fact right not to do so. On the first score, Geras succeeds completely. His main target here is the (then) widespread influence of Althusserian 'anti-humanism' in disseminating the belief that Marx's emphases on historical specificity and historical change preclude him from holding any general conception of human nature. In the face of a lot of evidence to the contrary from the whole body of Marx's work, those who wish to deny the existence of a human character that is constant have relied mainly on Marx's Sixth Thesis on Feuerbach (Marx and Engels, 1998). And it is to an extended discussion of this text that Geras devotes the first third of his book. The relevant part of the thesis reads: 'The essence of man is no abstraction inherent in each single individual. In its reality it is the ensemble of the social relations.' Geras separates out three possible interpretations of Marx's meaning: (1) that in its reality the nature of man is conditioned by the ensemble of the social relations; (2) that in its reality human nature, or the nature of man, is manifested in the ensemble of social relations; and (3) that in its reality the nature of man is determined by, or human nature is dissolved in, the ensemble of social relations. And his argument is that the first sense does not exclude a concept of human nature in that the dependence declared by it is not complete and that therefore the character of human beings must depend on something else as well and can be due in part to stable, natural causes. Nor does the second sense carry the implications that the opponents of human nature would want to see: for the reference to a social and historical diversity in no way tells against the concept of a human nature since there is nothing in the thought to say that such diversity does not contain permanent characteristics inherent in each human being. But the third sense above *does* involve the denial of a human nature and this is the reading of the Sixth Thesis that Geras is concerned to contest. He does not deny that the words *could* bear this interpretation, but insists that, in the context of Marx's other writings, such an interpretation is totally implausible. Given that Marx has held the view as early as 1843, well before he was a historical materialist, that 'man is the world of man, the state, society' and the insistence on basic human needs in *The German Ideology* (Marx and Engels, 1998) itself, Geras has no difficulty in establishing his point. More interestingly, he also shows convincingly that Marx does not depart from the view in his later writings.

The final chapter of the book is more open to question. Here Geras wishes to demonstrate not only that Marx did not reject a concept of human nature, but that he was in fact right not to do so. This is a large topic. Although Geras successfully refutes a variety of objections to the view that there is a constant human nature – e.g. that this is an inherently reactionary opinion – the very brevity of his treatment raises a number of questions. The central one is the distinction between facts and values. This distinction is part of the main Anglo-Saxon philosophical tradition and one that Geras subscribes to – though this is never stated very clearly. Since Marx himself evidently did not subscribe to such a view, there is inevitably a certain amount of reconstruction to be done in giving an account of Marx's theory involving such terms – and this would demand much more space than Geras allows himself. Thus he claims that any genuine materialism must insist that human beings are 'absolutely continuous with the rest of the natural world'. But at the same time he admits that they have linguistic, productive, and reasoning capabilities that 'make possible a transformation of the environment that no other earthly species is capable of'. More importantly, Geras's espousal of the fact/value dichotomy leads him to suppose that important claims about human nature can be construed as empirical non-normative hypotheses. As an example, he suggests that people will in general be happier if they have the opportunity to give vent to the breadth and variety of activity that Marx thinks to be characteristically human. But it is difficult to interpret statements involving the concept of happiness without supposing that they involve value judgements. For happiness is not a value-free concept such that one can first define it and choose whether to consider it a good. Geras argues that 'if one places a value on human life and happiness and there exist universal needs that must be satisfied respectively to preserve and promote these, then this furnishes, the fact and value conjointly, a basis for normative judgement: such needs ought to be satisfied *ceteris paribus*' (Geras, 1983: 101). It is the word 'conjointly' here that involves a certain slipperiness. This approach leads to a separation of theory from moral judgement that is quite uncharacteristic of Marx. To say of *Capital* that 'whatever else it is, theory and socio-historical explanation, and scientific as it may be, that work is a moral indictment resting on a conception of essential human needs, an ethical standpoint, in other words, in which a view of human nature is involved' (Geras, 1983: 83–4), is surely not an accurate description of how Marx at least conceived his work. In what is primarily conceived of as an exegetical commentary this divergence should be made a lot clearer.

This 'divergence' is addressed in Geras's later substantial contributions to the interpretation of Marx, where he discusses the question already posed in the book on human nature: 'did Marx, as some philosophers affirm and other philosophers deny, condemn capitalist society in the light of a conception of justice?' (Geras, 1983: 101). In a fifty-page article published in 1985 and entitled 'The Controversy about Marx and Justice', Geras gives an emphatic and ingenious answer to his question. He begins with a careful and fair summary of the problems. On repeated occasions Marx repudiates any appeal to the idea of justice. He denies, for example, that the wage relation is unjust: the capitalist may exploit the labour power he has bought to create a greater value, but this 'is a piece of good luck for the buyer, but by no means an injustice towards the seller' (Marx, 1976: 301). Another example would be his letter to Engels, where he says that he was obliged to insert a phrase about 'truth, morality, and justice' into the preamble to the Rules of the First International, but that 'they are placed in such a way that they can do us no harm'. Finally, in the famous passage in the *Critique of the Gotha Programme*, Marx contrasts (1) the lower phase of communist society in which each receives in proportion to their labour contribution, which he characterizes as 'still stigmatised by a bourgeois limitation', with (2) the 'to each according to their needs' principle where 'the narrow horizon of bourgeois right' has been crossed. If 'right can never be higher than the economic structure of society and its cultural development thereby', this seems to imply that standards of justice are relative to successive modes of production and not trans-historical. On the other hand, Marx frequently writes of the capitalist's appropriation of surplus-value as 'robbery' or 'based on theft' – and such stealing seems to involve an injustice. Moreover, the very talk of higher and lower stages of society equally seems to appeal to a standard which transcends history.

In the face of this apparent contradiction, Geras proposes 'some measure of reconstruction beyond mere exegesis' (Geras, 1986: 28). He claims that 'a reconstruction along these lines, however, broadly vindicates the view that Marx thought capitalism unjust, because it is better able to explain the apparent evidence to the contrary than are those who gainsay that he did able to explain what speaks against them'. Geras's reconstruction is based on the proposal that 'Marx did think capitalism unjust but did not think he thought so'. In elaborating on this (as he admits) paradoxical proposal, Geras claims that 'in so far as he indeed thought directly about and formulated any opinion concerning justice, which he did only intermittently, he expressed himself as subscribing to an extremely narrow conception of it' (Geras, 1986: 36). In other words, Marx tended both to associate justice with prevailing judicial norms and also, when thinking about justice, to focus on the process of exchange in the market. But, in Geras's reconstruction, what Marx says elsewhere leads to the conclusion that 'implicit in his work is a broader conception of justice than the one he actually formulates, notwithstanding the fact that he never himself identifies it as being such' (Geras, 1986: 37). Marx's critique of capitalism in terms of freedom and self-realization is thus held to be a critique which incorporates a conception of distributive justice. Even the higher phase of communist society, based on the satisfaction of needs, is said to embody a principle of equality – though some might think that this is to make the principle of equality so wide as to be almost vacuous: both equality and justice have connotations which spring from a bourgeois society, and a communist society would need concepts more appropriate to its own social arrangements. But Geras of course needs to be able to characterize communist society as involving the principle of distributive justice in order to be able to maintain that Marx's concept of justice is trans-historical.

Geras's attempt to, as it were, have his cake and eat it on the question of Marx and justice aroused, not surprisingly, a certain amount of criticism. He returned to the charge some five years later with a robust defence of his views. He reiterates his thesis here in a blunter way than previously, which is worth quoting at length:

> if generally capitalists and workers have and get what is theirs by right, what belongs to them, as they do according to Marx's own overt, relativist conception of justice; and if this relativist conception yields the only serious perspective on what properly belongs to whom by right, as Marx insists is so; then there is no *other* serious perspective from which one can find the distribution patterns of capitalism improper, those patterns being determined by people's various ownership entitlements. But Marx did think those patterns were improper – even though the concept of justice he affirmed forbade him from thinking so. He was, therefore, confused. His explicit concept of justice contradicted, and was contradicted by, the broader concept of justice implicit in his thought. (Geras, 1992: 65)

It is to be noted that Geras is more explicit here in taxing Marx with being confused and contradictory than he was in the first article. Also that, in tidying up this confusion, Geras perhaps tries to be a little too neat. This neatness is linked to the fact/value distinction outlined in his previous book on human nature and reiterated here: 'that something is going or probably going to happen, does not show why, or that, it should be valued or fought for' (Geras, 1992: 44). To show this, we have to have recourse to 'ethically pertinent criteria'. To elucidate these, he refers to 'the thinkers of liberalism who developed a rich and impressive philosophical literature on the subject of justice' and recommends that Marxists who have thought that the principles of distributive justice were not an essential part of the eventual communist enterprise now have to learn about these things 'in liberalism's more advanced school' (Geras, 1992: 67). The only direct reference here is to Kymlicka, but presumably such thinkers as Rawls are envisaged. This, ironically, sounds more like Bernstein than Luxemburg. And it is also in some contrast with the end of the first article with its criticism of those who indulge in 'minute analysis of the right, the good, the just and what have you, conceptually *nice and far* from the messy throng, the scarred history of toil and comfort, power and protest, fear, hope, struggle'. He continues: 'The contemporary discussion of precisely justice provides ample illustrative material, in the several conceptions of just social arrangements proffered in conjunction with more or less nothing, sometimes actually nothing, on how these might conceivably be achieved' (Geras, 1986: 57).

The second article ends on a note which presages Geras's later development: socialism is for him now a 'utopian' project – and utopian 'in the way Marxists used to mean that'. In Marx at least, the term was invariably pejorative.

During the 1990s, Geras continued to produce a stream of articles with the same acumen, but with the same 'liberal principles' mentioned above coming increasingly to the fore. In two articles preceding the second one on justice, for example, Geras offers an extended discussion of revolutionary ethics. Here he returns to his treatment of means and ends in the book on Rosa Luxemburg. He rejects both a utilitarian consequentialism and, more specifically, the view that virtually anything goes as long as it works in favour of an approach based on just war principles. His conclusion is that, however much revolution may involve violence and war,

> none of this can legitimate a way of thinking, or at least of speaking, which would relax all moral limits by making the activity of war itself the culprit for anything that the participants in it might do. If there are indeed circumstances to make some moral crimes unavoidable, it is still necessary to have the rules and restraints which define them as crimes and which serve as a barrier against the avoidable ones. (Geras, 1990b: 50)

In the second of these articles, entitled 'Seven Types of Obloquy', Geras is in his element, dissecting with clinical accuracy some of the more egregious dismissals of Marx by writers such as Elster, Hindess, and Keane. He is particularly good here on how close attention to Marx's texts would show that his conception of a communist society involved neither the idea that it would be completely harmonious nor the claim that it would enjoy unlimited abundance. Interestingly, too, Geras here says that 'the argument against privileging the working class is unconvincing'. On a broad definition as victims of economic oppression, the working class is here said to be 'the primary constituency of socialism' (Geras, 1990a: 30 f.). This is in some contrast to Geras's view in the second article on justice, published some two years later, where he says that, whereas in much previous Marxist writing workers were taken to be the real core constituency of socialism, there is no good reason why, for example, the homeless or those generally in need 'should not be regarded as part of the core in their own right' (Geras, 1992: 69). Mention should also be made of Geras's splendid demolition of the airily 'discursive' version of socialism offered by Laclau and Mouffe (Geras, 1990b).

The centrality (or otherwise) of the working class to the Marxist project is referred to in Geras's last substantial piece on Rosa Luxemburg. In this 1994 article, he takes her to task for her emphasis on the proletariat and writes that 'the least that can be said is that this was a particularism which did not always strengthen, in theory or in practice, the democratic and humanist sensibilities of Marxists' (Geras, 1994a: 104). Indeed it is on democratic grounds that Luxemburg is here found to be wanting in her rather determinist view of the inevitable triumph of the Marxist revolution. The discussion of 'socialism or barbarism' is interestingly different here from the discussion in his 1976 book. Now Geras sees Luxemburg's determinism as a threat to democracy in that it precludes citizens from freely choosing the path ahead, since only one outcome is truly thinkable. Given the strictures, it is not surprising that Geras should conclude that Marxism will now continue as a 'programme of research' and a 'tradition of enquiry'.

During the 1990s, Geras's research turned increasingly to Holocaust studies, but without abandoning his commitment to what he calls a kind of Marxism. One of his most interesting contributions in this field is his discussion of the anti-foundational liberalism of Richard Rorty (Geras, 1995a). Although agreeing that 'Rorty's values, the values of a radical liberalism, are somewhere close to mine' (1995a: 4), Geras claims that Rorty's opposition to universalist modes of moral thinking is not conducive to democratic ways of thought. In particular, in examining the motives of those rescuing Jews in Nazi Europe, Geras impressively deploys the universalist concept of human nature put forward in his 1983 book.

Finally, two short articles deserve mention. In the first, published in 1995, Geras returns to the question of universal moral standards, claiming that a belief in progress involves a commitment to such standards, and reiterates his view that distributive justice is vital as a foundation for any future socialist/communist society. In the second article, published in 2004, Geras repeats his insistence on there being a universal human nature and retracts his view of the future possibility of a 'differentiated but freely, non-coercively, self-regulating society' (Geras, 2004: 623). The conclusion has to be that 'a socialist utopia, if one is possible, will have to be a liberal utopia' (Geras, 2004: 626).

It might be thought that the evolution of Geras's thought over three decades as described above represents something of a volte-face or at least an example of the familiar modification of youthful radicalism by age and experience. Although there is obviously some truth in this suggestion, such a description is an over-simplification. For there are striking continuities and consistencies in Geras's work. As he himself rightly says, his later (1995a) discussion of Rorty is a 'sequel and companion' to his 1983 book on human nature. And he is perfectly prepared to say he has changed his mind, while castigating the 'shameless flight from and denigration of Lenin's political legacy that are the norm and fashion today [1986] with so many on the left and so many who used to know better' (Geras, 1986: xiv). Thus the seeds for the Euston Manifesto[1] view that the overthrow of the Baathist regime in Iraq should be seen as 'a liberation of the Iraqi people' were sown early. For Geras's Marxism has always been of a specific kind: this specificity hinges on the distinction between fact and value. The concept of human nature, central to Geras's work, is, for him, an empirical construction (Geras, 1985: 98 ff.). He is thus keen to stress 'the necessary logical distinction between the sociological question of the genesis of a thought and the epistemological question of its truth' (Geras, 1986: 140). This is reminiscent of the approach of Austro-Marxists such as Max Adler, who combined a view of Marxism as strictly scientific with a neo-Kantian account of values. These self-standing Kantian values can be pretty robust. The 'categorical imperative' is just that – categorical. Unmediated by history, these sorts of values have a tendency to become, in some sense, absolute.

It is significant here that Geras has little time for Hegel, for whom the only absolute was history itself. Most commentators on Marx have given his Hegelian inheritance a large place in their interpretation – the exact nature of this inheritance being, of course, contentious. Not so Geras. He makes no reference to any influence Hegel may have had on Marx, and the few references he does make to Hegel are almost all in the context of Althusser's negative views on the subject. It is therefore no surprise that Geras has little time for any 'dialectical' method. He rejects any dialectical approach to ethical principles (Geras, 1992: 66), and claims that 'often the dialectic only muddies the water' (Geras, 1986: 27) and that the path to Marx's confusion over justice 'is certainly smoothed by his use in this context of the language of the dialectic' (Geras, 1986: 28).

At the centre of Geras's use of the fact/value distinction is his insistence that justice is, in Marx a 'trans-historical' concept. He claims that the distinction relative/trans-historical is not the same as the distinction relative/absolute, but many would see a distinction here without much of a difference. Values that are not relative to historical circumstance tend to be absolute. Geras's view is that liberal principles are, at least, a necessary starting point for socialists (Geras, 1992: 67), and his version of these, as in, for example, the Euston Manifesto, is couched in pretty non-negotiable terms. At the same time, a dialectical (!) approach to Geras's impressive contributions must stress also that it is precisely this either/or stance that gives his prose its splendid clarity and its analytical, and sometimes rhetorical, edge. For which we are all in his debt.

Note

1 The website for the Euston manifesto can be found at
   http://eustonmanifesto.org.

3

Professor Geras and Blogger Norm

Nick Cohen

Late in his life and perhaps much to his surprise, the left-wing journalist James Cameron found that he preferred the familiarity of the
old to the shock of the new. 'There is much to be said for retaining
the past', he admitted to himself as much as to his readers. 'I suppose
I am at heart, in everything but politics, a rooted conservative.'

The many admirers of Norman Geras might have thought that
Cameron's words applied as well to him. His love of his family shines
through, and his uxorious example is a living refutation of Auden's
aside

> To the man-in-the-street, who, I'm sorry to say
> Is a keen observer of life,
> The word intellectual suggests straight away
> A man who's untrue to his wife. (Auden, 1966: 190).

He adores country and western, the folk music of the English-
speaking world, and bows to no man (and few women) in his
knowledge of Jane Austen. Above all, he loves cricket, that most
traditional of sports, and loves it all the more when, as was once
traditional, Australia win. Geras is to my knowledge the only political
philosopher who could begin a treatise on our responsibilities to
prevent torture and genocide after the Holocaust with, 'The idea
which I shall present here came to me more or less out of the blue. I
was on a train some five years ago, on my way to spend a day at
Headingley, and I was reading a book about the death camp
Sobibor.'[1] Admittedly, he goes on to explain to 'those who may not
know this', that Headingley is the home of Yorkshire County Cricket
Club, but the dismissive use of the auxiliary 'may' suggests that he
finds the ignorance of 'those who may not know this' incredible and
reprehensible in equal measure.

And yet on Monday 28 July 2003 at 11.29 am, the apparent small 'c' conservative embraced a dynamic new technology, ignored by the media executives who justified their lavish salaries with claims to possess clairvoyant powers. Norman Geras, Emeritus Professor of Politics at the University of Manchester, dispensed with his titles and became Norm. 'In the immortal words of Sam Peckinpah, "Let's go"', he declared.

As Geras is most certainly not a conservative in his politics, his embrace of the freedom the new medium allowed is not as surprising as it seems. 'I only really got wise to the blogosphere earlier this year during the lead-up to the war in Iraq', he explained in his first post. 'I began to acquaint myself with other blogs, following the links from one to another in pursuit of the debate that was taking place on this subject. My desire to do so was strengthened by the fact that, since September 11 2001, I'd come to find much of what was appearing on the opinion and letters pages of my daily newspaper of choice [the *Guardian*] repellent. And as a supporter of the war for regime-change reasons I was also less than comfortable with the balance of views I was encountering in the circles, professional and social, in which I move.'

I could fill the rest of this book with describing what was wrong (and remains wrong) with the liberal consensus which turned Professor Geras into Blogger Norm. A short list includes: its unwillingness to support the victims of psychopathic regimes and movements if their suffering cannot be blamed on the West; a concomitant and inevitable failure to hold onto the old leftish virtue of solidarity with those who share your principles when they are suffering at the hands of ultra-reactionary forces; a preference for the status quo, even when it is intolerable; and a relativist willingness to tolerate abuses in other cultures you would never tolerate in your own, which is really just parochialism dressed up in its Sunday best.

Plenty to argue about, but where to argue? As Geras half-recognized when he described the discomfort he felt about the arguments he was hearing in his circles, social pressure can be the most powerful and debilitating force in intellectual life. If everyone you know, every newspaper you read, every person you once admired are all saying the same thing, it takes an effort of will to argue back. As important – and I speak from experience here – it is hard to disagree rationally, to break from a consensus with intelligent arguments rather than instinctive revulsion. Unreflective consensual thinking is,

I believe, more prevalent in England than in any other European democracy because the media are centralized in the capital. Everyone knows everyone else; talks with, works with, socializes with and, on occasion, sleeps with members of their tribe. The result is stale conformism. For instance, many Conservatives in industry and the City are pro-European because they can see the business case for the Union, but you would never know it from reading the Conservative press. Not one columnist on the *Mail* or *Telegraph* treats the European Union (EU) with anything but scorn. The conspiratorial may say that editorial and proprietorial pressure explain the failure to argue, or even admit the possibility that an argument might be justified. Although I have no doubt that career considerations play their part, the main explanation for uniformity is cultural rather than economic. In the newspapers and think tanks that make up the clubs of Conservative London, saying a good word about the EU is an unforgivable breach of etiquette.

Dissident leftists often say that the vitriol against those who break the party line is worse on the left than on the right. I am not sure that is true: ideologues of all colours treat heretics with equal loathing. But the vitriol is certainly as bad on the left as on the right, and it is dispensed with a level of personal abuse rarely matched elsewhere for a reason those who are not part of the liberal-left club regard with amusement.

Despite the evidence of history, leftists assume they possess an intrinsic goodness. Even if their theories turn out to be spurious or projects unworkable, they assure themselves and others that their ideas are offered with good intent; that, to put it another way, the world would be a better place if their theories turned out not to be spurious and their projects delivered as promised. It follows that anyone who breaks with the leftish consensus is not just mistaken but wicked, mad, crooked, a tool of capitalism, or, more recently, a Jew. The heretic is worse than a life-long Conservative, who cannot be expected to know any better, because he has seen the liberal-left's goodness – been a good man once himself – and rejected it. The only plausible reason for breaking with the club must be some form of personal corruption. The whiff of the witch-finder rises from much left-wing writing because its authors cannot accept that opponents can disagree with them in good faith. They must be in the pay of Rupert Murdoch or the Israel – ahem – 'Lobby'. There must be an ulterior motive.

The conditions for conformism in an already centralized media could not be better. On the one hand, the assumption of leftish benevolence stops people from taking on the proponents of bad arguments with the necessary rigour. On the other, the fear of denunciation keeps the nervous in line. It is for these reasons that you can know what an opinion piece on virtually any subject in the liberal press will say without reading it.

The great service *normblog* and its comrades on the Net provided was to break down the gates and allow fresh arguments in new intellectual spaces. New alliances brought contrary opinions and new sources of information to the reader. For someone writing from a similar position at the time *normblog* began, I cannot over-emphasize how important it was to realize that I had comrades out there.

Put like this, it sounds easy. Norm recognized faster than most that the old media world was breaking down and embraced the possibilities the Web was offering. But the sleek media executives who ignored the technology which was to undermine their business models were not quite the fools they seem in retrospect. At the time, it appeared reasonable to wonder why anyone would want to read the thoughts of a blogger sitting in his or her living room. The media long ago replaced their dismissal of Web 2.0 with a frantic embrace of the new technology. Yet their original question remains: why should anyone care what Norm thinks?

Both the enthusiasts for and denigrators of the blogosphere miss the point that it simply consists of writers. As with most of what appears in the press or on television, much blogging is low grade. More often, it is a private conversation conducted in a public space by friends for friends. Outsiders have no more interest in reading them than they would have in listening into the phone calls of strangers. Observers have argued that the blogs which rise above online chats stand out because they provide what the mainstream media isn't giving – in the case of *normblog*, an anti-fascist critique of the alliances with or an indifference to theocracy. Although I am sure there is truth in this, the real explanation is surely simpler. Like the best journalism, the best blogs survive because of the quality of their thought and prose.

Norm's has so well expressed his ideas, and I have so ingrained them, that I now probably do not realize how many principles which I take for granted came to me from him. If I examined them honestly I would realize that my notions that the deliberate killing of civilians is always a war crime, or that anti-Semitism cannot be explained away as an understandable reaction to intolerable Western provocations, or that human rights can only be universal are … well, perhaps, not as original as I would like to think.

'Academic' is almost an insult in English, conjuring up images of narrowness and status-consciousness. Norm is the opposite of Dr Casaubon, a true intellectual who explains himself to the wider public without compromising his ideas or avoiding complexity when it is necessary. This is in my view at once the hardest and most admirable writing style for a serious journalist.

To pick an example at random, here is Norm taking apart Karen Armstrong:

> Karen Armstrong wants to be able to eat her cake and at the same time keep it whole, unbitten into, let alone chewed and swallowed. Religion, she argues, is misconceived when it is thought of as being about beliefs rather than about practices:

> *[R]eligion is something you do, and … you cannot understand the truths of faith unless you are committed to a transformative way of life that takes you beyond the prism of selfishness.*

> Religious narratives deal in myth, she says; they're 'a programme of action', 'a species of practical knowledge'. Let's leave aside that a person may lead a life going beyond selfishness without signing up to any religion, either belief- or practice-wise. But notice that little phrase 'truths of faith'. What are these now if religion is about practice rather than belief? Why still call them 'truths'? Because when all is said and done Armstrong is holding on to something of the usual referent of the word 'belief'. Thus:

> *Skilled practice in these disciplines ['yoga, prayer, liturgy and a consistently compassionate lifestyle'] can lead to intimations of the transcendence we call God, Nirvana, Brahman or Dao. Without such dedicated practice, these concepts remain incoherent, incredible and even absurd.*

> Practices, then, lead to 'intimations' of the transcendence we call God. But this latter, this transcendence, isn't itself a practice, and the affirmation that it is some sort of reality looks, willy-nilly, like involving belief. Likewise here:

> *When a mythical narrative was symbolically re-enacted, it brought to light within the practitioner something 'true' about human life and the way our humanity worked, even if its insights, like those of art, could not be proven rationally.*

Something true about human life that is called an 'insight' just does bring back beliefs about the world, however dependent these might be, for their acquisition, upon practices.

Armstrong's is a form of special pleading. No one would buy it were they to be told about the practices of dusting, roller-skating and blogging that these yield special insights which can't be expressed and rationally defended as propositions within a system of beliefs. (http://normblog.typepad.com/normblog/2009/07/id-have-baked-one.html)

Notice how Norm takes no cheap shots. There are no jokes about Armstrong being an ex-nun or criticisms of her other writings, deserving of criticism though they are. The argument in front of him is all that matters. Notice, too, how he takes the reader through the distinction between practices and truths, and allows us to grasp a complicated idea through the clarity of the writing. Observe finally, that Norm's avoidance of polemical bitterness and his observance of the normal rules of polite debate does Ms Armstrong no good: she still ends up in pieces on the floor.

In this as in so much of his writing, he is muscular without being intimidating, forthright without being insulting. He speaks to his readers as intellectual equals, and although, alas, we rarely are his intellectual equals we are flattered into a better understanding of the struggles of our time.

As Sam Peckinpah nearly said, 'Keep going!'

Note

1 All quotes and comments attributed to Norman Geras can be found in *normblog*, http://normblog.typepad.com/normblog/.

4

Socialism or barbarism: Marxism and the Holocaust

Philip Spencer

The twentieth century witnessed an explosion of state-organized violence against entirely innocent civilians that is so overwhelming it can sometimes be hard to believe. The political scientist R.J. Rummel has estimated that what he calls 'democide', the killing of citizens by governments, runs to some 260 million, a figure he himself found hard to credit (Rummel, 1994). As he points out, 'just to give perspective on this incredible murder by government, if all these bodies were laid head to toe, with the average height being 5 feet, then they would circle the earth 10 times'.[1]

In the midst of this catalogue of catastrophe lies an event that, in the eyes of a number of social theorists, has been understood as a pivotal turning point. The attempt by the Nazis to annihilate the Jews has seemed to stand out as a point at which something fundamental shifted, some boundary was crossed. For Jürgen Habermas, for instance, 'something happened there that up to now nobody considered as even possible. There one touched upon something which represents the deep layer of solidarity among all that wears a human face; notwithstanding all the usual acts of beastliness of human history, the integrity of this common layer had been taken for granted ... Auschwitz has changed the basis for the continuity of the conditions of life within history' (Morgan, 2001: 281). From a very different perspective, the French postmodernist Philippe Lacoue-Labarthe has identified it as a 'caesura ... which, within history, interrupts history and opens up another possibility, or else closes off all possibility of history' (Milchman and Rosenberg, 1996: 10). Whilst Hannah Arendt insisted that the extermination camps had 'exploded our traditional categories of political thought and the standards of our moral judgement in every area' (Arendt, 1994: 403).

But among the many voices that have sought to come to terms with what happened in the middle of the twentieth century to the Jews, there is one striking absence. There has been almost nothing from historical materialists. This silence is striking because it is surely one of the defining characteristics of Marxism that it attends to transformative moments in the history of humanity. Marxists have written not just about tectonic shifts in social and economic structures, such as the move from feudalism to capitalism, but also about major political events that have (of course not unrelatedly) changed the world, such as the French or Russian Revolutions. But there has been almost no Marxist response to the Holocaust. In his essay on this question, Geras identifies only a brief, albeit very striking, comment by Trotsky, and a couple of pieces by Ernest Mandel. It is true that we now have Enzo Traverso's valuable work, although again this is more in the form of essays on particular themes (Traverso, 1999; 2003). But beyond that we have almost nothing to go on, before, during, or after the event.

This silence has been more than a theoretical one; it has also been political. As the Nazi persecution of the Jews gathered momentum in the 1930s, the response of both the social democratic and the communist parties was feeble and evasive. Until *Die Rote Fahne* headlined a protest against *Kristallnacht* in November 1938, what was happening to the Jews was not a priority for the party, and it did not remain one. According to Jeffrey Herf, 'the persecution of the Jews ... played only a minor role in communist thinking about the resistance' (Herf, 1994: 262). The German socialists, as David Bankier (2000) has shown,[2] never mounted any direct action against Nazi anti-Semitism from the outset; its leadership systematically refused to give any direction to party members (Niewyk, 1971); and there is no evidence of any illegal material being produced or smuggled into Germany on anti-Semitism. After the event, the German communists, now in power, swiftly suppressed those few who wished to raise the question of the Holocaust and its historical significance. The one leading figure, Paul Merker, who made any serious effort to think about what had happened to the Jews was marginalized and then arrested (on a trumped-up charge as a supposed American agent) and jailed for eight years (Herf, 1999). The social democrats of course abandoned Marxism entirely at the end of the 1950s, eliminating any possibility of a coherent Marxist political reflection from that quarter.

Some obvious questions arise at this point. *Can* Marxists have anything meaningful to say about this event? What kind of approach to history do we have here, if historical materialists cannot register the significance of an event of such magnitude? What kind of radical politics is it that cannot respond to an almost successful attempt to eliminate a whole group of people from off the face of the earth, and cannot think after the event about what this might have meant?

I do not pretend to provide here a comprehensive answer to such questions, but rather to look for sources within the Marxist tradition that might enable a more meaningful response. In particular, I want to argue that in the work and to some extent the life and fate of Rosa Luxemburg, the subject of one of Geras's early works (1976), there lie the seeds of a better understanding for Marxists of what was involved in the Holocaust, and of at least part of an explanation of how it came to pass; and that this has implications for how Marxists might think more seriously about what can be done in the face of genocide more generally.

My starting point is the old socialist phrase – 'socialism or barbarism'. Many today would object, of course, to any use of the term 'barbarism', as a merely pejorative expression of hypocritical Eurocentric values. It has been argued that it has been repeatedly deployed especially by Western powers to denigrate the culture of the 'other', to justify exploitation and slaughter (Salter, 2002).[3] More recent histories of its usage, however, suggest an altogether more complex picture. Roger Pol-Droit (2007) in particular has deconstructed very different usages over time, with many cases in which those identified as barbarians have been seen to hold virtues that civilized societies have forgotten. Value-laden projections clearly cut both ways.

It is also a term whose application has been particularly hotly disputed in relation to the Holocaust, where some have argued that it is a fundamental error to see it in terms of a regression from civilization. The main proponent of this thesis in recent years has been Zygmunt Bauman (1989), who argues that what he calls 'the morally elevating story of humanity emerging from pre-social barbarity' is a myth which obscures how central features of this same civilization contributed to the Holocaust. There is an obvious difficulty with Bauman's essentially Weberian approach (which would not, rightly or wrongly, commend itself as such to historical materialists). As Yehuda Bauer (2003) has pointed out, it cannot account easily for the fact that not all civilized societies have committed genocide.

But, in any event, the term 'barbarism' is not one that the founders of Marxism found they could do without. As heirs to the Enlightenment, as moralists, despite their own denials (whose implausibility Geras [1985] has also highlighted), Marx and Engels were committed to a conception of a future for humanity in which people would live side by side in peace and justice; but they were also aware that there were other possibilities, states of existence which were its very opposite. The contrast between socialism and barbarism was fundamental: there is a profound sense in which barbarism was, for them, the opposite of socialism, conceived of as the highest stage of civilization.

This is not to say that they always used the term 'barbarism' consistently. In one usage (Engels, 1970: 206–9), drawing on the work of the anthropologist Lewis Henry Morgan, they used it to refer to an earlier stage of history held to have occurred (at different levels – 'lower', 'middle', and 'higher') somewhere between savagery and civilization. In another sense, however, barbarism is used by them to refer to particularly brutal aspects of contemporary, capitalist society, which clash with that society's self-image. Here (Marx & Engels, 1976a: 196) they cite the utopian socialist Charles Fourier, who argued that barbarism is not confined to some far-off, distant past, but is very much present within what passes for civilization itself.[4] A third meaning has to do with a possible outcome of class struggles, not only that apparently between capital and labour but other, earlier ones. Here the struggle does not yield an unambiguous victor; the two sides rather pull each other down to a state of mutual ruin (Marx and Engels, 1976b: 484). Yet a fourth reference is to barbarism as a state to which society can regress, in moments of crisis (Marx and Engels, 1976b: 490).[5]

It is this latter, most radical formulation which is Rosa Luxemburg's starting point for some reflections which provide, I want to argue, the basis of a Marxist approach to this question. They are to be found in a remarkable document, the *Junius Pamphlet*, which she wrote in prison during the First World War. Geras quotes from this pamphlet at some length, as it happens, in his own book on Luxemburg, and so shall I, although for different purposes:

> Friedrich Engels once said: 'Capitalist society faces a dilemma, either an advance to socialism or a reversion to barbarism'. What does a 'reversion to barbarism' mean at the present stage of European civili-

sation? We have read and repeated these words thoughtlessly without a conception of their terrible import. At this moment one glance about us will show us what a reversion to barbarism in capitalist society means. *This world war* means a reversion to barbarism. The triumph of imperialism leads to the destruction of culture, sporadically during a modern war, and forever, if the period of world wars that has just begun is allowed to take its damnable course to the last ultimate consequence. Thus we stand today, as Friedrich Engels prophesied more than a generation ago, before the awful proposition: the destruction of all culture and, as in ancient Rome, depopulation, desolation, degeneration, a vast cemetery; or the victory of socialism, that is, the conscious struggle of the international proletariat against imperialism, against its methods, against war. This is the dilemma of world history, its inevitable choice, whose scales are trembling in the balance. (Luxemburg, 1970a: 269; emphasis in the original)

Luxemburg does not use the term 'barbarism' casually at all here. Barbarism, as she understands it in this text, has five quite specific elements: the destruction of culture, depopulation, desolation, degeneration, and the construction of a vast cemetery. And she accompanies this depiction of the menace it already provides with an ominous warning – that things might get even worse, if this world war is followed by another.

And of course it was. The second war was considerably more destructive than the first, and at its epicentre lay a particular and immense explosion of violence, of a state against a whole people, the Jews. In fact, if we look again at this extraordinary passage, the terms that Luxemburg uses seem to apply rather more directly, much more precisely, to what happened then than to what she saw around her in 1915.

Consider, firstly, the Nazi onslaught on what they deemed 'degenerate' culture – for instance the burning of books or the censorship of art and music. If this was not an attack on culture *tout court*, it was certainly on all culture associated with the Jews.[6]

Consider, secondly, the radical depopulation of whole villages, towns and countries, as Jews were violently removed by the Nazis from where they had lived for centuries, either by killing on the spot or by transportation first into mass ghettoes and then to the extermination camps.

Consider, thirdly, the desolation of the Jews in the face of this onslaught, a desolation which almost precisely matches the definition of the term by the *Oxford English Dictionary* as 'without means; destitute of inhabitants, uninhabited, deserted … laid waste … forlorn, disconsolate, wretched … abandoned'.

Consider, fourthly, as a deeply shocking instance of degeneration, the extraordinary inversion of morality by the Nazis as they planned and justified their attempt to annihilate the Jews. Recall the extraordinary speech given by Himmler in 1943 before high-ranking SS officers, in which he openly and proudly acknowledged the nature of the crime being committed: 'the hard decision … that this people should be caused to disappear from the earth … we have taken the responsibility for it on ourselves – the responsibility for an act not just an idea'. Indeed, he made a virtue out of it, as 'a glorious page in our history' (if one that could not be written). This was, as Berel Lang (2003) and Saul Friedländer (1993) in particular have argued, a consciously chosen, deliberate embrace of what was known to be fundamentally wrong, if not of evil itself.

And consider, fifthly, the vast cemetery into which the Nazis turned so many sites in Eastern Europe, a cemetery this time without markers, as they sought to eliminate almost all trace of their victims, first systematically turning corpses into ashes, then trying to burn those previously buried in unmarked mass graves in an effort to cover up the crime.

We may perhaps put it, starkly, like this. If this was not barbarism, what would count? Was not this combination – of the destruction of culture, of the depopulation of whole areas, of the almost unimaginable desolation of the Jews in the ghettos, the transits and the camps, of the inversion of morality – was not this barbarism?

I do not want to suggest there that Luxemburg was possessed of uncanny abilities, that she was a clairvoyant of any kind. But there is nevertheless something striking about her definition of barbarism and its applicability to the Holocaust that promotes some further questioning.

Was this, to begin with, a merely literary achievement, a fine piece of writing which just seems to fit, as one might want to use a poem or a quotation at the beginning of a book? There seems more to it than this, some more profound sources of intuition of the kind that Geras has himself seen in Trotsky's own remarkable prediction in 1938 that 'the next development of world reaction signifies with certainty the physical extermination of the Jews' (Trotsky in Geras, 1998: 139). Geras suggests this had to do not just with Trotsky's profound understanding of fascism but also with a deeper 'human sensibility', an ability to see into the depths of human destructiveness. In Luxemburg's case, I want to suggest we have a similar and arguably rather more concrete, more developed, understanding, for reasons that have to do with Luxemburg's life and even her death.

For Luxemburg was herself directly confronted by enemies who were to be closely connected to the architects of the Holocaust. Those who hunted down and killed her were drawn from the ranks of the anti-Semitic, anti-Marxist far right. The forces mobilized in Germany in 1919 to put down the revolutionary threat from the left were the nucleus in important ways of Nazism. This was not only a matter of personnel, the fact that, as Hannah Arendt noted, her 'murderers were members of the ultra-nationalist and officially illegal *Freikorps*, a paramilitary organisation from which Hitler's storm troopers were to recruit their most promising killers' (Arendt, 1968: 35). It was also a matter of ideology.

Before 1914, anti-Semitism had become what Geoff Eley (1997: 125) has called a 'vital sub-plot' in the coalescence of old and new elements on the German right. Between 1917 and 1919 this anti-Semitic element became more virulent and unrestrained, providing the 'vocabulary of counter-revolutionary desperation'. Rage and resentment focused on a particular ideological amalgam, an imagined internationalist republican Marxist conspiracy led (supposedly) by Jews, almost perfectly personified by Luxemburg. What the Nazis were able to provide for such elements was less a new ideology than an effective way of organizing what had hitherto been fractured groupings. The ideological matrix within which this counter-revolutionary right operated did not fundamentally alter.

Now it is undoubtedly the case that anti-Semitism was not a pressing concern for Luxemburg. She could indeed be, as Geras has reminded us, particularly dismissive of those who sought to alert her to this issue.[7] Could she have continued to be so as a radical anti-Semitism emerged as the core, central element to the political project of the Nazis? There is, obviously, no certain answer to this question. Some revolutionaries, who perceived themselves as having broken with any Jewish identification, did go to their deaths refusing to recognize the centrality of anti-Semitism to the Nazi project; others did not.

But what we can say surely is that Luxemburg understood something profoundly important about what was at stake in the struggle with such forces. She understood in particular that masses of people can be mobilized one way or another, for diametrically opposed purposes. In her writing about the First World War, there is a graphic depiction of what happens when a toxic nationalist ideology overwhelms socialist beliefs, how large numbers of workers were mobilized by an ideology of hatred to engage in what became quite quickly a mass slaughter of denigrated others.

This was an historic defeat for socialism but not quite yet a terminal one. Going to (world) war was one thing; winning it, another. Germany's subsequent defeat, for a brief moment, seemed to vindicate those who had opposed the world war from the outset, to give an opportunity to renew the movement for socialism. The faltering of this project, the divisions on the left, which allowed the reactionary right to regroup and ultimately to wreak its revenge, are well known. But the hatred that lay behind this revenge was even greater than before. The conclusion drawn from Germany's defeat was that the only way to ensure victory next time was to become radically more violent and murderous. The mass killings perpetrated then, not just by the SS or the *Einsatzgruppen*[8] but in collusion with and by the German army, were justified to a large extent in these terms, as Omer Bartov has argued. 'Repeatedly exhorted to remember that this was a war of ideologies aimed at exterminating the Judeo-Bolshevik enemy who had caused the collapse of 1918 ... the troops came to view their criminal actions ... as exacting a just and necessary retribution for past defeats and humiliations and thereby ensuring the final victory ... to portray mass killing of civilians as a glorious and final reckoning with foes who had been poised to inflict untold barbarities on the German *Volk*' (Bartov, 2000: 28).

But these troops were not the Nazi elite. They were soldiers recruited from the German population, including the German working class. The Nazis had been able to mobilize large numbers of ordinary people to kill without restraint. This is of course a huge problem, which has (somewhat surprisingly), only come to exercise historians of the Holocaust relatively recently (Matthäus, 2005: 206),[9] since the publication in particular of Christopher's Browning's (1992) study of Reserve Police Battalion 101 and of Daniel Goldhagen's (1997) *Hitler's Willing Executioners*, which (amongst other things) looks at the same evidence but draws radically different conclusions. The debate turns in some ways on what noun to affix to the adjective here – were these 'ordinary men' (as Browning insists) or rather 'ordinary Germans' (Goldhagen's conviction)? But the noun that needs to concern Marxists is neither of (or not only) these. The question that Marxists have to answer is: how is it possible for *workers* to engage in genocide?

I want to suggest here that Luxemburg's treatment of the idea of barbarism, counterposed to socialism, can provide us with some elements of an answer to this question. There was, immediately after the Nazi take-over of power, a violent assault on the organized left: political parties were banned and mass arrests made, creating what Detlev Peukert calls a 'terror-induced split between the activists and the politically passive proletarian community' (Peukert, 1991: 41). Even those activists who might have been willing or able to resist were overwhelmed (Gellately, 2001: 14). At best, there was audible resistance until about 1935–36, but ruthless persecution of those involved made its continuation impossible (Lüdtke, 1999: 158). As Allan Merson, who generally takes the most optimistic reading of the extent of communist resistance, notes, 'by 1935 a large part of the original mass membership was either dead, imprisoned or in exile' (Merson, 1985: 305).

The German working class had suffered a defeat on a far greater scale than that of 1914 which, in Luxemburg's view, had opened the way to barbarism. The question is what happened *after* a defeat of this kind. The Nazis were now able to mobilize those who had or might have previously been mobilized by the left. They had now been subjected to Nazi rule for several years. In that time Nazi ideology and indoctrination had wrought its effect on those workers. They were in some sense not the people they had been or, in the case of younger workers, not the people they might have been. The cumulative effect in Germany between 1933 and 1941 of persistent, increasingly radical anti-Semitism had brought them to a point at which they could well have *become* 'willing executioners' in the absence of any plausible, coherent political alternative. No worker could reasonably have believed by 1941 that the regime could be overthrown from within, let alone that any kind of socialist revolution could take place. Collective, organized, politically conscious resistance by workers was impossible by then. No alternative socialist vision of society could now be articulated inside Germany; no agency could meaningfully be identified that could bring it about. Socialist ideas would have appeared to have almost no purchase on reality at all.

The Nazi project, by contrast, might have seemed to have a vibrant future. Not only had it delivered full employment, the war in its initial stages went better than anyone could have dreamed. Even when casualties began to mount, it would still have seemed invincible; there would, moreover, have been extensive opportunities for promotion (Bartov, 1994: 61). Now, after any kind of socialist prospects had been eliminated for the foreseeable future, workers could be recruited for a project which *was* radically anti-Semitic, to the point of genocide. This other project indeed *required* their mobilization. Without it, the full implementation of barbarism would have been impossible. Killing on the scale that was to be imagined, planned and executed had after all, in the end, to involve very large numbers of people,[10] many of whom must have been workers. But this mobilization was of a qualitatively different kind to that called for by socialism, in either its reformist or revolutionary version. They had been remobilized, not as a universal class but as a mass, to form a very different kind of collective, a *Volksgemeinschaft*,[11] which could then in turn take a military and truly murderous form, a *Kampfsgemeinschaft.*

How much of this Luxemburg herself could predict is perhaps then neither here nor there. What I have tried to suggest rather is that her depiction of barbarism may not be merely rhetorical. It is not just that the terms she uses to define barbarism are quite precise. It is also that her understanding of barbarism comes out of a sense of what might ensue if the struggle for the self-emancipatory socialism in which she believed was defeated.[12] (I say nothing here about alternative conceptions of socialism which are not grounded in notions of such freedom.) And such a defeat was not only possible but real, its catastrophic implications involving the transformation of even workers into agents of barbarism, into genocidal killers.

Thinking along these Luxemburgist lines does not of course provide a complete explanation for what ensued by any means. There are many aspects of even this partial and limited explanation which require filling out and correcting in both detail and substance. And in any event it only takes us so far, to a point at which even Luxemburg's version of Marxism necessarily falters. Once we enter (theoretically, that is) into the world of the extermination camps, it is reasonably obvious that serious problems arise there for anyone wishing to hold fast to Marxism. It is not at all clear, for example, what the dynamic of this (not so micro) society could have been, in the long run. Even allowing for the presence within this society of some appallingly exploitative industrial sites in which Jews were used as dispensable slave labour by impeccably capitalist firms like IG Farben (Allen, 2002), it is clear that its major function was not the production of commodities. It was rather a factory system in which the central product was death itself. To use Marxist terminology, we need to analyse it not as a mode of production but a mode of destruction. The tools we need for analysing such destructiveness cannot easily be found within a theory which assumes the existence and need for a surplus to be produced and distributed in different ways. Even if we recast our focus to consider the society of the camps within a wider totality, which remained capitalist to some considerable degree, we would probably begin to run aground quite quickly on the rocks of the irrationality of the determination of the Nazis to continue to prioritize killing Jews over anything else as the war was being lost.

But there is one other question which also arises and which, with the repeated recurrence of genocide since the Holocaust, remains a pressing concern. This is the question of how exactly it is possible to move out of such a state, to escape from barbarism once it has been established. If it is the case that those who had previously opposed the regime have been decimated; if opposing organizations have been destroyed; if their leaders have been killed or imprisoned; if their followers have been recruited for a diametrically opposed project, that of genocide itself: what hope can there be for change coming from within?

This question is, of course, not merely historical. It applies not only to the Holocaust but to subsequent genocides, of which there have been all too many since that catastrophe. Different though they may be the one from the other in certain respects, they share these characteristics in common, that the state is able to mobilize large numbers of people to kill whole groups of their fellow citizens. To name only a few – Ibos in Biafra (1966–69); Guayaki Ache Indians in Paraguay (1974); Kurds in Iraq (1987); Tutsis in Rwanda (1994); Muslims in Bosnia (1992 and 1995); Albanians in Kosovo in 1998–99; Black Africans in Darfur since 2003. In each case (and there are arguably many more [Rittner et al., 2002; Mazower, 2002]) those targeted for killing have no effective recourse internally. Opposition to what the state is now bent on has been eliminated earlier; alternative political projects command no significant internal support.

I do not mean to suggest here that in each case there had been an earlier struggle between socialist and counter-revolutionary forces, as was the case in Germany. More depressingly, perhaps, most if not all of the time, no socialist project of any recognizable kind had been on the agenda at all. In this sense we live in a radically different epoch. But what does need thinking about on the left is how to respond when the internal possibilities for resistance, for an alternative in the foreseeable future, have been eliminated.

Clearly, at this point, a central Marxist premise has been removed, one in many ways at the core of Marx's and also Luxemburg's conception of socialism, the notion of *self*-emancipation. What is needed now is rescue from without, intervention from outside the society to save the lives of those threatened with annihilation. But note that what we are talking about at this point is not emancipation in the classic Marxist sense but rescue, which is something much more basic: safety and survival, not a grander more ambitious project of creating a radically different kind of society to anything that has gone before. Those faced with annihilation need to be kept alive before they can even begin to think about reordering the world. The removal of the threat of annihilation, taking away the power of those with the capacity and intention to kill them (all, in the case of the Jews) is a precondition for emancipation in the sense in which Marx and Luxemburg understood this term. This is not in any way to minimize the significance of such a step. It is, clearly, of the most critical importance, a matter literally of life and death right now for millions of people. At best, it puts them back, as survivors, in a position in which and only in which they may begin again to consider and to organize for more far-reaching alternatives. In that position, they may (indeed are very likely to) find themselves again exploited and oppressed in various ways, some of which may very well also be deadly, particularly if we think of the second Marxist definition (above) of barbarism as referring to aspects of barbarism which are continually present in class societies. But this position (survival) nevertheless leaves open the possibility of self-emancipation.

But that survival, once genocide has begun, can only be safeguarded by intervention from outside. It cannot be achieved from within, by those under sentence of death themselves, at least not in significant numbers. This is a very difficult thing for Marxists to contemplate, especially as was the case in the Holocaust, when the agent of rescue was not any kind of socialist force (at least as

Luxemburg would have understood it) but something else – the Allied states of liberal capitalist America and Britain, and the Stalinist regime in the East. This is not of course, tragically, the only such case. The same considerations would apply, to give only a few examples, to the Bengalis in East Pakistan (liberated in 1967 from without by the Indian capitalist state), to the Cambodians (liberated from without by the Stalinist regime of North Vietnam), and to the Kurds in Iraq (liberated from without by the United States, albeit in two stages). Contemplating such instances of rescue requires Marxists to accept that there is, actually, a worse (genocidal) state of things even than capitalism or other forms of class exploitation. Liberation from a genocidal state is an imperative that takes priority over even the imperative of self-emancipation. This raises the question perhaps of whether Marxists need to rethink the concept of emancipation itself, either to include this other, more pressing element as a form of emancipation or to distinguish it more clearly from self-emancipation, perhaps as 'liberation' rather than emancipation.

But this is a consequence of the reality of barbarism. Barbarism (in the form of genocide) changes everything, at least for the time being. As the absolute opposite of socialism, right at the other end of the spectrum, it creates a very different set of imperatives. There are times when even the most radical socialist has to contemplate such realities, as Geras has elsewhere himself compellingly argued (Geras, 1998)[13]. Indeed, radical thinking surely requires the ability to focus unflinchingly on such possibilities, on what Luxemburg described as the 'terrible import' of the concept of barbarism.

What happens to the prospects for socialism *after* barbarism is not easy to think about. It may be that there has to be quite a long period of recovery, whilst the social forces that can fight again for a socialist society are rebuilt, that at some fundamental level social confidence has to be restored, belief in a common humanity revived after an experience that is deeply demoralizing. It may be, conversely, that some people could be even more motivated than before to fight for socialism, although we should be under no illusions that suffering (especially on such scale) is necessarily or inherently ennobling.[14] What is clear is that a failure to understand and accept what barbarism is and what it does to all those involved, not just to the victims but to those who have been remobilized as perpetrators, does not make the argument for socialism more convincing, but rather the reverse. After more than a century of extreme state-sponsored violence, in which Luxemburg's fears appear to have been borne out (more than once), perhaps it is time for Marxists to take more seriously the alternatives that she laid out with such clarity and prescience. The struggle for socialism, as she understood it, mobilizes forces around a radical vision for a more just, egalitarian, radical democracy in which people are free to develop themselves to their fullest potential. If that struggle is defeated, if not terminally then for a generation or for an epoch, by forces mobilized for a radically opposed vision of society, by forces driven by hatred, rage, and a desire for revenge, then a very different prospect opens up. That prospect is barbarism – the dehumanization and systematic murder of millions. It is the prospect of genocide.

Notes

1 www.hawaii.edu/powerkills/NOTE1.HTM (accessed 17 May 2009).

2 Bankier argues that the party's attitude was a compound of distrust of Jews, resentment, and fear that it would be over-identified with or even as Jews, and that there was also an element of overt anti-Semitism to be found amongst some of its own membership at all levels.

3 All too conveniently, Salter focuses exclusively on the history of the West and traces the term only back as far as the Greeks, whose complex uses of the term he grossly simplifies.

4 Where they quote Fourier's assertion that the 'civilised world raises every vice that barbarism practises in a simple form to a compound, equivocal, ambiguous'. Or, as Marx himself puts it, 'barbarism is created in the lap of civilisation itself' (Marx and Engels, 1976a: 434).

5 'Society suddenly finds itself put back into a state of momentary barbarism.'

6 They did of course promote what they called authentic German culture, although its products were entirely mediocre and superficial, what Herman Glaser (1978) calls 'culture as façade'.

7 See the rather sharp retort to her friend Mathilde Wurm, 'what do you want with this particular suffering of the Jews' reported (and reproved) by Geras (1998: 168–9).

8 The *Einsatzgruppen* were mobile killing units sent in behind to shoot Jews (men, then women, children, and babies too) and other designated racial enemies in astonishing numbers. See, amongst others, Langerbein (2004), who provides some very disturbing evidence about the educational and class background of their leaders.

9 According to Jürgen Matthäus (2005: 206), 'Browning's book ... put

the problem of perpetrator motivation where it had never been before: at the top of the historiographic agenda'.

10 There are varying estimates. Goldhagen (1997) argues that the numbers involved, one way or another, may have been as high as 800,000. Berger (1998) puts it about half a million.

11 The *Volksgemeinschaft* was the Nazi ideal of a racialized national community. The *Kampfgemeinschaft* was the militarized version, a community of soldiers.

12 My own view, for what it is worth, is in line with Luxemburg's, that socialism cannot exist without freedom and the exercise of an active radical democracy, underpinned but not restricted by a substantive egalitarianism, in economic and social terms as well as political ones. Whilst this undoubtedly begs very many questions, particularly about the institutional mechanisms needed to protect and nourish these and to resolve the tensions between them, I have not myself found the socialist ideal much better expressed than in Luxemburg's essay on the Russian Revolution. She praised the Bolsheviks (highly) for their courage in daring to 'pose the problem' of socialism, even if they could not solve it. But she insisted that socialism requires full participation ('the mass of the people must take part in it') by free, self-determining individuals, each with their own ideas. 'Freedom is always and exclusively freedom for the one who thinks differently ... socialism by its very nature cannot be decreed ... New territory. A thousand problems. Only experience is capable of correcting and opening new ways. Only unobstructed, effervescing life falls into a thousand new forms and improvisations, brings to life creative force itself, itself corrects all mistaken attempts' (Luxemburg, 1970b: 391).

13 In, for example, his essay on 'Socialist Hope in the Shadow of Catastrophe' (in Geras 1998) but also more generally in much of his 'blogging' about genocide in the context of debates about the Iraq War.

14 But the creation of, for example, the Ghetto Fighters kibbutz in Israel, founded by members of the Jewish underground, partisans and Holocaust survivors, may be a good example.

5

What is it like to be a blogger?

Ophelia Benson

Hume famously observed that it is not contrary to reason to prefer the destruction of the whole world to the scratching of his finger. He wasn't expressing a whimsically inflated sense of his own importance, but pointing out that logic doesn't determine how we weigh the world versus our finger. We have to love the world in order to be able to weigh it properly. Looking it up in a table of weights and measures won't do the job – we could see the arithmetic and still shrug and say yes but it's *my* finger, the world is none of mine and I don't care. We have to care in order to make choices properly – to make them in such a way that we don't place our own petty desires above everyone else's deepest needs. (We have been learning lately, if we didn't already know, that bankers and investment wizards could use some intensive training in this.) Morality is rooted in feeling, Hume told us, and researchers such as Antonio Damasio and Jonathan Haidt have been elaborating on the idea recently.

To be moral we need feeling, we need the right kind of feeling, we need educated feeling – we need to do what Martha Nussbaum called 'cultivating humanity'. It is arguable (and many people have argued) that the education of the feelings, and in particular sympathy, is one thing that literature and story-telling can do better than anything else. Numbers, by themselves, don't tell us enough; '100,000 women raped and killed' has less force than a pain in our own finger; but a story about one woman raped and killed can turn us inside out. In a world where '100,000 women raped and killed' is no invented paradigm but a brute fact, along with row upon row of similar facts, clearly anything that can help to cultivate sympathy and empathy is of the highest value.

The primatologist Frans de Waal notes in *Our Inner Ape* (2005), citing research on children and empathy by Carolyn Zahn-Waxler, that empathy precedes language. Zahn-Waxler has found that children a little over the age of one year respond to feigned sadness, pain, or distress in family members, and attempt to comfort them. Cognition and feeling mix, and the mixing is all important. Few animals can do it, even a little, as de Waal observes:

> All scientists who've set out to find consolation in monkeys have come up empty-handed ... Monkeys fail to provide reassurance even if their own offspring has been bitten. They do protect them, but show none of the cuddling and stroking with which an ape mother calms down an upset youngster. (de Waal, 2005: 193)

Monkeys, it appears, are more like the autistic narrator of Mark Haddon's novel *The Curious Incident of the Dog in the Night-time* (2003), who describes human anguish as one might describe a cloud-burst.

> And then Mother said, 'Oh my God.'
>
> And then she didn't say anything for a long while. And then she made a loud wailing noise like an animal on a nature programme on television.
>
> And I didn't like her doing this because it was a loud noise, and I said, 'Why are you doing that?' (Haddon, 2003: 236)

Empathy is all-important (yet, de Waal notes, until very recently scientists lumped it 'with telepathy and other supernatural phenomena' (de Waal, 2005: 181)) and anything which promotes and strengthens and expands it is of the greatest importance. The haunting final book of *The Iliad* illustrates this, when Priam begs Achilles to remember his own father and in doing that to pity Priam's grief for his own son – and it works: Achilles consents to let Priam retrieve Hector's body, and the two of them mourn together.

Literature and the liberal arts have long been seen as one way, or *the* way, to cultivate these capabilities – to awaken and foster what the eighteenth century called 'sensibility'. Hardness and indifference were thought to be incompatible with a taste for Cowper. That is far too easy, of course; we know all about the cultivated slave-owner or colonial administrator or Nazi officer who read Aeschylus or Goethe in the morning and had someone whipped in the afternoon. But the effect needn't be as reliable as a prescription to be real. In a world where lapses into brutality seem to beckon on every corner, *anything* that gives people experience of empathy and compassion must be of value.

Story-telling is not the only thing literature can do, however, and literature is not the only source of story-telling. Movies and television are full of stories (though often ones that convey the thrill of violence and leave suffering and empathy out of the picture). Journalism relies heavily on stories to build a bridge between '100,000 raped and killed', and felt human misery. Parallel to journalism, another rich source of an inward, subjective view of human experience and suffering is the personal diary. It is a great pity that Western literature took so long to come up with the idea – wouldn't we love to have a diary of Euripides, Augustus, Shakespeare, of merchants, soldiers, farmers going back many centuries? Historical novelists have been inventing some, but how we would love to have the real thing.

We don't have the real thing going far back in time, but we do have a new abundance of contemporary diaries in the form of blogs: they travel only a few years back in time but they reach out widely in space. Blogs can't tell us anything directly about the inner life of a victim of the Inquisition or the Black Death or a sixth-century invasion, but they can tell us a lot about the inner life of someone in Khartoum or Baghdad or Peshawar right now.

There is a lot of journalistic condescension towards the genre, which is perhaps inevitable between the paid and the unpaid, but it overlooks the usefulness (to put it crudely) of this new window.

Many writers prefer the formal, finished, professional, impersonal work to the loose unbuttoned conversational essay or diary. None but a fool ever writes except for money, Samuel Johnson said with characteristic bluntness, and his young friend Boswell *was* a bit of a fool, artlessly filling his diary with his furtive sexual bargains, his toadying, his dreams of glory. But how fortunate for us that he did. Another way of looking at the blog is that it is not merely a slovenly intrusion on the guild, but a vast sample of our contemporaries' inner lives of a kind that no one has had before.

One of many recurring themes on Norm Geras's blog is the myopia of critics of the genre – the genre as such rather than particular instantiations of it – who focus on potential or actual flaws while ignoring potential and actual virtues. Of course, a genre with no barriers and no editors is just that – but boring, badly written self-obsession is not the only outcome. It turns out not to be true that none but a fool ever writes except for money.

But we already knew that. Pepys wasn't paid to write his diary, nor was Kilvert paid to write his, nor was Keats paid to write his letters. What of it? They are now valued a good deal more highly than any number of salaried works.

The flaw in Johnson's dismissal is that not everything worth saying can command a market. Voluntary writing, writing done for its own sake, *may* be mere self-indulgence, or incompetent, or of interest to no one but the author, but that is not the only possible outcome. The great advantage of voluntary writing is freedom from other people's agendas and constraints, and some people – many people, in fact – make good use of that freedom.

Just for one thing, paid commissioned writing has a pre-determined size and shape, which conform to existing conventions – the short article, the long article, the story, the novel. There is little if any market for a single paragraph – but it is perfectly possible to have an interesting single paragraph to say. There is no law of nature that says a single paragraph is inherently too small to bother with; it is just not a publishing convention. (The *New Yorker*'s 'Talk of the Town' is one home of the very short piece, but that's an exiguous niche.) Weblogs (to give them their full baptismal name) offer a capacious platform for brief observations, thoughts, overheard remarks; they make it possible to think, dreamily, that nothing is lost.

They also offer a platform for long pieces, and middle-sized ones, and any combination of short and long and medium one chooses. The weblog is, in short, a new literary genre, a new branch of the liberal arts – an expansive, flexible, always-evolving, shape-shifting, liberating genre. It is like the novel in this. The novel has always been the antithesis of Aristotelian rules governing dramatic unities – capable of jumping from continent to continent, from century to century, from narrative to reflection to dialogue, with an involved author or a distant one. Blogs have the same ability to make their own rules on the fly.

In that sense blogs have a kind of natural alliance with human rights. It is *possible* for conservatives and theocrats hostile to the concept of human rights to be bloggers, but the fit is inherently uneasy. The two endeavours fight each other. Blogging is an undeferential activity, so a deferential mindset or an authoritarian one will feel out of place practising it. This intuition is backed up by the fact that authoritarian regimes make a habit of arresting bloggers – China, Saudi Arabia, Iran, Egypt, Burma to name a few.

Norm Geras's blog fits into this situation as a key fits a lock, by being just the kind of blog that authoritarians fear most, because it is everything that the authoritarian mind is not: broad, curious, reasonable, argumentative, inquiring, thoughtful, ironic, secular, and adamant about the importance of human rights. It is in short a conspicuously liberal blog, and this in more than one way, yet the ways are interconnected.

It is liberal in the obvious sense in that it is very often focused on issues to do with human rights, interventionism, tyranny and what to do about it, international law and justice, war crimes, universalism, and the like. But it is also liberal in the way it approaches such issues: via measured argument as opposed to vituperation and misrepresentation, and via open unfettered inquiry rather than by peremptory demands for conformity or silence. And in the broadest and most basic sense it is liberal in the breadth of its interests. Along with discussing liberal politics it also converses about the liberal arts – literature, jazz, cricket, films, popular music.

Cricket at first blush may seem to have nothing to do with human rights (although in fact authoritarian terrorists have recently been targeting, precisely, international cricket matches), but games and recreation and play are part of an expansive rights-based conception of human beings. Other ideas conceive of humans as tools or slaves or disobedient subjects, whose pains and pleasures don't register on the tyrant's meter. A universalist egalitarian liberal picture of our species empathizes with and relishes its pleasures, its achievements, its works of art, whether the poem, the film, the well-played match, the song.

To put it another way, a somewhat therapeutic way: it seems plausible that fostering an enthusiasm for a variety of kinds of human accomplishment is one way to foster a profound reluctance to smash human beings in large (or small) numbers. Norm Geras's blog is one place where a new branch of the liberal arts shows how a passion for various human games and concern for human rights can join hands and work together.

6

Aurum de stercore: anti-totalitarianism in the thought of Primo Levi

Alan Johnson

Introduction

In Primo Levi's writings we find a warning, a hope, and an invitation.[1]

Auschwitz was the 'dark centre of contemporary history', (Levi, 2005: 27) and because it happened, it can happen again. That is the warning.

But a politics of hope in the shadow of the catastrophe is possible. We can protect ourselves against ourselves by strapping on a 'truly solid moral armature' (Levi, 1988a: 49); that is, a set of culturally embedded and institutionalized practices – witnessing, reasoning, judging, resisting, and advancing liberal democracy.[2]

Philip Roth was struck by the fact that Primo Levi could find ordinary life 'exquisite' despite having stared into the abyss. Levi's invitation is that we do the same.

Warning, hope, and invitation, each precious, were mined by Levi from the dung of Auschwitz: *aurum de stercore*.[3]

In *The Truce*, a memoir of his return to Turin from Auschwitz, Primo Levi wrote of how each of us develops a *personal* philosophy of life 'in the wake of our experiences or those of others we have taken in' (cited in Gordon, 2001a: 31). If we 'take in' Levi's own work we find a *public* philosophy, a rulebook of sorts regarding the broad ideals and ethics that civic cultures should live by, and the models of conduct and habits of heart they should inculcate in their citizens.[4] Primo Levi is not a theorist, of course, and I do not find in his work the 'comprehensive, viable alternative to other modern works of political philosophy' that Homer does (2001: 5). But I do find 'elements that are wanted' (i.e. lacking) in the public philosophy of liberal democracies that again face a totalitarian foe against which they must defend themselves while preserving their values.

Anti-totalitarianism is a political persuasion or sensibility denoting more than simply opposition to totalitarian regimes and movements.[5] Pierre Rosanvallon has defined it as the 'complete renovation of the conceptualization of the political' that follows necessarily from 'taking the recognition of totalitarianism as [the] point of departure' (2006: 51). At its core is the conviction that we must, as Robert Fine has written, 're-read the political tradition through a lens darkened by the Gulag and Auschwitz' (2007: 187). If the anti-totalitarian is the person who knows we need an answer to the Psalmist's question, 'How can we sing the Lord's song in a strange land?', then Levi is a better guide than much political philosophy which, even during its renaissance in the late twentieth century, remained largely uninterested in the totalitarian experience. Levi, by contrast, insisted it was in Auschwitz that he 'learned to know the facts about people' (in Camon, 1989: 60), one of that small but vital group of writers who 'dr[ew] it into the interiority of their thinking' (Fine, 2007: 189).[6]

The name of Levi's desire was 'socialism without prison camps'. 'I am basically a socialist', he declared; 'I don't see any contradiction between democratic socialism and Judaism' (in Belpoliti and Gordon, 2001: 196, 33). He was an Italian liberal-socialist, at home among his left-wing and trade union friends (Thompson, 2003: 432–3), and a Turinese anti-fascist who recalled with pride that his commitment went 'back ... to the years of my adolescence' (see Anissimov, 1998: 379). He was formed politically by friends such as Bianca Guidetti Serra whom he accompanied to striking factories (Angier, 2003: 219), Sandro Delmastro, his climbing companion and hero, an anti-fascist who founded the Justice and Liberty Partisan Formations in Turin, and his second aunt Ada Della Torre, who helped Levi smuggle anti-fascist propaganda out of Milan (Ward, 2007: 13–14). In 'those few convulsed months' of 1943, the militants of the Partito d'Azione (which grew out of the anti-fascist movement Giustizia e Libertà) taught Levi that 'mocking, ironic intolerance was not enough' as they talked to him of 'unknowns: Gramsci, Salvemini, Gobetti, the Rosselli brothers' (Levi, 1984: 108). It was as a Partito d'Azione militant that he joined the partisans in autumn 1943 and was captured, and it was the anti-fascist heart he acquired in their ranks, combined with his experience in Auschwitz, that formed the warp and weft of his thought, and from which emerged the stark warning, defiant hope and joyful invitation which the rest of this chapter will now discuss.[7]

The warning

'I ask that we meditate', wrote Levi in his last book, *The Drowned and the Saved* (1988a: 43). He warned us to 'sharpen our senses' (1988a: 167) because what the Nazis demonstrated, they demonstrated 'for all centuries to come' (2005: 5). To view humanity in the perspective of Auschwitz – which is what it means to take totalitarianism as 'our point of departure' – is to cultivate a tragic sensibility that views human beings as 'ill-constituted', civilization as fragile, and evil as real.[8]

We are ill-constituted

Primo Levi thought we were centaurs, a 'tangle of flesh and mind, of divine inspiration and dust' (1984: 8). In us '[c]ompassion and brutality can co-exist in the same individual and in the same moment, despite all logic' (1988a: 39). Subjected to tension we evade judgement, 'just as a compass goes wild at the magnetic pole' (1988a: 46).

Frederic Homer has shown that Levi came to feel that the very things that make us human contain the seeds of our destruction. First, as Aristotle said, we are 'social animals', gregarious and forever forming groups, but there lies our tendency to simplification and Manichaeism; categorical thinking, prejudice, scapegoating, hostility to the outsider, and racism (See Belpoliti in Levi, 2005: ix–xi; Levi, 2005: 105–20). Second, although hierarchy can be natural, even useful in human relations, and striving is part of what makes us human, therein lies our tendency to vie for prestige, to dominate, and to create master–slave relations between ourselves (Levi, 1988a: 25). Levi struck a frankly conservative note in this regard: 'The ascent of the privileged, not only in the Lager but in all human coexistence, is an anguishing but unfailing phenomenon: only in utopias is it absent.' We must push this tendency to the margins, but ours will be 'a war without end', he thinks (1988a: 27).[9] Third, assertion, even aggression, has been necessary for our survival. But from it has grown violence, and our astonishing creativity in its use. In 1955

Levi warned that 'unsuspected reserves of viciousness and madness lie latent in man' (2005: 5). Our individuality can degenerate into a possessive individualism, or, worse, Nietzsche's 'Superman' (see Homer, 2001: 137–8). Fourth, we are distinguished from the other animals by reason, but human reason is far from being synonymous with wisdom, a baleful fact explored in Levi's moral fables about science. From chemistry, he pointed out, we got dynamite, and from the genius of Einstein and Fermi, Hiroshima.[10] We are bathetic creatures, always capable of 'hatching the cobra' (1990: 172–6).

Levi is not saying that these morbid potentialities of ours must dominate. As centaurs we contain other potentialities – for cooperation, altruism, and solidarity. He is warning us that *both* potentialities are there, and that 'we hold in our hand the key to maximum benefit and maximum harm: two contiguous doors, two locks, but only one key' (1991: 23). His writing is all about helping us to find the right door.

Civilization is fragile

The second part of Levi's warning is that from time to time Western civilization 'descends into hell with trumpets and drums' (1988a: 50).[11] As a chemist he knew that all living substances have a 'fragile stability' and in his essay 'Stable/Unstable' he extended that quality to 'our social behaviours', arguing that 'all of mankind today [is] condemned and accustomed to living in the world in which everything seems stable and is not, in which awesome energies (I am not only speaking of the nuclear arsenals) sleep a light sleep' (1991: 99). The Nazi genocide had demonstrated the 'essential fragility' of our civilization (1988a: 51) and just 'how easily good gives way to evil, is besieged and finally overwhelmed' (2005: 84).

Although the lack of state power can deliver the unprotected weak into the hands of the unrestrained strong, it has more often been the totalitarian state-movement that has banged the hellish drums. Aleksandr Solzhenitsyn showed this for Soviet Russia, Kanan Makiya for Saddamist Iraq and Primo Levi for Nazi Germany. 'Wittingly or otherwise' Levi observed, '[t]otalitarianism, any totalitarianism, is a broad path that leads downwards' (2005: 80).

Evil is real

A Catholic critic, Lorenzo Mondo, accused Levi of having an 'obsession with evil' (Thompson, 2003: 504). He certainly believed that with Auschwitz something evil had been 'introduced irrevocably into the world of things that exist'; something that showed Kant's moral law is not natural or 'within' us. For Levi, argues Angier, understanding evil meant 'understanding how ordinary people could do the evil ordinary Germans did' (Angier, 2003: 511). That the German perpetrators were 'ordinary men' *should* be existentially deflating and the cause for obsession. As one survivor put it to Robert Jay Lifton when interviewed for his seminal study of the Nazi doctors, 'It is demonic that they were not demonic' (Lifton, 2000: 5). Levi's own 1959 description of Rudolf Höss, the Commandant of Auschwitz, anticipated the baleful findings of Stanley Milgram's obedience experiments by registering the terrible ordinariness of evil. Höss, noted Levi, 'is not a bloody sadist or a hate-filled fanatic, but an empty man, a tranquil and diligent idiot, whose purpose is to carry out with the utmost care the bestial initiatives entrusted to him, and in this obedience he appears to succeed in appeasing every niggling doubt and anxiety' (Levi, 2005: 6).

Dragged down, Levi did not come back from hell empty-handed. As Gordon has pointed out, Levi's heroic achievement was to mobilize his 'sensory or involuntary memory' for over forty years, allowing it to erupt in his work but only after he had done the work of filtering and transforming 'pathological testimony' into a usable 'ethical memory' *for us* (Gordon, 2001a: 65). Evil appears as 'the Gorgon' he did not see, and the 'useless violence' he did. It is there in Doktor Pannwitz's look – 'as if across the glass window of an aquarium' – at Haftling 174517, and in the way Alex the capo uses Levi's shoulder – 'without hatred and without sneering' – to wipe some engine grease from his hand (Levi, 1987a: 111–14). It lies in the 'demonic' invention of the Sonderkommando and in the 'bestial power' which excluded the child Hurbinek from the world of men (Levi, 1987a: 198). It is the demolition of the human in man prior to his death. Enclosed in one image it was 'the musselman', the drowned.[12]

By seeing evil plain in this way and by rejecting as false the hope for a 'global universal answer' that could forever 'bring peace to the spirit' (Levi, 2005: 62), Levi supplied elements that are badly wanted in the liberal imagination. That which has been irrevocably introduced into the world *should* redefine the tasks of politics and ethics. As Paul Gilroy has argued, from Levi we learn that to be 'alive to the camps out there now and the camps around the corner, the camps that are being prepared', and so cultivate a 'concentration camp mentality', is the foundation for a 'planetary humanism' (cited in Cheyette, 2007: 81).[13]

Expressed negatively, Levi's warning amounts to what Giuliani (2003: 43–4) calls a 'nontotalitarian ethics' that is alert to the distance between knowledge and conscience, and to the danger of the search for a 'perfect man' that can close that gap and so transcend the ideal–real split. The split is in us, says Levi, and efforts by the prophets to get it out of us can only lead to enormity (Giuliani, 2003: 43–4).

Expressed positively, Levi's warning is captured in his amendment to Theodor Adorno's famous remark that 'to write a poem after Auschwitz is barbaric'. No, wrote Levi, 'after Auschwitz it is no longer possible to write poetry except about Auschwitz' (cited in Cicioni, 1995: 139). In other words, thinking about poetry (or politics) after Auschwitz is impossible, or at least inadequate, if it is not also thinking 'about Auschwitz' – that is, about the warning. In other words, our duty to 'meditate that this came about' is peremptory and absolute. It must be carved in our hearts, to be undertaken lest our house fall apart and our children turn their faces from us.[14]

Towards a politics of hope

Primo Levi's children, Lisa Lorenza and Renzo, are named after Lorenzo Perrone, a hired worker, mason, and fellow Italian who saved Levi's life in Auschwitz.[15] From the summer of 1944 when he overheard Primo speaking in his own Piedmont accent, Lorenzo brought aid. Despite the dangers – if he had been caught he would have been severely punished at the very least – Lorenzo brought Primo soup every day for half a year and a vest to keep him warm, sent postcards out of the camp, and was the conduit for Levi's mother to send chocolate, cookies, powdered milk, and clothing.

Their last meeting in the camp occurred after a heavy Allied raid. A bomb had burst one of Lorenzo's eardrums and thrown sand and dirt into the bowl of soup he was carrying for Primo. Lorenzo apologized for the state of the soup but did not mention his ear because he did not want his friend to feel indebted to him. 'He asked me once in very laconic words,' recalled Levi, '"Why are we in the world if not to help each other?"' (Levi, 1995: 214).

Can Lorenzo's dutiful altruism within Auschwitz be made central to a public philosophy outside the camps? Can 'the duty to bring aid' be routinely pitted against 'the contract of mutual indifference'?[16] Levi thought the effort must be made, and it must be founded on hope, for without 'a certain amount of optimism ... one doesn't accomplish anything and one lives badly' (Levi, 1990: 103).[17] And we have reason to hope. We humans have learnt to transgress against our biological inheritance, building shelters rather than hiding in the caves, and we can also build *social* shelters, 'obstacle[s] in the way of certain instincts that are our animal inheritance' (Levi, 2005: 111). Levi's writings can be read as gently urging on us the social practices, sensibilities, and institutions we need to succeed.

I now discuss these 'social shelters': witnessing, reasoning, judging, resisting, and advancing democracy.

Witnessing

Primo Levi had an intense need to testify about what had been perpetrated in Auschwitz, both to secure his own internal liberation and because 'remembering was a duty' to the dead. Positioning himself, as Gordon observes, 'between the necessarily horrific memory and the cognitive and ethical dividends paid by holding on to that memory with awareness' (Gordon, 2001a: 66), Levi made of his witness an anti-totalitarian ethics; 'laic', rooted in memory and history, and infused with the overwhelming sense of humility and frailty that both instilled (Giuliani, 2003: 39–40, 43). In his poem *Shemà* Levi made witnessing nothing less than a secular commandment, the first clause of a moral constitution for post-Auschwitz societies.

Reasoning

Levi was sure that many twentieth-century intellectuals simply failed to reason things out. Instead we 'found it convenient, economic, to put our faith in a ready-made truth' and for this 'human but mistaken choice', this 'delirium of delegating', this seeking of 'golden and distant idols' a heavy price was paid (Levi, 1991: 94–5).

The intimacy that exists between high and low forms of unreason is a powerful theme in Levi's work. When the intellectuals offer up words to answer each and every 'why?', once and for all, it always ends with the words the prison guard crushed Levi with on his arrival at Auschwitz: 'hier ist kein warum' (there is no why here). The combination has been constitutive of every form of totalitarianism, the dream of man-perfected ending up as man-demolished, Sayyid Qutb giving way to Mohamed Atta.

It was during his chemistry studies that Levi began to take the measure of these totalitarian forms of unreason. He discovered that zinc would not transform into zinc sulphate when very pure, and realized that two different philosophical conclusions could be drawn from this discovery. 'The praise of purity ... I discarded ... for life to be lived, impurities are needed ... Dissension, diversity ... Fascism does not want them, forbids them, and that's why you're not a Fascist' (Levi, 1984: 28).[18]

'Distrust the prophets, the enchanters [who] write "beautiful words"', he pleaded (1988a: 167). After Auschwitz he hoped the appeal of the prophets had been eclipsed – none 'dares any longer to reveal our tomorrow to us'. Levi even dared to think that 'perhaps the last ill-omened specimen is Khomeini and he won't last long' (Levi, 1991: 94–5). In place of the dreams of the prophets Levi recommended a more modest understanding of who we humans are (ontological deflation), what we can know (epistemological deflation), where the proper centre of a moral life lies (ethical deflation), a feeling for the limits to reason (temperamental deflation), and what the appropriate mode of intellectual work is after Auschwitz (the 'anti-barbaric intellectual').

Ontological deflation

The first story Levi wrote was titled 'Uomo' (Man). Uomo has a godlike quality in the story, but only as long as he is not part of the world. Once he is 'tested and worn by the desperate complications of human affairs' Uomo-as-God quickly fails (in Angier, 2003: 215). And so, he thinks, must the totalitarian ambition to create from man a 'perfect meta-ethical humanitas' (Giuliani, 2003: 43). When Norberto Bobbio praised the 'human measure' of Levi's prose it was surely a political as much as an aesthetic judgement (Thompson, 2003: 371).

Epistemological deflation

Levi stressed 'the extreme unknowability of the future' and distrusted 'whoever "knows" how to improve the world' (Levi, 1991: 94, 65).[19] 'The human condition is incompatible with certainty' so '[w]e must build our own tomorrow, blindly, gropingly; build it from its roots without giving in to the temptation to recompose the shards of old shattered idols and without constructing new ones' (1991: 95). Between anti-human scientistic progressivism and anti-human Luddism, Levi proposed a third way. 'We cannot continue to "progress" indefinitely,' he wrote, 'but neither can we stop or retreat on all fronts. We need to deal with the problems one by one, with honesty, intelligence and humility: this is the delicate and formidable task' (2005: 122).

Ethical deflation

From the totalitarian experience Levi drew a secular commandment: 'It is the difficult task of every man to diminish as much as he can the tremendous bulk of this substance which contaminates every life – pain in all its forms' (Levi, 1991: 184). Gordon points out that not the maximization of happiness but 'the avoidance of suffering or cruelty as a prime moral claim … emerge[s] at several points in Levi as a foundation for his ethical deliberations' (Gordon, 2001a: 26). In Judith Shklar's terms (2006), Levi believed we should 'put cruelty first'.[20]

Robert Gordon's essential book, *Primo Levi's Ordinary Virtues: From Testimony to Ethics*, establishes that Levi's ethic 'stands against the *Lager* but can never forget the *Lager*' (Gordon, 2001a: 37) for it is built upon the 'bond of a dense, but active kind between the extraordinary *univers concentrationnaire* and the ordinary world of Levi's here and now'.[21] By moving between those two worlds Levi produced new 'vistas of comprehension' (2001a: 271), not least that against the anti-ethics of the *Lager* we could pit the 'proper centre of moral life … [the] ordinary life … of marriage, family, and the home, of work and production', and cultivate there the 'ordinary virtues' – in Gordon's happy phrase, these are all the 'feints towards fixed value' we need (2001a: 26, 32).

Temperamental deflation

'[W]e should reject our innate tendency towards radicalism, because it is a source of evil' advised Levi. We should spurn 'the zero and the one' (Levi, 1991: 93). A sense of measure or 'limit', observes Gordon, is one of Levi's ordinary virtues (Gordon, 2001a, 113–32), while Homer notes Levi's intuition that single-mindedness, by detaching reasoning from consequences, can open the door to enormity (Homer, 2001: 73). Giuliani praises Levi's tendency to deploy irony whenever '[a] sense of limit is lacking', and argues that this was an expression of his conviction that 'wisdom ... should preside over [human] reason' (Giuliani, 2003: 4, 96).

The anti-barbaric intellectual

The term is Bernard-Henri Lévy's, coined during the French anti-totalitarian moment of the 1970s to dramatize his alternative to the prophetic-transcendent-reckless mode of intellectual life that had so disfigured the French left and left it so very vulnerable to totalitarian temptation. Against all that, the anti-barbaric intellectual is a democrat who sets out to 'testify to the unspeakable and hinder the horror, save what can be saved and refuse the intolerable', knowing that 'we will not remake the world, but at least we can see to it that it does not fall apart' (Levy, in Christofferson, 2004: 188). Levi was an anti-barbaric intellectual, an underlabourer to a post-Auschwitz world, seeking to build up its moral and political armature against enormity.

Judging

'Another lesson to be learned', argued Levi, 'is that although it might be difficult, it is necessary to judge ... to take a position' (Levi, 2005: 81). It is a genuine historical irony that the experience which made us think all acts of genuine discernment were just too close to acts of prejudice to be worth the risk was ... totalitarianism. The 'global labelling so dear to totalitarian regimes repels us', noted Levi, but we should not confuse it with *authentic judging*, which must be conducted with 'extreme caution, and on a case-by-case basis: precisely because we are not totalitarians' (cited in Gordon, 2001a: 8). One of the central lessons of chemistry, he pointed out, was that 'differences can be small, but they can lead to radically different consequences, like a railroad's switch points'. The ability to identify these differences was vital, and 'not only [for] the chemist's trade' (Levi, 1984: 51).

One such switch-point was the difference between democratic and totalitarian societies. When graffiti began to appear in Turin stating

'Factory = Concentration Camp', Levi was disgusted. It was 'not true' he said, and it marked a hysterical refusal of authentic judgement. 'There is no gas chamber at Fiat', he pointed out, and you can go home at the end of the day (in Camon, 1989: 20). When his daughter put up a portrait of Mao on her bedroom wall Levi bluntly told her that Mao was a 'dictator' and words were exchanged. (Thompson, 2003: 339).

He had a visceral identification with those who had been through the Soviet Gulag or suffered at the hands of communist totalitarians. He never failed to point out the differences between the Nazi camps and the Soviet camps – 'nothing appears that is even close to Treblinka or Chelmno' he wrote, against the revisionists (Levi, 1990: 165) – but neither did he fail to point out the parallels (Levi, 1988a: 3, 76–7, 81, 96) noting sardonically that 'The translation into German of *The Gulag Archipelago* cannot have presented many difficulties' (1988a: 77). On his release from Auschwitz he was questioned by a polite Soviet official in great detail about the camp. Later Levi said, 'I was naive enough to assume that my very courteous Russian inquisitors were collecting historical data rather than information on how to run the Stalinist camps' (see Thompson, 2003: 348).[22]

Resisting

Levi understood that there are times when we have no alternative but to take up arms against totalitarianism, another central feature of the anti-totalitarian sensibility. Despite being personally tormented at the thought of picking up a gun he decided to join the anti-fascist partisans in 1943 because it was 'my overpowering duty to take part in the fight' (Levi, 2005: 77). One night, after a successful raid to capture arms, Levi talked to his friend Aldo as they walked back to the partisan camp carrying hand grenades, rifles and revolvers. 'How sad', he said, 'that a man must seek weapons to use against other men' (in Angier, 2003: 246). This coexistence of the sadness but, *nonetheless*, the seeking, sums up the tragic – rather than therapeutic or militaristic – sensibility that he commends to us. He resolved the tension between what the theologian Reinhold Niebuhr called 'moral man' and 'immoral society' by placing his public duty above his personal feelings.

And yet, as always with Levi, he qualifies a first thought – fight! – with other complicating thoughts: the need for prudence, the threshold of last resort, and a fear of the unintended consequences or genealogies of violence. Politicians, Levi advised, should 'learn to live like chess players ... meditating before moving, even though knowing that the time allowed for each move is limited; remembering that every move of ours provokes another by the opponent, difficult but not impossible to foresee and paying for wrong moves' (Levi, 1991: 134). He felt violence should be a last resort because war is 'the worst type of school' (Levi, 2005: 85) and was sure 'there do not exist problems that cannot be solved around a table, provided there is good will and reciprocal trust' (Levi, 1988a: 168).

In *The Drowned and the Saved* he even argued that '[f]rom violence only violence is born', even a just war being liable to pulse out violence in uncontrollable ways, 'in a pendular action that becomes more frenzied' (Levi, 1988a: 168). Valuable as these second thoughts are for our own times, Levi's formulation 'from violence only violence is born', it seems to me, is excessive, and the locus of a contradiction in his thought, the place where moral man loses touch with the realities of immoral society. An example of the problem is the reception of his story 'Force Majeure' (Levi, 1990: 62–5). In the story a man enters an alley with high walls and no way out. He encounters a bigger and stronger man dressed as a sailor, with a dog. The sailor bars his way, forcing him to the ground, face down, and then deliberately walks on him, along his length from head to toe, before leaving. During the encounter, no words are spoken and no reason is offered. Someone else, a prostitute, walks past, and the sailor lets her through. As a parable about psychic demolition it is brilliant. But as a parable of the Holocaust, or the totalitarian situation per se, which is how it is often read, the story is radically incomplete. For the sailor rarely walks away. Men like my father had to pick up a gun, go into the alley and kill the sailor. And that brute truth is one more 'element that is wanted' in many parts these days.

Elsewhere Levi strikes a different note. He recalls those days after D-Day when the English prisoners 'saluted us with the V-sign of victory' because 'freedom seemed within reach' (Levi, 1988a: 80). Other soldiers were coming into the alley to rescue the man on the ground, and from *their* violence would come something other than 'more violence'. For Levi, liberation would come. More: Levi praised the 'desperate heroism' of the Warsaw ghetto fighters who threw themselves from balconies rather than surrender, and valorized the women who 'shot pistols with both hands' and so saved 'together with [their] own dignity, that of future generations' (Levi, 1990: 171). He paid homage to men like Baruch, a docker from Livorno who struck back against the guards in Auschwitz and was swiftly massacred, as typical of those who 'died not in spite of their valour but because of it' (Levi, 1988a: 63). His novel *If Not Now, When?* was a form of 'homage to all Jews [who] ... had found the strength to oppose the Nazis, and who had rediscovered their dignity and liberty in this unequal combat' (Levi, 2005: 167) and he thought the resistance inside the death camps was among 'the most heroic deeds of human history' (2005: 17). One of the lessons of the Holocaust is surely that when the drums and trumpets start up one fights back, immediately, and with everything, precisely because we, unlike them, do know 'that it was so'. The cliché that 'from violence only violence is born' is at odds with that insight.

The incident Levi relates as definitive of his own demolition as a man in Auschwitz concerns the execution of a prisoner who had helped blow up a crematorium. The condemned man shouts from the scaffold, 'Comrades, I am the last!' but Levi is unable to muster either an act of revolt or words of defiance. He was rightly 'oppressed with shame' to be part of an 'abject flock' and he knew himself at that moment not to be a man (Levi, 1987a: 156). That is why, at the age of 54, he raced to the gates of a school on Via San Seconda to confront knife-wielding fascists who were threatening the students (Thompson, 2003: 362). For there are times when to be a person is to fight.[23]

Advancing liberal democracy

Levi fought for liberal democracy as the breastplate of our moral and political armature against enormity. He quoted the Auschwitz resistance leader and historian Hermann Langbein: 'The lesson of Auschwitz is that the very first step, the acceptance of a type of society that seeks to dominate men in total fashion, is the most dangerous one' (cited in Levi, 2005: 80). The 'lack in Germany of solid democratic roots' Levi believed to have been an 'indispensable' factor that helped 'set off' the Holocaust (Levi, 1988a: 66).

We need the restraints of liberal democracy not least because 'we are all mirrored' in Chaim Rumkowski, President of the Lodz ghetto. Each of us is liable to be 'so dazzled by power and prestige as to forget our essential fragility' (Levi, 1988a: 50–1). For power, Levi insisted, 'is a drug, we need ever larger doses, and soon enough we get a syndrome: a distorted view of the world, dogmatic arrogance, need for adulation, convulsive clinging to the levers of command, and contempt for the law' (1988a: 49). Any society will produce such politicians, but only a liberal democracy can get rid of them without violence. As Homer puts it, Levi thinks liberal democracy is simply 'our best hope to stave off carnage' (Homer, 2001: 225).

The freedoms of an educated public, exercised through institutions in which they deliberate, educate, publish, and organize are the very best social shelters against totalitarianism, for here grow the civic cultures inhospitable to prophets. But Levi was no romantic. He knew democracy to be a fragile social and cultural institution that required much more than periodic elections to flourish. 'Where law turns out to be lacking, the law of the jungle is established', he warned, while without freedom of communication 'all other liberties soon vanish' (Levi, 1988a: 66). Toppling the dictator was very far from mission accomplished.

So, witnessing, reasoning, judging, resisting, and advancing liberal democracy are the components of a chastened politics of hope practised in the shadow of catastrophe. Judith Woolf claims that 'the fundamental motivation for all Levi's writings about Auschwitz' was to inculcate in us a shame without which 'we cannot perform the crucial task he has laid on our shoulders' (Woolf, 2007: 48). And that task, to take up the burden, is set out in his late poem *Delega* (Delegating) (see Cicioni, 1995: 165).

> Do not be frightened if there is much to be done.
> We need you, who are less tired.
> ... Reflect again on our mistakes:
> ...
> ... Do not be appalled at the rubble
> And the stench of rubbish tips: we cleared them with bare hands
> When we were as old as you are now.
> Maintain the pace, as best you can. We have
> Combed the hair of comets,
> Deciphered the secret of genesis,
> Stepped on the sand of the Moon,
> Built Auschwitz and destroyed Hiroshima.
> See, we have not been inactive.
> Take up the burden, puzzled as you are:
> Do not call us teachers.

The invitation

Il n'y a pas de honte à préférer le bonheur. (There's no shame in preferring happiness) (Camus, 1960: 170)

But is the disillusioned life *worth* living? Can we live *well* carrying that burden? Levi's answers were affirmative. Soon after the liberation he wrote to his friend and fellow survivor Jean Samuel to say that although he vowed each day that 'we are witnesses and we must bear this burden', nonetheless 'I rejoice in all the small things in life which familiarity used to let by unnoticed' (BBC, 1992). Is there anything wiser that seeps out of Levi's life and writings than that coupling?

The capacity to find sublimity and intensity in the 'small things', the prosaic and the ordinary, is the sense and sensibility of anti-totalitarianism. 'If you are happy with daily life, living the life of a *mensch* freely, then yes, you can describe it as my paradise', he said (in Belpoliti and Gordon, 2001: 32). He invited us to cultivate our own capability to extract 'those instants of happiness, of enjoying them fully, as though we were extracting pure gold from the dross' (Levi, 1988a: 53).

He came close to rendering sacred the world of play in essays that are pervaded by a very Turinese kind of hedonism, civilized and intelligent (see Gordon, 2001a, chapter 12). Although he praised very highly the intense camaraderie of work, he seems to see us at our most human when we are simply enjoying ourselves. In play, he wrote, we find again 'the savour of childhood, delicate and forgotten', for to enjoy play is rather 'like receiving, free of charge or almost, a rare and beautiful object' (Levi, 1991: 173). Play helps us express not only pleasure but also freedom, and a political freedom at that (Gordon, 2001a: 285). '[T]he substantially non-verbal civilisation of play', he pointed out, can cross political frontiers 'with the happy freedom of the wind and clouds' (Levi, 1991: 169).

Levi loved the mountains. His story *Bear Meat* begins 'Evenings spent in a mountain hut are among the most sublime and intense that life holds' (Levi, 2007: 31). But he was also at home in the valleys, through which he would walk, fearing no evil, amusing Norberto Bobbio with his 'Talmudic hair-splitting, Jewish jokes and witticisms', all the while pointing out to his companions 'the marvels of the natural world' (Thompson, 2003: 371).[24] But Levi also enjoyed the city, praising the humble pavement as a 'civilised institution ... full of surprises' (Levi, 1991: 177).

'The vocabulary and imagery of friendship is everywhere in Levi's work', Gordon reminds us (Gordon, 2001a: 221). And in his life too, we might add. He enjoyed 'the poetry of chess', a game at which he was 'execrable' but played in a 'dreamy and festive spirit'. He had a chess computer but preferred the flesh-and-blood opponent because 'he is your blood brother, even if you met him only a few hours ago. You see his face, you measure yourself against him, you know him to be as capable as you are of happy inventions and off-the-wall mistakes. At the end of the match, as if at the end of a life, you can talk to him with the familiarity that is born from a contest' (Levi, 1991: 192, 195).

Levi could be wondrously impressed by the 'instantaneous and prodigious' leap of the flea. He wrote a whole essay on that (1991: 33–7). He wrote another about the beauty of the butterfly and recalled with poetic reverence the moment when he read of 'an Antiopa with its brownish-purple wings' landing on the hand of Hermann Hesse, before it departed again, according to Hesse, 'in the great warm light' (1991: 9). He really noticed things, did Primo Levi. Actually, he noticed everything twice. His aesthetic enjoyment of 'the vivacity of birds', for instance, was not lessened but doubled by his scientific appreciation that this explosion of colour is 'an obligatory solution to the problem of survival' (1991: 83). Has any other writer better bridged the two cultures of the sciences and the humanities?

In one essay, Levi describes his deep feelings for the plain house in which he has spent his entire life, bar a year in Auschwitz and a brief stay in Milan (Levi, 1991: 1–5) Levi called it 'a machine for living' but by directing his memory to that living, he enchanted even its nondescript little spaces. 'The next corner, between the wall and the walnut closet, was coveted as a hiding place when we played hide-and-seek; I had hidden there, on some unspecified Sunday of the Oligocene, and knelt down on a sliver of glass and still bear the scar on my left knee. Thirty years after me, my daughter hid there, but she laughed and was found immediately; and after another eight years my son, with a flock of his friends, one of whom lost a baby tooth in that very spot and for mysterious magical reasons shoved it into a hole in the plaster, where it probably still is' (1991: 3).[25]

Family (a very big thing, lived as a series of very small things) was extremely important to Levi. His mother Ester lived with him and his wife, and he cared for her even when those duties oppressed him. (After all, 'Why are we in the world if not to help each other?') He writes beautifully about a childhood memory of a day spent with his grandfather, who 'had a store selling fabrics on the old Via Roma'. At carnival time, he would invite all the grandchildren 'to watch the procession of allegorical floats from the store's balcony'. Levi closes his eyes and recalls the view in a prose poem of precise, astringent writing: 'At that time Via Roma was paved with delightful wooden tiles on which the iron hoofs of the draft horses did not slip, and along it ran the tracks of the electric trolley' (1991: 62).

The political point, I think, is this. If we were to stop listening to the 'beautiful words' of the prophets and instead cast our eyes down to those beautiful horses click-clacking their way along the delightful wooden tiles of the Via Roma, we might all be better off. Perhaps then we could finally get on with living the life of a *mensch*, freely, in a festive spirit.

This need not be a recipe for political quietism. Remember Lorenzo Perrone's words: 'Why are we in the world if not to help each other?' And think on Levi's too: 'Man is, must be, sacred to man, everywhere and forever' (Levi, 2005: 7). What more than those convictions do we need? Inspired by them we can fight not just to fend off enormity, but to extend to each other, everywhere and forever, the capability to enjoy the exquisite. As for the rest, it is just a matter of details, and we democrats can work them out as we go.[26]

Notes

1 Primo Levi was born in Turin in 1919 and grew up a preternaturally shy and intelligent boy. In late 1943 he was captured while fighting with the anti-fascist resistance and as a Jew he was sent to Auschwitz. His knowledge as a chemist saved his life: he became a slave labourer in the Buna rubber factory at Auschwitz-Monowitz. After liberation, with 'a torrent of things to tell the civilised world' and 'the tattooed number on my arm burning like a sore' he wrote his series of remarkable books and essays. He died in 1987, probably by suicide, a complicated subject outside the scope of this chapter.

2 'Socialist Hope in the Shadow of Catastrophe' is the title of an essay by Norman Geras, first published in *Are There Alternatives? Socialist Register 1996* and then reprinted in his 1998 book *The Contract of Mutual Indifference: Political Philosophy After the Holocaust*. In my reading the essay sets out the case for a necessary deflation of the socialist project in the shadow of the Holocaust, albeit one that retains a commitment to a politics of hope and a dream of a 'minimum utopia'.

3 I have taken the Italian expression 'aurum de stercore' (or 'gold from

dung'), from Carole Angier's biography of Levi (2003: 174) and I agree with her that alchemy of a sort was 'his dream in writing and his achievement'. In doing so I do not ignore Levi's plea that his readers avoid treating him as 'the prophet, the oracle, the seer' (1990: 3). I share Bryan Cheyette's concern about 'flattening appropriating discourses that have enveloped Levi' (2007: 79), not least the effort to impose an affirmative and redemptive frame upon him in the USA by changing the titles of his books, from *If This is a Man* to *Survival in Auschwitz*, from *The Truce* to *The Reawakening*, from *Lilith and Other Tales* to *Moments of Reprieve* (see Langer 1998: 23–4). But Levi accepted that there was 'a sort of wisdom that seeps through from my books that I don't feel within myself' (in Belpoliti and Gordon, 2001: 174). My sense is that Levi is right here, and then some. Norman Geras has also been struck by Levi's 'extraordinary wisdom … not only about the camps, but about life and the world' (2004). It is this wisdom, and the unusual conditions of its emergence, that I seek to capture by using the phrase 'aurum de stercore'.

4 See Gordon, 2001a; Homer, 2001; Belpoliti and Gordon, 2007.

5 Totalitarianism refers most obviously to Italian fascism, German Nazism, and Russian Stalinism. The Ba'athism of Iraq (Makiya, 1989) and global Islamist-Jihadist networks (Berman, 2003) can also be read as forms of totalitarianism. Levi believed totalitarianism had three weapons: 'direct propaganda or propaganda camouflaged as upbringing, instruction and popular culture; the barrier erected against pluralism of information; and terror' (1988a: 16). Anti-totalitarianism should hold more than an antiquarian interest for us because, as Clive James has it, 'Totalitarianism, however, is not over. It survives as residues, some of them all the more virulent because they are no longer hemmed in by borders' (2007: xxi).

6 I cite Robert Fine's praise for the achievement of Claude Lefort here, but I think it also describes Levi's achievement. Norman Geras's later work demonstrated the value, perhaps the necessity, of testing our normative theoretical conceptions 'against the worst calamities of our time' (1998: 26).

7 For Levi's involvement in Turinese anti-fascism see Ward, 2007: 3–16; Angier, 2003: 116–33; Belpoliti and Gordon, 2001: 59–63; Gordon, 2001a: 15, n.25; and Cicioni, 1995: 12–16. In 1985 Levi supported Bianca Guidetti Serra's candidacy for Democrazi Proletaria (Thompson, 2003: 477). The political philosopher Norberto Bobbio was 'utterly devoted to Levi' according to Thompson (2003: 371), their relationship founded on political agreement as well as a mutual love of the mountains.

8 The expression 'ill-constituted' is Frederic Homer's (2001: 48) and it captures superbly Levi's view of the tragic imperfections of the human condition.

9 There are affinities between Levi's chastened yet hopeful view of human possibility and Norman Geras's claim that any 'feasible conception of progress today needs to come to terms with the likely persistence of some of the less pleasant tendencies and potentialities that are lodged within the characteristic make-up of human beings' (1998: 135).

10 See also Levi's 'Preface to L. Cagliati's *I due volti della chimica* (*The Two Faces of Chemistry*)' in 2005: 121–5.

11 Levi's reference is to Book 1 of his beloved Dante's *Divine Comedy* (Canto XXII). 'I have seen horsemen in the past break camp, muster their army and open assault, and at times even beat a quick retreat; I have seen outriders roam your countryside, O Aretines, and seen raiding-parties charge, tournaments clash and jousters galloping, some called by trumpets and some by bells, by drumrolls and by flares from castle-walls, by homemade and imported instruments; But never before have I seen horsemen, footsoldiers, or ships that sail by sighting of land or stars move to a stranger bugle' (Dante Alighieri, 2000).

12 Hurbinek was 'a nobody, a child of death, a child of Auschwitz … he could not speak and he had no name'. Levi encountered him after the liberation, paralysed from the waist down and atrophied. He died in March 1945, but only after he had 'fought like a man, to the last breath, to gain his entry into the world of men, from which a bestial power had excluded him' (Levi, 1987a: 197–8). The term 'musselman' was used by 'the old ones of the camp to describe the weak, the inept, those doomed to selection'. These 'men in decay … drag themselves along in an opaque intimate solitude, and in solitude they die or disappear, without leaving a trace in anyone's memory' (1987a: 94–5).

13 Levi's was no uncritical Western humanism but was alert to 'the dangers inherent in a categorizing science and a falsely universalising European culture' (Cheyette, 2007: 82).

14 I make use here of some lines from Levi's poem *Shemà* (1988b: 9). See Geras's acute discussion of the poem in Geras 1998: 16–17.

15 Judith Woolf (2007: 45) discusses Levi's writing on those others who retained their humanity in Auschwitz, such as Schlome, Steinlauf, Alberto, and Jean, the Pikolo. She notes 'Levi's Dantean ability to invest [them] with paradigmatic meaning', and that too is *aurum*.

16 The terms 'contract of mutual indifference' and 'duty to bring aid' are Norman Geras's. He claims that the heart of a progressive politics after the Holocaust must be a 'positive universal right to aid and a universal obligation to bring it' (Geras, 1998: 48). For Levi's reflections on Lorenzo Perrone's life in Auschwitz, and sad death in Italy, see Levi, 1987b: 149–60 and 1995: 213–14.

17 Levi's optimism, he said, came up 'from my roots' and was 'constitutional'. But it was also based on a historical consciousness: 'Since there

is a very real risk of ruin, the only remedy is to roll up our sleeves' (in Belpoliti and Gordon, 2001: 130).

18 See Giuliani's essay 'Reactions: Primo Levi's Chemistry and His Fascist Education' (2003: 17–26).

19 For discussions of Levi's problem-solving approach see Belpoliti and Gordon, 2007: 61, 135; Giuliani, 2003: 97; and for a particularly subtle discussion of Levi's 'pragmatic, constructive, solution-led *Weltanschauung*', see Gordon, 2001a: 89.

20 Levi is not here embracing a flatly consequentialist view of morality, often thought to be one source of the abandonment of those moral constraints which prevent us from becoming barbaric. Each deflation conditions every other, and here the dangers of a rigorous consequentialism are offset by a temperamental deflation which is suspicious of rigour and valorizes moderation, and an epistemological deflation which recommends pragmatic flexibility not axiom as our guide to action.

21 Similarly, Norman Geras (2004) has noted Levi's ability to use 'common experience to illuminate the experience of the Nazi universe of death, and vice versa'.

22 Levi was willing to see Stalinism plain. 'The massive exploitation of slave labour was learned by Hitler in the school of Stalin' was not an untypical observation (Levi, 1988a: 168). This was most uncommon among European left-liberal intellectuals. After the fall of the Berlin Wall, the Polish dissident Adam Michnik asked the West German social theorist Jürgen Habermas why he had never attacked Stalinism head on. Habermas explained he did not want 'applause from the wrong side' (see Rabinbach, 2006: 82). Levi did not seek it, but he knew there were worse things in this world than receiving 'applause from the wrong side'. Another piece of *aurum* he brought back from the *stercore* of Auschwitz.

23 Levi thought the search for understanding could get in the way of the imperative to act. Yes, the prisoner could 'drown in a sea of non-understanding' but he or she could also sink beneath our efforts to fathom the unfathomable. Homer draws from Levi the maxim that sometimes '[t]he prisoner was better off reacting alertly to circumstances than trying to fathom what was happening; the latter would lead to despair, futility and further confusion' (Homer, 2001: 34).

24 For a discussion of Levi's humour see Cicioni, 2007.

25 For a discussion of Levi and the ethics of home see Gordon, 2001b.

26 I presented a version of this chapter as my inaugural lecture as Professor of Democratic Theory and Practice at Edge Hill University on 13 December 2007. I would like to thank my students on the course I have been teaching on the Holocaust since 2004, and those who have taken part in the Primo Levi Reading Group.

7

Evil and the norms of society

Laurence Thomas

Recall the extraordinarily poignant words commonly attributed to John Bradford: 'There but for the Grace of God go I'. Applied to evil behaviour, the implication is this: insofar as most of us are not given to committing evil behaviour or, in any case, to the toleration of such behaviour, this is not so much a testimony to our strength of moral character, but to the good fortune of our not having been born in an evil climate, where we belong to the group of individuals who are perpetrating the evil in question. From the genocide in Rwanda to the Holocaust to American slavery, the facts certainly seem to bear out the Bradford view. Precisely what we know, beyond any shadow of doubt, is that most members of these societies did not stand up to the atrocities being committed in their societies. Nowadays, of course, we would all like to believe that the Bradford view does not apply to us. Unfortunately, there is no reason whatsoever to think that this is so. My aim in this chapter is to offer an explanation for why the Bradford view is correct. I shall argue that the Bradford view makes reference to the social nature of human beings, on the one hand, and to the significance of the moral baselines of the society in which we are raised, on the other. It might seem that the Bradford view points to the problem that arises when people are not autonomous. As we shall see, though, this line of thought is mistaken.

One of the problems with explaining the Bradford view is that doing so might seem to excuse wrongdoing. I think not, however. For the view is not that people are naturally evil or good, but that the environment makes the fundamental difference. Both Plato and Aristotle held this thesis. The Bradford view does not excuse evil. Rather, it brings into sharper relief some of the important things that we must do in order to ensure that evil does not occur. What is more, we do not take seriously the reality that evil can occur unless we take equally seriously the reality that, in many cases, people never imagined that they would end up committing the evil in question or, in any event, tolerating its occurrence in others (see Zimbardo, 2007).

Morally right behaviour and the question of autonomy

It is very tempting to think that the Bradford view brings out the fact that most people are not autonomous; and that, if most were, then it is highly unlikely that evil would occur on a grand scale. There are two ways of understanding this line of thought. One is that in virtue of being autonomous most people would not be much concerned with fitting in with other individuals. The other line of thought is that there is a connection between being autonomous and doing what is right. I shall speak to the first concern in the following section. What I want to draw attention to in this section is that there is no connection at all between being autonomous and embracing morally right views. Of course, one can always define autonomy so as to mean that an autonomous person is one who is independent and who embraces the morally right views as delivered by the facts. Alas, this would be a pyrrhic victory at best.

Alex de Tocqueville, Thomas Jefferson, and Immanuel Kant surely stand as models of the autonomous person.[1] Yet, all three thought it obvious that blacks were intellectually bereft. It is true that Kant opposed slavery and that Jefferson thought it better for blacks and whites to live separately. This just shows, though, that opposing slavery and embracing equality are not the same. John Stuart Mill's view of blacks stands in stark contrast to the view of the three intellectuals just mentioned. Whatever the explanation for the difference here, it surely cannot be that Mill was either more intellectually gifted or more autonomous than de Tocqueville or Jefferson or Kant. Nor can the explanation be that Mill had at his disposal a richer set of facts about human nature than did any of the three.

Now, let us look at things from a quite different direction, namely the people of Le Chambon (Hallie, 1979). In this small town in France, people did what seemed to have been the impossible. In their commitment to protecting Jews, they stood up to the might of Hitler's army. In modern times, there is no better testimony to the unity and commitment of a people to what is right in the face of evil.

Yet, in our characterization and description of the people of Le Chambon, their being autonomous is not what invariably heads the list of commendable things that are said about them. The regret voiced by most people is that throughout Europe the Christian faith did not take the expression that it took in the people of Le Chambon. Notoriously, the Catholic Church was hardly at the forefront of the opposition to Nazi ideology, which is particularly striking since Jews had enjoyed very favourable relations with the Holy See in of all places Rome itself.[2] In any case, autonomy does not take centre stage.

Now, as is well known, Jews were thought to be inherently evil owing to their rejection of Christianity. As a purely formal point, if Jews were inherently evil, then cooperation between Jews themselves would be impossible, since it is not clear how there can be ongoing cooperation between any two inherently evil individuals. And yet it was abundantly evident that there was considerable cooperation and goodwill between Jews. Clearly, the people of Le Chambon had no trouble whatsoever seeing this, although most of the world did not see it. Once more, notice that as an explanation for why the people of Le Chambon did not accept the view that Jews are evil we do not first invoke the autonomy of the Le Chambonnais people.

I want to end this section by returning to the intellectual giants mentioned at the outset. The following is a very significant formal point: even if it were true that (a) no black is as intelligent as the most intelligent white, what simply does not follow from the truth of (a) is that (b) all blacks are less intelligent than any and every white. Indeed, the truth of (a) is compatible with the truth that (c) the typical black randomly chosen is no less intelligent than the typical white randomly chosen, where by hypothesis the typical white did not include, for example, a person like Jefferson. Surely, Jefferson did not think whites generally were on the same intellectual plane as he; and at the very least that consideration would have pointed to (c). The same holds for de Tocqueville and Kant. Yet, it is only Mill among these four who rejected the intellectual inferiority of blacks.

In this section, I have mentioned the names of four individuals whom we rightly regard as autonomous if indeed we regard anyone at all as autonomous (see Dworkin, 1988; Hill, 1991).[3] They were all tremendously capable of critically examining *on their own* the facts at their disposal and the ideas presented to them. What is more, they all understand that both misguided feelings and popular opinion, as such, can be a grave impediment to arriving at the right assessment of matters; and, in this regard, they all had very good reason to believe that they were indeed better than most at avoiding either one of these snares. They understand that few, if any, surpassed them in intellectual stature. Yet these four did not handle the same commonly known facts about blacks in the same way. Only one of them rejected the view that blacks were intellectually inferior to whites. These considerations suggest that it is not plausible to hold that it is autonomy as such that gives us the bridge to morally right behaviour. And the people of Le Chambon serve only to underscore this very point, for we begin with courage rather than autonomy as the explanation for the willingness of these villagers to stand up to the might of Hitler's army in order to save the lives of Jews. And the fact that everyone was willing so to behave was surely relevant to the fact that each was so motivated. So this story is about extraordinary moral interdependence and not breathtaking moral independence.

The web of the social nature of human interaction

A natural reading of the Bradford view is that there is a proclivity on the part of human beings to behave like the general members of their community, even when it comes to committing acts of evil. Coercion cannot be the explanation here, since that leads to an infinite regress. If group Alpha will commit evil against group Beta only if the members of Alpha are coerced, then we will need another group, namely the group Zed, to do the coercing. And we will need yet another group, namely the group Omega, to coerce the group Zed. And so on. Coercion cannot be the only explanation. There is what H.L.A. Hart referred to as the internal point of view (Hart, 1961), namely the idea that people internalize the norms of society, be they evil or otherwise.

So what is the explanation for this proclivity? Part of the answer is the very nature of humanity. Proper human development is inextricably tied to being affirmed by others. From the parent–child relationship to the formation of ties of friendship and romance, human beings seek affirmation. It is also the case that our sense of self, from appearances to abilities, is tied to the ongoing affirmation that we receive from others – not just our friends and loved ones, but people in general. At a basic level, human beings can be said to have a thirst for affirmation. We spend much of our lives in pursuit of it in various ways.

What is more, the sense of self that we have is dynamic rather than static; accordingly, it stands in need of regular affirmation. For example, if a person generally thinks that she is quite talented, this is because the reactions of various people, many of whom are not in her circle of close acquaintances, to the views that she expresses warrant that assessment. The same holds if a person thinks that he is rather attractive or that he is an excellent cook, and so forth. A single assessment can indeed go a long way if it is from the right person, such as Madame Marie Curie who received two Nobel Prizes. However, it will not sustain anyone forever.

Among the standard ways of affirming people are expressions of admiration, praise, and confidence in their abilities; and these various ways of affirming people can take particular forms depending upon the context, the persons involved, and so forth. For instance, a person can understandably find it very affirming that people turn to her with questions pertaining to maths and science. Far more subtle, of course, is a glance. Just so, a simple glance of the right sort can be a considerable indication of physical attractiveness. And if such glances are common enough, then a person has good reason to believe that she or he is a physically attractive individual. The right look may reveal that one is seen as physically attractive or that what one is saying is indeed quite interesting. And so on.

Although it is often the case that affirmation is verbal, a sublime truth is that even with verbal utterances the non-verbal delivery is in most cases extremely important.[4] The words 'I trust you' are typically meaningless in the absence of the appropriate non-verbal behaviour. And as we all know, what the words 'I love you' mean has just about everything to do with who is saying them, and how and when the person is saying them, and to whom the person is saying them. Of course, misunderstandings of any utterance sometimes occur. The fact of the matter, though, is that we get the intended meaning right vastly more often than we get it wrong.

Now, if all goes well, we benefit in the following ways from growing up in a community. On the one hand, we have considerable familiarity with how the network of affirmation is configured. We know the sorts of behaviours that occasion affirmation and the various ways in which they do so. On the other, we have enjoyed a sufficient amount of affirmation from different sources in the community. Indeed, this is true in part owing to our familiarity with the community's social network of affirmation.

In terms of doing things that are conducive to our attaining affirmation, we sometimes make a trade-off. Thus, we may make a point of showing up in one context, such as a meeting or a religious service, because it will result in our being viewed in a more favourable light in another context. A very different kind of example in this regard pertains to ethnic identity. For example, a Muslim woman may not particularly like wearing the hijab. However, she may do so upon occasion because it affords her a standing that she would not otherwise have among various members of the Muslim community.[5]

While the preceding remarks are no doubt obvious, a most fundamental consideration that is ever so relevant to the Bradford view is that we do not choose the social network of affirmation in which we are born and raised. Accordingly, we do not begin our social development by choosing a framework of values. Rather, we grow up being taught a framework of values (by parents, family friends, clergy, and teachers) and then affirmed for displaying in various ways our mastery of those values. Part of the moral upbringing of every child includes statements about who is good and who is bad. So, from a child's point of view, adding ethnicity to the mix hardly seems out of place. In a community of blacks, the claim may be that whites are generally racist and so are to be mistrusted. In a community of whites, the claim may be that blacks are generally less intelligent and so are not to be relied upon for insight. In either case, the community has the greater credibility in the eyes of the children of that community owing in part to the fact that it is its members who are providing the affirmation. What we get is not just a belief, but a deep evaluative attitude – the forging of a set of sensibilities. What we get is a way of believing and a way of being valued that are inextricably bound together.

It is, of course, possible for people to bring themselves out of this grip. Some have in fact done so. Alas, what is unquestionably true is that, in the absence of a defining experience that forces a re-assessment, or some fact that gives a person enormous standing vis-à-vis the members of her or his community, it is extremely difficult for people to do so unless there is some minimal social network that replaces the affirmation that they lose. Thus, exercising the freedom to walk away from the affirmation that one has may not be worth the price one pays in the loss of affirmation. Another way of putting this point is that being autonomous, as wonderful as it may be, is no substitute for the affirmation that comes from those around us. A great many of us are prepared to forgo a measure of autonomy for the sake of affirmation. This should come as no surprise, for we do not enter the world as (well-developed) autonomous beings who then seek affirmation here and there. Instead, things are just the opposite. As psychological creatures, we enter the world as individuals who are rather like sponges to water in terms of the importance of affirmation in our lives; and the importance of such affirmation remains ever so salient for quite some time before we even have the psychological capacity that is a prerequisite for acting autonomously. Our psychological health and happiness is much more tied to being affirmed than it is to being autonomous.[6] It is this truth that underwrites the Bradford view, and so explains why the environment in which we are born and raised makes so much of a difference in the moral character of our behaviour.

The difference between the town of Le Chambon and other cities in France where anti-Semitism manifested itself, such as Cannes and Toulouse, is not marked by decisively more autonomy on the part of the people of Le Chambon. Rather, it is marked by a stark difference in the ends that were publicly affirmed in each community, and so in the kind of behaviour on the part of individuals in the community that brought affirmation from others in the community (see Poznanski, 1997). And if the people in Le Chambon had all been more autonomous, there is no guarantee at all that, on that account alone, they would have been free of racial bias towards Jews. This is a point that we can extract from the parallel case of blacks and the fact that three of the most autonomous individuals ever to walk the face of the earth did not see blacks as the moral and intellectual equal of whites.

Moral baselines

One important way to see the significance of the Bradford view is to consider the reality of moral baselines. A moral baseline refers to the expectations that the members of a society (or community) have regarding how people should behave in a given context. There could be no moral baseline at all with regard to a given piece of behaviour, such as whether or not one should give money to someone on the street who is begging for money. Or, a moral baseline with respect to a given piece of behaviour could be de rigueur. Needless to say, moral baselines can apply to society at large or to a well-defined segment within society. That is, such a segment of society may have moral baselines which do not exist in society at large. The people of Le Chambon are an example par excellence of this being the case, since the moral baseline for altruistic behaviour on the part of these villagers was much higher than it was in France generally. Extremely well-defined social groups such as fraternities or sororities may also have baselines for various kinds of behaviour (see Nuwer, 1999). Obviously, the moral baseline for the same behaviour may vary with locale. Though certainly a common enough greeting in France between adult males who are either close friends or family members, males in North America who have like ties with one another most assuredly do not *faire la bise* (the kiss on each cheek) as a way of greeting one another. Finally, moral baselines can shift upwards or downwards. I shall begin with a few remarks about that.

As an example of a moral baseline that has shifted upwards, it is increasingly the case that men are very much expected to take greater responsibility in the day-to-day care of their children. Concerns with the daily well-being of children that were once deemed to belong only to the domain of women are now held to be an integral part of being a responsible and loving father, and so not at all incompatible with a man's masculinity. Although the greater responsibility still falls upon women, a very substantial shift towards men being more responsible has certainly taken place.

As an example of a moral baseline that has shifted downwards, there was a time when on crowded public transportation with standing room only a healthy young adult man gave his seat to an elderly woman. If such a man failed to do so, an air of disdain towards him filled the public transportation vehicle in which everyone was travelling. The moral baseline that I have just described no longer exists. A young adult male might still give up his seat to an elderly woman. His doing so, however, would flow from his own moral convictions, and not from a concern on his part not to be an object of public moral disapprobation. Notice that the original moral baseline did not expand to include either young adult women so acting on behalf of elderly women or young adults generally acting on behalf of the elderly, be they women or men. Rather, it simply disappeared entirely.

When the moral baseline of behaviour pertaining to a given context is low, there are people who will nonetheless behave with considerable excellence in that context unless doing so jeopardizes their own well-being. Unfortunately, the moral behaviour of most individuals will veer towards the level of the lowered-baseline even if their own well-being is not jeopardized. Noting the difference in impact between a high moral baseline and a low one will help to bring out why this is so.

When the moral baseline is high with respect to a given mode of behaviour, all the members of society have continuous indications of the morally excellent behaviour that is expected of them; accordingly, when a person misses the mark, there are reminders from a multitude of directions that she or he has failed to measure up morally. What is more, in order to block criticism for not behaving as required, a person needs to have a very good excuse. Thus, in the era when it was understood that, on public transportation, a young adult male gave up his seat to an elderly woman, a male who failed to so behave could not just be tired or busy reading a book. Rather, he needed to have a physical affliction, say, that got in the way of his doing so.

No matter how committed any of us are to exhibiting a given excellence, the reality is that we all become tired or overwhelmed by various concerns or have moments of discouragement. In moments like these, an environment with a high moral baseline roundly reinforces our commitment to behave in accordance with the ideal that we embrace. This commonly happens on a number of different levels, from wishing to avoid feelings of public shame to being inspired by the memory that someone who is even worse off than we are nonetheless found the wherewithal to do the right thing, to recalling that we are setting an example for others. And so on. By contrast, when the moral baseline is low, none of the factors just mentioned are in place to motivate persons whose resolve to exhibit the moral excellence in question has weakened. What is more, even the most morally vigilant person knows that she or he will not be criticized. In particular, she or he knows that people will understand that they lack the leverage to raise criticism. This is because the uptake of moral criticism is tied to sincerity, and a person who routinely fails to exhibit a moral excellence cannot possibly claim to be sincere in holding that other individuals should exhibit the behaviour in question. This is the force of the utterance 'You are in no position to criticize me'. The point of the remark is more about the person as the source of the criticism than the criticism itself.

Given this social backdrop, it is a rare person whose moral behaviour will not slide towards the lower moral baseline with respect to the behaviour in question.

The above considerations offer insight into how otherwise decent people can come to engage in evil behaviour or, in any case, and as is more likely, how they come to be sufficiently tolerant of the evil or morally inappropriate behaviour that is going on around them. In the absence of being a part of a very strong and well-defined sub-community that reinforces the excellent behaviour in question, the odds are that the typical denizens of society will find themselves at the very least numb or indifferent to the wrongdoing going on around them.

To live in a society is to be affected by the moral baselines that prevail. Yet, it is obvious that we do not choose the moral baselines of our society. Moreover, moral baselines are rarely, if ever, set in place, eliminated, or re-defined by a formal act, such as legislation. Indeed, how a baseline will be applied can rarely be predicted. Here is a rather stark illustration of these remarks. When we think of lynching in the United States, what readily comes to mind are racist whites inflicting unjust violence upon blacks. We do not imagine that blacks might upon occasion have lynched blacks. Yet, this is precisely what did happen (see Michel, 2008). It happened infrequently, to be sure; but the fact that it happened at all tells us a great deal about how people are impacted by the moral baselines of their society.

To state the obvious, the practice of lynching was a most effective practice for ensuring that blacks complied with the norms imposed by whites regarding the way in which blacks should behave and, in particular, the ways in which blacks should comport themselves around whites. Both blacks and whites alike understood that reality; and, alas, it was precisely this understanding on the part of blacks that led to the rare, but no less real, cases of blacks lynching blacks. Indeed, one of the most interesting cases is that of several black women having a black male lynched for the lascivious behaviour that he exhibited towards them. While we might wonder how these women could have done such a thing, they were no doubt utterly indignant over the fact that this black man was showing them less respect than he would have shown any white woman. From the basis of that indignation, it does not take much to arrive at a quite discon-certing argument from equality, namely the conclusion that he deserves to be punished in precisely the way that he would have been punished had he so disrespected any white woman.

Unlike nowadays, vigilante justice was the norm in the late 1800s and early 1900s, as was the idea that death was an appropriate punishment for sufficiently heinous behaviour. From our present vantage point this is all rather horrifying. Alas, a most sobering truth is that virtually none of us would have thought otherwise were we living under those social conditions. What is more, and this brings us to the very point of the example, lynching was certainly not introduced by whites in the hope that blacks would employ it as means of controlling black behaviour towards blacks. Surely whites never imagined that it would be used in this way.

In modern times, the cell phone stands as a striking example of the way in which, within the space of a mere decade, the baselines of social interaction in society have been impacted in ways that no one could have foreseen.[7] The cell phone has evolved from a device that afforded an important layer of security in the event that a person became lost or otherwise had a crisis to a device that commands our attention no matter what else we might be doing or where we might be. Accordingly, the very politeness and courtesy that were once deemed de rigueur and the mark of a civilized society have been seriously eroded.

Equality and tolerance as the moral baseline

In view of the fact that the evil committed against groups has invariably entailed an inappropriate rejection of the group in question on morally indefensible grounds, it seems reasonable enough to think that the problem of evil of this kind will surely disappear if the moral baseline is one of equality and tolerance for differences between groups. Unfortunately, this is not so, as I shall show in what follows.

If there are any inconvertible truths about human beings, one of them, surely, is that from an evolutionary perspective ethnic differences are entirely inconsequential in terms of any set of abilities that any and all ethnic groups have vis-à-vis one another. We know this truth now in a way that Plato could not have known it – indeed, in a way that even Darwin could not have known it. Alas, although we all seem to pay lip-service to this truth, it remains a fact that in the name of such values as ethnic pride and cultural heritage enormous importance continues to be attached to ethnic differences.

Significantly, ethnic pride is not analogous to personal pride based upon accomplishments. With personal pride, any two people can take pride in the very same accomplishment. Indeed, when another does not think well of herself or himself for an accomplishment, it is common for people of good will, including those who have achieved the very same accomplishment, to point out to the individual that she or he should feel a sense of pride. Ethnic pride, by contrast, would seem to attribute 'essences' to people based upon their ethnicity: people of ethnic group G and only people of ethnic group G can exhibit quality Q or, in any case, do so with more finesse than any individual who is not a member of G. Some will go so far as to say that a member of G who is not exhibiting Q is not being true to himself or herself as a G.

For some the idea of ethnic pride has little, if any, significance vis-à-vis our common humanity. For others, the idea is deemed to be an important component of self-affirmation given a history of racial injustice. In any case, ethnic pride is an accepted part of most Western cultures. Unthinkingly, it is extolled and embraced as something akin to a self-evident truth. Those who would dare to challenge its validity are often dismissed as either racist or self-hating, depending upon the ethnic group of the person making the challenge.

So what could be more disturbing than the reality that this widely embraced view has a striking affinity to Adolf Hitler's view of racial purity? In *Mein Kampf* we find the following words:

> Any crossing of two beings not at exactly the same level produces a medium between the level of the two parents. This means: the offspring will probably stand higher than the racially lower parent, but not as high as the higher one ...

> The consequence of this racial purity, universally valid in Nature, is not only the sharp outward delimitation of the various races, but their uniform character in themselves. The fox is always a fox, the goose a goose, the tiger a tiger, etc., and the difference can lie at most in the varying measure of force, strength, intelligence, dexterity, endurance, etc., of the individual specimens.

From considerations such as these, Hitler concludes:

> Historical experience ... shows with terrifying clarity that in every mingling of Aryan blood with that of lower peoples the result was the end of the cultured people. (Hitler, 1941, vol. 1 ch. 11)

I take it as a given that no one who defends the idea of ethnic pride need hold that any ethnic group is superior to any other.[8] Yet, the formal thesis that

(a) For any ethnic group G, there is no group G* to which G is in any way biologically inferior

is compatible with the thesis that

(b) For any ethnic group G, G will be worse off in virtue of the members of G forming intimate ties with any non-G, where being worse-off need not mean that G will disappear but only that the wherewithal of G to exhibit the attributes said to be definitive of G will diminish owing to 'dilution', if you will.

Difference does not entail inferiority. Hitler clearly thought that non-Aryan groups were sufficiently inferior to Aryan groups. And while he thought that there were differences between non-Aryan groups, he was not committed to rank-ordering all non-Aryan groups just so long as they were all inferior to Aryans.

With (a) and (b), we have a conception of equality. It should be painfully clear, however, that what we also have is a most obnoxious conception of equality – one that veers towards a Hitlerian conception of ethnic differences because ethnicity is privileged above our common humanity. Without asserting superiority, it can nonetheless be asserted of non-members of a group that 'They are not like us'. And that assertion has been the handmaiden of evil, serving as a basis for unwarranted distrust and suspicion.

There are many reasons, some of which are indeed laudable, for why modernity has ended up embracing a view of ethnicity that bears an uncomfortable affinity with Hitler's view regarding race. The important point, though, is that modernity has ended up here notwithstanding the fact that equality and mutual respect for all are among the pillars of modernity. Here the influence of the moral thought of Kant is extraordinary. The idea, which was given its most eloquent contemporary expression in John Rawls's *A Theory of Justice* (Rawls, 1971), is that every human being has, and should also be able to see that all other human beings have, an equal and absolutely non-negotiable claim to moral respect from any and all human beings. The surprise is that we went from a world that did not embrace this Kantian ideal of personhood to one that very much veered in that direction to one that has powerfully gestured backwards; for in the name of diversity people are now said to have significant attributes of excellence that flow not just from being a human being, but from being a human being who belongs to a certain ethnic group. And this line of thought has among its advocates many well-informed and independent thinkers. Most unfortunately, attributing essences to people on the basis of their ethnicity too readily opens the door to attributing shortcomings to them on that very same basis.

Together, the foregoing considerations tell us something very significant, namely that arriving at the right moral baselines in society is not easy, even when we have as an ally a fundamental set of truths about human nature. I shall conclude this chapter with a few remarks regarding the significance of this reality.

Plato versus Mill: constructing a moral society

Both Plato and Mill were equally committed to morality. Broadly construed, the difference between them is as follows: in the *Republic* (Plato, 1966), Plato is a staunch foundationalist, who held that unless individuals are instilled with the right moral values and sensibilities from the outset then it is rather unlikely that they can be counted on to do what is right in the face of the temptation to do what is wrong. By contrast, in his essay *On Liberty* (Mill, 1859) Mill embraced the ideal of living truth which he contrasted with dead dogma; and he held that when living truth is given pride of place in society, then society will veer towards moral and intellectual excellence. Both agree that merely being in possession of the truth is no guarantee that one will do what is right with it. Where they differ, it would seem, is that Plato would contend that in the absence of the right upbringing we cannot become the kind of individuals who will engage in rigorous debate and self-examination in the way that Mill deemed necessary in order for our beliefs to be living truths rather than dead dogma. Let me briefly suggest why I believe that Plato is right, although there is a respect in which I accept the priority that Mill accords to liberty.

It is a given that human beings have a social nature and that affirmation plays a fundamental role in the psychological development and well-being of human beings. This truth supports Plato's contention that how things proceed at the beginning of our lives is of the utmost importance. No conception of liberty will alter this fact. Although Plato does not make the analogy, it would appear that the development of our moral and social self has a strong parallel to the acquisition of fluency in a language (which is very foundational). Anyone can learn to say basic things in a given language. However, being able to do that still leaves one a very long way from being fluent in that language. And it is very rare for people to achieve anything like native fluency in a language if they were not raised speaking that language. What is more, it is extremely difficult for people to forget their native language.

The preceding section makes it abundantly clear that Mill's idea of living truth will not come about in society simply in virtue of people being free to say whatever they please. Freedom of expression is perfectly compatible with privileging ethnic identity in a way that is not only inimical to the idea of living truth but has a most disturbing affinity with an evil ideology.

Now, if we agree that no child could flourish morally or intellectually if accorded complete freedom at the outset of her or his life, then we are conceding a point that is at once most profound and very far reaching, namely that the backdrop of excellence is not freedom. There is no inconsistency at all in holding, on the one hand, that adults should have liberty of belief and maintaining, on the other, that it is only in virtue of having the right upbringing that as adults individuals are most likely to embrace beliefs in a way that is characteristic of the ideal of Mill's conception of living truth, and so to embrace beliefs that veer towards moral and intellectual excellence. What is more likely to deliver that excellence: the right upbringing or rational reflection as such? History and the arguments of this chapter (the previous section in particular) would suggest that the former is much more likely to do so. And that I believe is Plato's point in the *Republic*.

With rare exceptions, *rationality all by itself* is no match for beliefs that have been tied to a lifetime of affirmation and to attitudes sustained by moral baselines of inequality. It was not the grip of rationality alone coursing through the thought of citizen after citizen that led to the end of apartheid in South Africa or the end of the Holocaust or to the end of American slavery. Nor, again, has equality between women and men advanced simply upon rational reflection alone. Although history has been replete with the extraordinary accomplishments of women, far less capable men have insisted that it is natural for women to be subordinate to men.[9]

The challenge for postmodernity is this: how can humanity

inexorably veer towards moral and intellectual excellence by privileging liberty in the way envisioned by Mill without embracing a Platonic conception of upbringing and so the development of the self? I believe that Plato saw more clearly than anyone else that (i) we must choose to privilege excellence above liberty or to privilege liberty above excellence and that (ii) if we choose to privilege liberty over excellence, we thereby assure that evil shall have a place in society.

In a remarkably perceptive essay entitled 'Human Nature and Progress' Norman Geras writes the following:

> Whatever else the goal of socialism might be held to be about, I do not believe it would be worthy of the commitment of morally mature people if it did not include as a central feature the aim of conquering – of radically reducing and eventually, if possible, getting rid of – the kind of evils I have begun here by enumerating. (Geras, 1995b)

Is Norman Geras suggesting that if we sacrificed a little liberty to ensure the demise of evil, then we would be left with all the liberty that any decent human being could ever want? An affirmative response is more plausible than one might suppose, as I shall briefly sketch in what follows.

In 'Language, Truth, and Justice' (1995a) Geras is adamant in his inexorable commitment to truth, observing that there can be no justice in the absence of truth. Then in his essay 'Our Morals: The Ethics of Revolution' (Geras, 1989) he is clear that it is morally permissible to fight in order to attain justice for all. I submit that the moral lesson of 'Human Nature and Progress', when taken in conjunction with the other two essays just mentioned, is that an inviolable duty to enhance justice for all is an ineliminable part of the very same struggle.

Nothing makes justice more secure than a world in which, in the first place, the desire to do what is evil does not obtain a purchase upon our lives. In such a world, individuals are free, but there are certain kinds of choices that simply do not occur to them, in precisely the way that it does not occur to any decent person to commit murder although there is a perfectly straightforward sense in which any decent person is often free to do so. Indeed, as Plato reminds us in the *Republic*, persons with a reputation for being just have an advantage that persons known to be corrupt do not have, since the former are less readily suspected than the former. The just person does not do what is wrong even if it is rather evident to her that no one would suspect her if she did.

A world in which no one thinks to murder or steal and so forth, although everyone has the freedom to commit such wrongs and to get away with doing so, is a world in which our social affirmation is tied to a very high moral baseline. It is this kind of world that Geras thinks we have an obligation to bring about in virtue of being, to use his words, morally mature people. This world does not trivialize the importance of freedom. Rather, it embodies the fundamental truth that the worth of freedom for all increases immeasurably when a society comprises morally upright individuals.

The reality is that a viable and self-sustaining justice society is not an event on the order of the movement of the stars in the galaxy. Rather, such a society is necessarily a moral choice; and, like any choice (moral or otherwise), this choice has consequences. Both a society rife with immorality and a society brimming with upright human beings configure or, at any rate, roundly influence the kinds of desires people have and the choices that people are likely to make. However, it is surely a society of upright individuals that gives us far more of the freedom that contributes to our well-being than does a society of immoral individuals. Both of these claims have centre stage in Plato's *Republic*. Thus, in holding that 'We should unashamedly embrace utopia' (Geras, 2000) Geras grasps better than most that, owing to the fragility of human beings,[10] we need to have Platonic moorings in place if Mill's idea of a living truth is to affirm majestically the humanity of all.

Notes

1 I have discussed these matters in 'Moral Equality and Natural Inferiority' (2005).

2 See Emmanuel Robocanachi, 1891. Robocanachi notes that, although there were exceptions, Jews lived with a tranquility in Rome that was difficult for them to find elsewhere in the world (p. 7).

3 Both authors marvellously illustrate the ways in which autonomy is taken to be important. Dworkin, though, takes a more critical stance regarding the value of autonomy than does Hill.

4 See, for example, the class work in this regard by Irving Goffman, 1959; also Nancy Henley, 1977.

5 It is, of course, understood that strictly speaking it is a divine command in Islam (Sûrah 33:59) for women to wear the hijab unless they must

fear for their well-being in doing so, as Anne-Marie Delcambre discusses (Delcambre, 2006: 201–7). In practice, however, many women have made wearing the hijab a personal choice. See, for example, the discussion of two sisters in the newspaper *Liberation* (20 January 2004), 'Alma et Lila: Tête voilée et obstinée', where one wears the hijab and the other does not.

6 John Deigh illustrates this point in a very interesting way by noting that the richness and closeness of marriage is not at all about maximizing autonomy (Deigh, 1996).

7 For a most illuminating discussion of this, see the group publication by Pièces et Main d'Œuvre (2008).

8 I am influenced here by Norman Geras's marvellous essay 'Language, Truth and Justice' (Geras, 1995a).

9 This point is masterfully illustrated by Paule Paganon (Paganon, 2009).

10 I have developed this line of argument regarding human fragility in chapter 1 of *Vessels of Evil: American Slavery and the Holocaust* (Thomas, 1993); and the idea of human fragility is masterfully developed by Michel Terestchenko (Terestchenko, 2006: chapters 1 and 9).

8

The case against forgiveness[1]

Eve Garrard

When I first started to work on moral issues connected with the Holocaust, the problem I was most concerned with was the idea of evil – what is its nature; do we need to appeal to it to talk adequately about the Holocaust; does the concept do any genuine explanatory work? I found at that time a surprising lack of serious analytical discussion of the concept (a state of affairs which certainly doesn't obtain now), and also a rather unexamined readiness among liberal thinkers to deny that we had any need of that hypothesis, and indeed to assert that appeal to the idea of evil was itself morally deplorable. The idea of evil was, so it was claimed, a way of essentializing human nature, of erroneously supposing that it is determinate; a way of pretending that the alleged evil-doers were somehow monstrous, different and distant from the rest of us; a way of declaring that we were better than them; a way of illicitly drawing on a mystical and unsupportable metaphysics. Some of these putatively objectionable suppositions, such as the appeal to a human nature which is not entirely plastic, not entirely the product of its environment, seemed to me to be obviously correct. Others of them, although objectionable, seemed not actually to be implicit in the appeal to evil at all. So, for me, discovering the work of Norman Geras was in the first instance an enormous relief – here was an avowedly secular thinker who was prepared to argue not only that there was such a thing as human nature, but also that it had some very dark elements indeed in it, elements for which the term 'evil' was the most appropriate one. And as I continued to try to think about these issues, and cognate ones, I constantly found that Geras's work helped me to see, not so much what to think, but more importantly how to think in this most troubled of areas. The moral seriousness of his work; its combination of deep moral commitment with a steady refusal to engage in platitudinous simplification of the evidence or argument; its sensitivity to the complexity of the terrible phenomena under investigation along with a total rejection of any relativizing of the moral implications of those phenomena, or dissipation of responsibility for them; above all its independence of thought: these were and remain a model of how to work on so morally intense and painful a part of the history of the inhumanity of our species.

One of the most obvious, and most troubling, issues raised by moral atrocities is the question of how we should respond to their perpetrators. One possible response is to banish them perpetually from the moral community, to exclude them from our communal concern; another, contrasting, response is to forgive them. Which do we have reason to do; which do we have *most* reason to do? I've argued elsewhere (Garrard, 2002; Garrard and McNaughton, 2002), and will try to do so again here, that we have reason to forgive perpetrators, even those who haven't repented of their crimes. But long-standing discussion with Norm (and others) on this topic has brought me to see how very strong the case is against this view. Any serious attempt to argue in favour of forgiveness must of course start by addressing the full weight of the arguments which tell against it. Most people readily acknowledge the *psychological* strength of the considerations against forgiveness, but it's characteristic of discussions with Norm that he's helped me to see just how *morally* weighty these arguments are.

The appeal of forgiveness

Forgiveness has generally had a very good press in our culture, and this is not surprising in view of the enormous cultural influence of Christianity, with its intense interest in sinners, their need for forgiveness, and its Divine availability. For those who are part of this religious tradition, forgiving our enemies is (among other things) a way of imitating, in so far as we are able to, the goodness and generosity and loving-kindness of God. Even those who are not directly part of this tradition have often been deeply affected by it, and a readiness to forgive is widely seen as not only attractive but also virtuous: an admirable character trait to which we should all aspire. To forgive those who have wronged us, even if (perhaps especially if) they haven't repented of their wrongdoing, is seen as displaying a commendable lack of rancour and malice, and a large-minded generosity of spirit.

In addition to these reasons for forgiveness, another set of more purely consequential considerations are often adduced. In the aftermath of the large-scale political horrors which so disfigured the twentieth century (and which show little signs of abating in the twenty-first) the wounds inflicted on the body politic can only be healed, so many people think, if there is reconciliation between the victims and their tormentors; and forgiveness, it is suggested, is the natural and perhaps necessary precursor of that reconciliation. And as well as these social benefits there are also, it is claimed, personal benefits for the victim: forgiveness frees her from the corrosive effects of bitterness and resentment, and hence enables her to move on from the crime and from her role of victim in it. Both at the social and at the individual level, forgiveness is seen as having a powerfully therapeutic part to play in restoring the equilibrium disrupted by the original offence, or in creating a new one.

We should not necessarily see these consequentialist considerations favouring forgiveness as being in some deep contrast to the moral reasons. It's quite plausible to suppose that the reason forgiveness (allegedly) has these therapeutic effects is closely related to the fact that it calls on character traits which are themselves virtues: kindness, generosity, tolerance, humility. It would not be surprising to find that the exercise of the virtues leads to human flourishing – this is, after all, exactly what virtue theorists claim. And this complex of moral and prudential considerations fits well into aspects of the prevailing cultural climate of the times, with its demand that we always be ready to see the point of view of the other person, that we recognize how difficult the circumstances of wrongdoers often are, that we understand our own weaknesses and see how easily we too might have been perpetrators of terrible crimes had our circumstances been different. Forgiveness stands in opposition, it is thought, to an arrogant certainty of our own moral superiority, and to the concomitant hypocrisy which overlooks our own moral shortcomings. So, irrespective of our background theoretical commitments, forgiveness presents a very appealing face to us: both on moral and on prudential grounds, there seem to be good reasons for forgiving wrongdoers, perhaps even those wrongdoers who haven't repented or shown remorse for their crimes.

Facing this rosily attractive picture of forgiveness, however, are a number of formidable arguments against it, and especially against unconditional forgiveness.[2]

The case against forgiveness

To see the strength of the case against forgiveness, we must first briefly remind ourselves what forgiveness actually amounts to – just what it is that we're being recommended to do in response to offences committed against us. Forgiveness is sometimes characterized as 'wiping the slate clean', but in so far as this means forgetting the crime, or behaving as if it had never happened, or allowing it to make no difference to how the offender is to be treated, then there are often situations in which these responses are neither desirable nor even possible. A mother whose child has been murdered cannot forget the crime, nor would it be right for her (or anyone else) to refuse to let the crime make any difference to how the murderer is to be treated – for a start, it might be important to alter the circumstances in which the murderer could come into contact with other children. Nonetheless, it would be possible for such a mother to forgive her child's murderer. (Psychologically, of course, it would be desperately difficult for her to do so. But the issue in hand is not whether it would be hard for her to do so, but whether it would be right for her to do so – whether she has an all-things-considered reason, or indeed any reason, to forgive such an atrocity.)

Wiping the slate clean doesn't capture what is at the heart of forgiveness, since forgiveness is possible, and may be desirable, even where wiping the slate clean isn't. A better account of forgiveness focuses on the mental states which are incompatible with it. Common, and very understandable, responses by the victim towards the offender include anger, resentment, indignation, rancour, contempt, bitterness, malice, and a range of other negative attitudes. Some, though not all, of these are incompatible with forgiveness: broadly speaking, those states which involve ill-will towards the offender are what must be overcome in forgiveness. Not all negative states involve ill-will: indignation, for example, need not; but resentment and rancour commonly do, and malice invariably does. The broad account of forgiveness which will be adopted here is that forgiveness is the overcoming of those negative attitudes which involve ill-will, most characteristically resentment and its cognates; and also the adoption of a stance of at least minimal good-will towards the perpetrator. Forgiveness, on this construal of it, is in most cases supererogatory: it can't be demanded of the victim, especially not by the perpetrator. (For a more detailed discussion of the nature of forgiveness see Garrard and McNaughton, 2002).

Perhaps there are some cases where it's true to say that we ought to forgive a person who has done us wrong – when the wrong wasn't very great, when the perpetrator of it has repented, has apologized and made restitution, when no harm to others will result from the restoration of good will towards the offender. To say that we ought to forgive the offender in such cases is to say that we have, all-things-considered, reason to do so. But such cases do not at all exhaust the rich and diverse range of human wrongdoings, many of which involve terrible and irreparable harm to the primary victim and to others (such as those who love her, for example), and in many of which the perpetrator has felt, and still feels, no remorse for his crimes. Here forgiveness, if it takes place at all, seems to be supererogatory – a gift given by the victim to the perpetrator. And it's not immediately obvious why victims should offer offenders that gift. It's unclear, to say the least, that they have reason to forgive, to adopt a stance of well-wishing towards, the wrongdoers who have caused such harm.

Just as there are two main kinds of reasons which are advanced for forgiveness – the (alleged) production of good consequences, either social or individual or both, and the (supposed) inherently moral considerations to do with generosity, solidarity, and the rejection of hate and malice – so there are two kinds of arguments against forgiveness. Firstly, there are the anti-therapeutic arguments, so to speak. Is it really so clear that forgiveness is what enables the victim to rise above (in a revealing but question-begging locution) the wrong that was done to her, and move on? Sometimes a quite different course of action, such as revenge, also seems to bring closure and allow the victim to let the wrongdoing subside into the past. Sometimes it is the passing of time, and the victim's growing indifference to the offence and the offender. Since other stances and attitudes can produce the therapeutic effect, it's not obvious that that effect yields an argument exclusively favouring forgiveness.

At the societal level, it may well be true that the maintenance of hatred and the pursuit of revenge will prevent any return to social equilibrium. But it doesn't follow that forgiveness is needed to ensure that return. It is notable that in the South African context what has been sought is truth and *reconciliation*, and though forgiveness has been encouraged it has not been an obligatory part of the reconciliation procedure. Forgiveness is not in fact necessary for reconciliation, and it is the latter rather than the former which is needed for social repair. (This argument doesn't deny that forgiveness could also heal social wounds; it's just that forgiveness doesn't seem to be necessary for that to take place.) It is also worth noting that the pressure on victims to forgive can itself be quite damaging to them (see Brudholm, 2008), by delegitimizing the resentment which they justifiably feel, and demanding of them a generosity which they may not wish to offer to the person who has done so much harm both to them, and to people whom they loved.

In any case, a stronger claim can also be made that it isn't clear at the societal level whether forgiveness does have the therapeutic effects which are so readily claimed for it. Victims who refuse to forgive offenders may be gripped by a desire not for vengeance but for justice, and in maintaining resentment they may be insisting that we should not lose our morally essential sense of the responsibility and the culpability of those who have committed terrible wrongs. The persistence of resentment may, as Améry thought, protect us all from the easy forgetfulness that would allow the horrors of the past to be recreated in the future.[3] It may be that what a broken society needs is justice rather than, or at least prior to, forgiveness, since without justice the embers of conflict are more likely at some point to burst into flame again. The suggestion here is that for social stability justice is at least as therapeutically important as forgiveness. Unless perpetrators are publicly brought to justice and punished for their misdeeds, we are unlikely to be able to prevent future atrocities of the same or worse kind from taking place. Not only is forgiveness unnecessary to restore social stability, it may be insufficient as well.

It is of course very hard to know what kind of evidence would settle these psycho-social claims, but it's safe to say that at the very least the therapeutic case for forgiveness is empirically unproven. But, in any case, even if forgiveness were more therapeutically efficacious than any of the alternatives, the arguments against it are not exhausted.

The second kind of argument against forgiveness puts therapeutic considerations to one side, and draws our attention to other morally significant features of our response to offenders. Some, perhaps much, of the pressure on victims to forgive implies that those who refuse to do so are morally defective – perhaps understandably, considering what has been done to them; but nonetheless (it is implied) in a condition which is morally inferior to that which they are being invited to occupy. On this picture, all the *moral* considerations are seen as weighing in on the side of forgiveness, in contrast to the (supposedly) more primitive and emotional reasons, such as a desire for revenge, which count in favour of non-forgiveness. As it stands, such a picture simply begs the question against the possibility of a morally legitimate maintenance of resentment. Contrary to that picture, there are in fact serious moral reasons for maintaining resentment and other hostile attitudes towards the perpetrator. Even if it were true that forgiveness is therapeutically efficacious for the victim by releasing her from psychological bondage to the past and enabling her to take up more positive attitudes, it is not always the case that victims put their own mental well-being first in these matters (see Amery, 1980). For some, at least, the demand for justice takes priority. Victims with this attitude may not be primarily concerned with their own healing or well-being at all – their demand for justice or retribution may derive from a duty they feel to those who died as a result of the perpetrators' crimes, or they may see the demand for justice as morally compelling in its own right, as necessary to rectify a violation of the moral order, irrespective of its effects on their psyches. An insistence that the importance of recognizing and acknowledging breaches of the moral order can outweigh questions of psychological health is not a morally negligible position.[4]

It is in any case a mistake to think of demands for justice driven by indignation at the offender's breach of the moral order as equivalent to demands for revenge. Revenge is private and personal; it relishes the suffering it inflicts on its object; it readily (though by no means invariably) aims for disproportionate punishment of the offender. Justice by contrast is public; it is constrained by considerations to do with equity and desert; enjoyment of the suffering produced in the offender is no part of it. If we have to choose between justice and forgiveness, then we are choosing between differing moral considerations, rather than between morality and some more self-interested or more primitive kind of reason for action.

It might be argued here that since justice for serious offences will normally require punishment, and since punishment normally involves some degree of suffering, then justice also seeks suffering for its own sake, and cannot be distinguished from revenge in this respect. But this too is a mistake: even where revenge is directed at a wrongful action (which isn't always the case), its focus is not on the rectification of that wrong. Rather, what the vengeful person seeks is the satisfaction of seeing the perpetrator suffer, whether or not that suffering serves justice. But in pure retributive justice, it is the rectification of the wrong that is the focus. No satisfaction is taken in the suffering of the perpetrator for its own sake, but only in so far as it serves justice. The attitudes of the vengeful person and the indignant person to the suffering imposed in just punishment will characteristically differ. The indignant person who is not vengeful will be pleased if the offender's punishment may rightfully be lessened, perhaps because the offender repents and reforms, or because we discover that the offence was less severe or was mitigated in some way. In so far as the justly indignant person seeks the offender's suffering, she does not desire it *qua* suffering but *qua* rectification of a wrong. That attitude, unlike the desire for vengeance, does not seek satisfaction in the suffering for its own sake, but for the sake of justice. The vengeful person, by contrast, will gloat over the downfall and even degradation of the one who has wronged him, and be frustrated if it turns out that the wrongdoer deserves a lesser punishment than the vengeful person would find satisfying. Demands for retributive justice are not, therefore, equivalent to demands for revenge, and the victim whose sustained resentment is a way of maintaining the demand for justice is not morally equivalent to one who purely seeks revenge for her own wrongs.

But in any case something which must not be overlooked is that the victim has a *right* to feel resentment, given what the perpetrator has done to her. It is true that she can if she chooses waive that right, but that fact doesn't invalidate the right itself. What the perpetrator has done warrants hostility, and too easy a readiness to forgive seems to overlook the moral significance of the original offence. Part of that significance resides in the way in which the offender has made light of the victim's standing, has treated her as if she and her interests are of no importance. Too ready a forgiveness runs the risk of colluding in that light dismissal, of implicitly endorsing the low status which the perpetrator has accorded to the victim. Forgiveness in these circumstances may betoken a failure of self-respect, and pressing a victim to overcome her resentment and hence to forgive may amount to collusion in the offender's dismissal of the victim's moral status, since it may tacitly imply the judgement that what was done doesn't really warrant the hostility which the victim is being urged to overcome.

We have reasons to provide justice, with its attendant publicity and punishment, for the sake of the victims, dead or alive. In subordinating these reasons to considerations of future personal or social flourishing we are treating the victims as if they, and their sufferings, weren't, in the end, of great moral significance. And this is, in general, one of the major arguments against forgiveness: in readily forgiving the offender, we fail to show sufficient respect for the victim. Where the offence is at the individual level, the victim's readiness to forgive the offender shows, on this argument, a failure in self-respect. Where the forgiveness is at the societal level, and hence where the main potential forgivers are the victims' families, and other members of their ethnic or religious groups, as well as those victims who have survived, then too easy a forgiveness fails in respect towards those who have suffered from the offenders' misdeeds. Ready forgiveness of the offender, acceptance of him back into the circle of good will for the sake of the benefit to the rest of society, doesn't seem to be a way of adequately respecting his victims: the justice which we owe to them is being traded off against social good – that is, the good of others. Even where we think there is reason to do this, we shouldn't deny that a price is to be paid: the victims (or their families) will be denied justice for their sufferings, and to that extent will be shown less than sufficient respect.

Closely allied to this objection is the claim that, in forgiveness, we often fail to grasp the full weight and gravity of what the offender did. It is that weight which justifies the victim in responding with hostility and resentment: if a perpetrator has dismissed my needs and interests as of no concern, then I am justified in resenting this, and it's reasonable for me to withdraw good will from such a person. One who fully grasps the nature of the offence and what it has done to the victim will respond with indignation at the very least, and often with ill-will; this is what has to be overcome in forgiveness. Too facile a forgiveness suggests that there wasn't much hostility to struggle with, which in turn suggests that the full weight of the offence hasn't been grasped, since, if it had, the natural response to it would have cost some effort to overcome. Here, as elsewhere, affective and cognitive responses are not fully separable, and the person who feels too little indignation is suffering from both an emotional and a cognitive deficit. Where resentment is minimal because indignation is minimal, forgiveness comes cheap; but it is bought at the expense of a failure to recognize and respond appropriately to the true gravity of the offence.

And these considerations are bolstered by the patently obvious fact that sometimes forgiveness is motivated by considerations which are less than morally respectable: people may offer forgiveness in order to demonstrate their moral superiority; or to put others at a moral disadvantage; or to curry favour with powerful offenders, or with others who approve of forgiveness; or to heap a burden of guilt on the shoulders of the offender or of other less forgiving bystanders. There can be a multiplicity of bad motives for doing good things, and forgiveness is no different from other actions in this respect

To sum up: the principal arguments against forgiveness claim that:

(1) it doesn't always have the therapeutic effects claimed for it, either at the individual or at the societal level;
(2) forgiveness is not the only route to achieving these desired effects;
(3) in some cases at least it is actually damaging, both at the individual and at the societal level;
(4) even if it does have strongly therapeutic effects, that alone doesn't settle the moral argument, since there can be good reasons for thinking that other things are more important than therapeutic considerations;
(5) one of these things is justice, which is morally important in its own right, and may also produce better outcomes than forgiveness;
(6) forgiveness often involves too little respect for the victim as a person;
(7) forgiveness often involves a failure to grasp the nature and extent of the victim's suffering;
(8) forgiveness can be and often is motivated by craven or self-serving considerations, which have no claim on our moral attention.

In defence of forgiveness

The case against forgiveness, especially unconditional forgiveness, is a formidable one. It is also in many ways a morally satisfying one; quite as satisfying, in its different way, as is the case for forgiveness. Where the case for forgiveness speaks to our desire for reconciliation, harmony, generosity, so the case against it satisfies our commitment to justice, to moral responsibility, to an uncompromising rejection of atrocity. It legitimizes our desire to bear witness to the iniquity of what has been done to the innocent, and to make explicit our refusal to collude with those crimes in any way. It is true that the case against forgiveness can be abused and exploited in various ways – it can be used to gratify what may sometimes be a very powerful and discreditable urge to condemn others and inflict punishment on them. There is a rancorous mean-spiritedness which can easily masquerade as a proper concern to uphold justice and ensure that people get what they deserve. But the case for forgiveness can also be abused: 'cheap boosterism' (see Murphy, 2003) about forgiveness can exploit our desire to seem generous, sympathetic, morally elevated; to embrace a hoped-for rosy future and to forget about the ugly and sometimes horrifying past, and about the inconvenient and often quite costly demands for justice from those who suffered in that past. Praise for forgiveness of those who have harmed others can readily slide into a light-minded dismissal of the weight and gravity of those harms. We can't judge either case by its vulnerability to abuse, since that exists so prominently on both sides; as always, we can only assess them on the basis of their actual strengths and weaknesses.

Although the case against forgiveness is indeed a strong one, it is not necessarily conclusive. Some at least of its objections to forgiveness can be met, and others can be defused by careful analysis of what is at issue.

Firstly, the defender of forgiveness can concede that it may not be as therapeutic as is sometimes claimed, and in some cases it may be less therapeutic than alternatives such as revenge or indifference. But she can readily concede this because she can also agree that therapeutic efficacy isn't always the most important consideration in establishing how victims, and the rest of us, should respond to perpetrators. Indeed, a defender of forgiveness can agree that much of the cheap boosterism about forgiveness is as shallow as it is facile, and that forgiveness is often a difficult and laborious project which might take a lifetime to complete.

Secondly, many of the morally important considerations which the case against forgiveness rightly emphasizes can be accommodated within a defence of forgiveness. It is often pointed out that offenders deserve punishment, and that this element of retribution is lost if we endorse forgiveness as a general policy. But that is not in fact the case: forgiveness is compatible with punishment, although it

doesn't necessarily demand it. The forgiver may, for example, see
that punishment is needed for the sake of other victims' well-being;
or for the sake of justice, to rectify the breach in the moral order
which the offence constituted; or to deter the offender (and others)
from repeating the offence; or to bring the offender to a realization of
the moral nature of what he has done – a realization that is an
essential part of his future flourishing. Each of these is compatible
with overcoming ill-will towards the offender, and adopting a stance
of good will towards him – that is, with forgiving him. It's true that
offenders don't (usually) deserve to be forgiven, and to that extent if
forgiven will not get what they deserve. But we do not generally
believe that people should always and only get what they deserve
('use every man after his desert, and who would 'scape whipping?')
And even where justice requires punishment it doesn't require ill-
will, so the demands of justice can be delivered, if that is what the
situation morally requires, even where there is forgiveness.

Thirdly, with respect to the explicit rejection of atrocity, the public
refusal to collude with it, and the bearing of witness to the iniquity of
what has been done to the innocent: all these are compatible with
forgiveness. What forgiveness requires is that we relinquish ill-will
towards the offender; it doesn't require that we abandon all negative
attitudes, only those which involve ill-will. One entirely legitimate
response to wrongdoing is indignation – outrage (or some similar but
less intense emotion) at a breach in the moral law. Indignation
normally involves the desire to protest against and to rectify that
breach, but it needn't involve ill-will, and hence forgiveness is
compatible with it. Indignation may, where appropriate, involve
explicit and public rejection of the offence and the full acknowledgement of its weight and gravity; but this is compatible with forgiving
the offender, though it will perhaps naturally involve taking steps to
prevent re-occurrence of the offence. And that too is compatible with
forgiveness: since forgiveness isn't a matter of wiping the slate clean,
it doesn't entail that the relationships which obtained before the
offence must be restored. Often they will be, but not always. Where,
for example, restoring the previous relationship might put the victim
at further risk of harm, she may forgive the offender without being
prepared to restore the *status quo ante*. There is nothing inconsistent
with abjuring ill-will towards him while refusing to return to the
previous situation.

Fourthly, forgiveness is entirely compatible with holding the offender morally responsible for what he did. Indeed, it actually requires that attribution of responsibility: if the offender isn't responsible for the wrongdoing, then there is nothing to forgive. (This is why it's so objectionable to be forgiven when you don't regard yourself as having been responsible for any wrongdoing.) Forgiving is not the same as either condoning the offence (that is, judging that it wasn't really a wrongdoing) or excusing the offender (that is, judging that the perpetrator wasn't really to be blamed for committing the offence). In forgiveness, we hold the wrongdoer to be fully responsible for his actions, and we maintain an accurate view of their moral gravity, and yet we overcome ill-will towards him, and adopt a stance of at least minimal good will. This is often a very difficult thing to do, which is why boosterism about forgiveness can seem so facile.

Finally, there is the question of self-respect. Many people think that a readiness to forgive the perpetrator betokens a failure of self-respect on the part of the victim (or a failure in respect towards the victim if the forgiveness is being offered by third parties).[5] Here the thought is that resentment is an appropriate response to the attack on one's standing which the original offence involves, and that abjuring resentment implies an acceptance of the low status which the wrongdoer assigns to the victim. Of course, such things are possible. But they are not an inevitable feature of forgiveness: another possibility derives from the fact that there is a form of self-respect, which (in the light of Darwall's (1977) distinction between appraisal respect and recognition respect) we might refer to as recognition self-respect, which is not earned from or bestowed by others, and cannot be lost by their failure to acknowledge it. Self-respect based on that ground is not threatened by offenders, and overcoming resentment towards them displays no failure in it. Someone whose self-respect had this basis could still have resentment to overcome, since we can properly be hurt by, and resent, being neglected, or slighted, or treated maliciously, even where we are sure that this treatment was unjustified and where our self-respect isn't eroded by it. This resentment needs to be overcome for forgiveness to take place, but doing so needn't involve any objectionable servility.

It should be noted that although all offences which wrong someone do involve a failure to treat them with sufficient respect, forgiveness doesn't imply acceptance of the verdict (implicit or explicit) in that failure. Abandoning ill will and adopting goodwill doesn't mean accepting the views or the verdicts of the one towards whom you take a benevolent stance. Silence does not imply consent or endorsement; in any case, forgiveness is compatible with protest. What seems to be doing the work in this concern about forgiveness is the implicit assumption that forgiveness involves some kind of *concession* to the offender's view of the matter. But this assumption is ungrounded: forgiveness can be seen as a gift, not a concession, and to assume that to forgive is to concede is to beg the question at issue.

It might at this point be suggested that the position being defended here no longer contains anything that is fully recognizable as a conception of *forgiveness* at all. I have argued that forgiveness is compatible with the maintenance of anger and indignation; also, in some cases, with the demand that the perpetrator be punished in full for his crimes; even, in some circumstances, with the refusal to re-establish prior good relations. But is the condition of a person who has been forgiven in this way any different from that of someone who hasn't been forgiven at all – is forgiveness really what's going on here? Surely, it might be said, this conception of forgiveness is just too remote from the usual understanding of forgiveness as wiping the slate clean, or forgetting along with forgiving.

It's true that there is a range of different conceptions of forgiveness, and the one being defended here is certainly at the more robust and unsentimental end of the spectrum. However, there are two things which tie it to our common core conception of forgiveness: firstly, on this account forgiveness comes out as being *difficult,* since it requires a full grasp of the violation of the moral order which the perpetrator has committed, and the overcoming of the resentment which this naturally and justifiably produces. This difficulty in getting oneself to forgive is acknowledged in much of the literature on forgiveness, and is a readily recognizable part of our common moral experience. Secondly, the focus here is on the rejection of ill will, and the re-establishment of at least a modicum of goodwill towards the forgiven person. The difference between ill will and even a modest degree of goodwill is enormous, a difference in kind, as anyone who has faced a serious case of the former can testify. A conception of forgiveness which has that difference at its heart is not one in which forgiveness is negligible or invisible. But nor is it one that lends itself to the easy reconciliations and cheap boosterism which others have rightly condemned, and which have diluted the general understanding both of what forgiveness really requires, and of the proper response to violations of the moral order.

The positive case

It looks as if the principal objections to forgiveness made in the case against it can be met. But this does not amount to a positive argument in favour of forgiveness. It remains the case that the victim may be warranted in resenting the offender – her resentment can be entirely legitimate. However, it doesn't follow that there can be no other reasons which overcome that one: it's possible that a legitimate reason for resentment may nonetheless be legitimately outweighed.

What reason can be offered for overcoming resentment and forgiving the perpetrator? There are two principal candidates for such a reason: respect for persons, and human solidarity. Promising though it looks, respect for persons does not in fact generate a convincing reason for forgiving unrepentant offenders, particularly since the resentment which is warranted by their actions is something which we only offer to persons anyway, and hence it itself involves a full recognition of their personhood and their concomitant ability to choose for themselves.[6] In the case of serious offenders, their use of their distinctively personal characteristics – their practical reason, for example – has been so distorted and degraded that it's quite unclear why respect for them as persons should generate any remission in ill will. A better bet as a candidate reason to forgive derives from the facts of our common human nature. Here the focus is on our shared humanity, and hence our shared human frailty and fallibility. In the case of the worst perpetrators, let's hope that it's true to say that we wouldn't have done what they did; but most of us believe, rightly in my view, that in certain circumstances we too could have acted like that. This isn't to provide any kind of excuse or condoning of what wrongdoers have done: in recognizing that I too could have acted like that I am recognizing that I too could be fully responsible for wrongdoing, and hence a fit object for resentment and hatred. This recognition follows from the thought (voiced among others by Primo Levi) that even the worst perpetrators aren't monsters, they're humans like you and me. Maybe another way to put that is that if they are monsters, then so too are we, at least potentially – there's a recurring streak of evil in the human blueprint.

(I am not here suggesting, and do most strongly not believe, that this involves any moral equivalence between the perpetrator and the victim. Responsibility belongs to those who perpetrate the wrongs; their victims are in this respect innocent. However counterfactuals about what we ourselves might have done in the perpetrators' circumstances can properly affect the attitudes we take to these truths about the perpetrator's responsibility.)

It might be argued here (see for example Griswold, 2007: 66) that these facts about human moral frailty, rather than grounding a commitment to forgiveness, warrant the view that a regime of the harshest punishments and explicit refusals to forgive is what's needed to keep us all on the straight and narrow. This is to treat the question of forgiveness as primarily a matter of producing the best consequences. But this is too narrow and impoverished a view of what's at stake here, especially in the light of the significance of questions of desert for this topic. In any case, we know in advance that nothing will keep all of us, or even most of us, permanently on the straight and narrow, so the question will still arise of how we should stand towards those who depart from it when deterrence has failed; and, as we have seen, forgiveness is compatible with the demand for punishment, so its deterrent power is not lost to those who endorse forgiveness.

In what way, then, do considerations about our common human frailty provide a reason for forgiveness? We could, of course, just write off the perpetrators of terrible wrongdoing – hate is not an unreasonable response to what they have done. But, given our common human nature, this will be a verdict on our possible selves as well as on them. And our sense of common humanity, the solidarity we may feel with the rest of the human race, our awareness that we too could be offenders and in need of forgiveness, whether or not we were to realize it at the time: all these give us reason to forgive the perpetrators of wrongdoing, who have failed to meet the moral demands of the human condition under which we all labour.[7]

There is also a more direct argument in favour of forgiveness. The specificities of the individual case, crucial though they normally are in moral matters, may not always be what settle the issue. Background commitments, to goodwill rather than to ill will, to love rather than to hate, may come into play here, and alter the interaction of the various considerations. Although many, perhaps most, moral issues are to be settled by a process of weighing and balancing the competing considerations present in the particular context which we're facing, this needn't always be the case – sometimes we feel ourselves called on to make a brute and fundamental choice, in which we commit ourselves to our broadest background values. What constitutes the best response in the particular case can be determined by a wider world-view involving a preference for love (and its cognates, such as goodwill) rather than hate (and its cognates of ill will and malice), even where hate is entirely legitimate. Such preferences are basic, and cannot be further defended. But many people share this one, at least in principle. Even Jeffrie Murphy, who defends resentment so persuasively, thinks that all of us would prefer to be inscribed in the Book of Love rather than in the Book of Hate (Murphy, 2003: 86), and that is a preference which may give us reason to choose forgiveness over even a fully justified, entirely legitimate resentment.

Even if there is, as I am arguing, always sufficient reason to forgive, it doesn't follow that all cases of forgiveness are admirable. Here as elsewhere, people can do the right thing for the wrong reasons. As mentioned earlier, forgiveness can be proffered for a variety of self-serving and discreditable reasons. In fact where such motives predominate it often isn't clear that forgiveness – the overcoming of ill will and the adoption of at least minimal goodwill – has actually taken place. If the desired outcome – recognition by others of one's own occupation of the moral high ground, the keeping of the peace, or the warm glow of self-admiration – fails to materialize, an uprush of resentment often reveals that the work of forgiveness is still to be done. But even where forgiveness has genuinely taken place, it may remain objectionably shallow and facile, having been undertaken for such self-regarding considerations. Nonetheless, in all such cases the possibility will remain of a forgiveness undertaken for good reasons, difficult though this will generally be.

The case against forgiveness derives much of its strength from the fact that there is more than enough evil in the world to generate good reasons to hate its perpetrators. If forgiveness is supererogatory, as I have suggested, then it follows that many cases of resentment and hatred are not morally blameworthy. More than that: they may be morally preferable to cases of facile forgiveness of the kind described above, where the actual considerations motivating the forgiveness are shallow and discreditable. The sustained resentment of a Jean Amery may be of far greater moral worth than the cheap forgiveness of a Uriah Heep. Nonetheless, so I have argued, there are always reasons available to us which tell in favour of forgiveness, reasons stemming from human solidarity, from a consciousness of our common moral frailty and susceptibility to evil, and from a commitment to the value of goodwill, and more broadly of love.

How strong are these reasons to forgive – do they amount to a duty? Surely not; the power of the case against forgiveness precludes it from being obligatory. Forgiveness is a gift, one which can't be demanded of the victim; since it is supererogatory, there is nothing blameworthy in choosing to withhold it. On the robust construal of forgiveness which has been offered here, it is compatible with indignation, the demand for punishment, and the refusal in at least some cases to restore the relations which obtained before the offence was committed. These features go a considerable way to satisfy the case against forgiveness, and in their presence it seems safe to say that forgiveness is always permissible, at the least. There is always sufficient reason to forgive, and we can always, without moral defect, choose to do so for those reasons.

Notes

1　I owe a primary debt here to David McNaughton, without whom this chapter wouldn't have been written. My thanks also to Steve de Wijze for very helpful comments.
2　See, for example, Brudholm, 2008; Griswold, 2007; Murphy, 2003; Amery, 1980.
3　See Amery, cited in Brudholm, 2008: 78.
4　See Brudholm, 2008.
5　Although it is sometimes argued that third-party forgiveness is either impossible or illegitimate, it seems clear that third parties can sustain ill will towards offenders on account of their offences, and hence it is at least possible for them to overcome that ill will and to adopt a stance of goodwill – i.e. to forgive them.
6　See Garrard, 2002.
7　For a more fully worked-out defence of this view see Garrard and McNaughton, 2002. For a criticism of this view, see Griswold, 2007: 64–7.

9

A fine site

Damian Counsell

Norman Geras is an emeritus professor of politics, with well regarded books to his name. However, it was not through these that I first became aware of him, but through his weblog. *Normblog* is now an institution, one of only a handful of UK blogs worthy of that description. I suspect that its regular readers number in the tens of thousands, and that hundreds of thousands have visited the site during its six years of existence. Although Norm is responsible for by far the greatest part of its content and he must be given credit for its extraordinary success, others have contributed to this achievement. Their contribution flows, in turn, from Norm's willingness to offer space to the opinions of others – even when those opinions differ from his own. As well as individual essays from friends, colleagues, comrades, opponents, and others, Norm publishes correspondence and runs regular slots – in which, for example, a different (dead-tree) writer each week writes about other writers, or a different blogger answers questions about him- or herself. Even without such contributions, *normblog*'s archive would still be a valuable scholarly resource in its own right.

Many people complain that, while the World Wide Web (WWW) overflows with data, little of its content is true or useful information, and still less of it embodies any kind of wisdom. The medium is used to spread myths, publish libels, perpetrate fraud, cultivate hatred, and celebrate violence. (This has also long been true of the written word. One of the earliest and most prominent blogging software companies, the one responsible for hosting Norm's blog in fact, refers to the earlier technology of the printing press in its trade name: 'Movable Type'.) Despite all this, the Web is a store of human knowledge unprecedented in its accessibility and scope. In return for its easy bounty, we have to apply more sophisticated forms of the skills we have had to cultivate since our ancestors first learned to speak: the ability to recognize accurate accounts of the external world, and the ability to identify worthwhile conclusions based on such accounts. There is both information and wisdom in *normblog*.

For most of my adult life, I worked in research institutions or universities doing biomedical science; but, although I have always followed politics, I have taken little interest in academic political studies. Scientists sip from a fire hose of current published research. They tend to specialize narrowly. When they venture outside their own area of professional interest, they also tend to restrict their intake to work that they think has wider importance, containing conclusions that meet their respective burdens of proof, and discussions that meet certain standards of argumentation. Many scientific research publications fall short of these criteria. So many non-scientific academic publications fall below this threshold that few scientists take them seriously or even attend to them at all. This is unfortunate. The history and taxonomy of political thought, for example, are important subjects for higher study, and fine scholars document valuable insights in these areas. Scientists are not by definition better thinkers, but, within the hard sciences, nature and computation widely impose an inescapable discipline upon those who report the outputs of their experiments and models to their peers in good faith. Outside these external constraints, many scientists are as susceptible to faulty reasoning as their non-scientific peers. It is a shame that our educational institutions, including those devoted to the sciences (and those devoted to philosophy), do not spend more time teaching students to think rigorously.

This last concern is especially important now that so many students and scholars research and publish online. The Web was originally devised as a means by which dispersed groups of scientists could share research data and collaborate over the Internet (Net). Given the Net's historical origins in the US and UK military, telecoms, and academic research and development, it is not surprising that its architecture and ethos owe much to the Western spirit of academic freedom and the First Amendment to the US constitution. The medium of the Web has low barriers to entry and, in much of the world, sets all-but-nominal limits on the quality of the messages it carries. For all the trouble this inherent openness has caused, it has been central to the dazzling growth of modern communications networks and the rapid evolution of the activities they mediate.

Virtual life develops so much more rapidly than life in the real world that some of the virtual world's citizens routinely refer to 'Web years', which are assumed to run an order of magnitude faster than years in real time.

I was early enough to the Internet to witness various protocols compete to occupy the space thereon that the Web dominates today – perhaps a few of those reading this will remember exploring the Net with something called 'Gopher'. For years of Web time, I failed to appreciate that blogging software was the catalyst of another revolution. Like that of the WWW before it, this revolution was as much a product of a step change in usability as it was of a step increase in computational power. The emergence of blogs attracted many new users to the Web – including people who had interesting things to say, but who had previously lacked not only the means to publish those things but an understanding of the technology that would allow them to do so at modest expense. Weblog software and weblog publishing companies made it possible for individuals to disseminate information, and then supplemented that gift by offering them means to *exchange* information. Weblogs are discussion machines. They enable humans to write, publish, read, comment, review, and annotate. They connect people.

As a life-long programmer, when I started my own Weblog, I began by opening a program designed for editing computer code: I shaped the text of my blog entries by hand, and then uploaded it to my own website, avoiding the basic commercial blogging services and software which existed then, and which were anyway cheap or free. Why would I need dedicated third-party software? If I became a more frequent blogger, I could always write my own code to do the housekeeping. How difficult could it be to weave text strings into a daily journal? For a living I wrote software for analysing the three-dimensional structure of protein molecules! Hubris. It was as though I had started to write a novel by hand-making my own paper. It was only when I took advantage of existing, collaboratively written, blogging programs (albeit running on my own website) that my efforts became productive and anyone paid attention to what I wrote.

It is one of the great strengths of *normblog* that Norm used a commercial hosted blogging service from the outset. This choice of his was one reason why, once I had joined this new conversation, Norm was among the first of the other participants I noticed; but there was a more important and telling one: other people I knew drew my attention to him. They thought that what he wrote on his blog was worth reading. Norm later became the first member of this new kind of Web tribe whom I met in person: in London in 2005, when he kindly bought me dinner, as he had done for other bloggers. This is typical of his generosity towards and interest in people. As an early and prominent UK political blogger, Norm was in a position to draw his many readers' attention to other blogs and send traffic their way. He did so even when he disagreed profoundly with what they wrote.

Later, another early adopter and mutual blogging friend of ours, Jackie Danicki, said to me: 'The trouble with Norm is that he's such a nice guy. I don't want people to get the idea that Marxists are like that.' The problem is worse: Norm is not only a nice guy, but a clever, thoughtful, and moral person; and he still describes himself as a Marxist. The writings of Marx and Engels are grandiose follies, monuments to the terrible consequences of uncoupling philosophical speculation from evidence, rigour, and test. They inspired enormities on a scale that is still hard to grasp. My disagreements with Marxism are deep and wide. My disagreements with Norm's liberal and humanist views, as expressed in his writings away from Marx, are relatively minor and narrow.

I dismiss much that is written about politics by contemporary academics, and condemn and oppose Marxism in every manifestation I have encountered, including the qualified and informed variant outlined by Norm. Given these facts, why do I take a self-confessed Marxist, his blog, and his own thinking seriously? Why do I believe him to be a good man? I reached my answer first of all through an appreciation of his blog: a public, digital manifestation of the person behind it. As it is increasingly common for scholars to research and publish on the Web, so it is increasingly common for private individuals to meet one another first via that medium. This trend extends those ancient real-world skills of social discrimination that we have taken into the asynchronous, mediated world of written publication in the virtual world of the Web. Not only does the Web provide a medium for accessing ideas, it allows its readers to obtain further useful clues about their reliability. Since daily life is difficult without the ability to make judgements about what and whom to believe, and since we spend more and more time on the Web, we need to find ways of judging online resources. In short, good judgement of online resources is something that every student and scholar must possess or acquire. I am going to use the specific and personal example of *normblog,* and of Norm himself, to address the more general, impersonal, and increasingly important question of how a reader can judge the worth of a resource on the Web.

The first and most immediately impressive quality of *normblog* is its scale. In the real world, if *normblog* were printed on paper and bound it would comprise several large volumes. One of the simplest definitions of a Weblog is 'online diary'. There have been very few days in the years of its existence when there hasn't been a new post on *normblog,* the overwhelming majority of them written by Norm himself; most days there are several. If, as I try to, you want to at least glance at each new item that he publishes, then you should take care not to let your gaze wander for more than a week or so. Quantity and quality are proverbially set in opposition to each other, but sites that are regularly updated by a human being not only tend to be more up-to-date, but also tend to contain more reliable information – and they offer more points of data upon which their veracity can be assessed. *Normblog* is one such site.

It seems almost trivial to point out that the content of *normblog* has human origins, but one of the curious phenomena of the growth of the Web into the World's biggest shopping mall (or red-light district) – and one of the things that makes it harder to assess material published there than material published in the real world – is that, online, much of what is presented as new, natural content is either auto-generated by software or spliced together from the unaccredited efforts of others. There are both financial incentives to do this (advertising income) and lower and lower costs involved (blogs make it easier for Web-native computer programs, 'bots', to publish too – and computer power continues to grow, alongside access to networks of zombie desktop PCs hijacked by malicious computer code). Many blog-hosting companies devote substantial resources to suppressing and removing spam blogs – so-called 'splogs' – assembled from fake or filched content.

Large volumes of real and original content are valuable things. The best way to identify such troves is to watch their riches accumulate over time, so that you can see they are coherent and consistent. This kind of long-term test is not always easy for an individual to conduct, but there are many eyes looking at the Web, enough that some of them will be looking in the same direction as you. The task of surveying an accumulation of content can be shared. This kind of passive collaboration takes place in the real world also, but it is so much easier online: you don't even have to ask a friend, 'I've just started following Site X. Is it any good?'; you can read reviews of Site X; you can follow existing links to Site X from other sites you already trust; you can use checks developed by search engine companies, checks that identify 'zombie' websites, to reassure yourself that not only is Site X a source of true and human content, but that it will not infect your own computer with malicious code if you interact with it.

So peer review and impact ranking exist online on a larger scale and more informal basis than in the 'real' world of academic publishing, and they serve at least one similar function. The views of others are our second useful metric. Indeed, 'Google Rank', the proprietary secret of the most successful search engine on the planet today, is built on that principle.

Most of those who are reading this will already know that the Web makes both plagiarism and testing for plagiarism easy: copy a sentence from a suspicious source, surround it with quotation marks (to ensure that you are searching for those particular words in that particular order), and paste it into a search engine. If it turns out to have been published elsewhere, then, often, something fishy is going on. So, when judging a blog, perhaps more than other kinds of website, a third step in assessing it is to check that content presented as original truly is indeed original and that the site presenting it is its original source.

Another obvious and excellent thing about *normblog* is the simplicity of its page design. It is rendered in only three colours, in a single font of a single family and, for the most part, is free of graphics, animation, or photographs. Because of this, it is easy to read it on a large screen on a desktop PC and it is easy to read it – as many do, I am sure – on a netbook, phone, or other mobile device. Elegance is anathema to the Internet huckster or hooligan; even before reading the content of *normblog*, you sense, rightly, that the site belongs to neither.

In the real world, flashy presentation is harder – a trivial example: it is more expensive to print a colour document than a monochrome one. But, like so many other things in the virtual world, the price of dressing up ugly lies online tends towards zero: entire website designs can be cloned in minutes. Indeed, it puzzles me that so many Web-based malefactors fail to take advantage of such possibilities.

For example, why do online paranoiacs so often telegraph the flakiness of their claims with the flakiness of their site layouts? This apparent tendency, then, offers us a fourth quick-and-dirty guide: if a website or blog looks a mess, then the thinking behind it is probably a mess too.

Bad prose need not signal bad thinking or untrustworthy content, but the link is a strong one. Superfluous apostrophes, confused tenses, and juvenile orthography flag the output of cranks. Norm takes great care with his grammar, spelling, and punctuation – especially commas: Norm's deployment of the comma extends beyond bare correctness, through craft, into pointillism. In the real world, this is a less useful guide. Academic authors often have co-authors. Scholarly publications have reviewers. Dead tree publications have editors. Grammatically correct gibberish is not rare. Online authors usually write alone, feel less reason to copy-edit their own output, and, even when they do, their fastidiousness is usually proportional to the quality of their deliberation. So here is a fifth indicator, one that can even help you to discriminate between the better and worse parts of a more generally trustworthy blog or website.

Just as good writing is no guarantee of good content, good manners are no guarantee of good intentions. There are individuals whose great politeness is matched by their great spite. *Normblog* not only has a civil surface, it also consistently appears – I do not presume to read Norm's mind – to be written without malice. This has been all the more telling when others have used hate-filled language to attack Norm for taking what he believed to be moral positions on certain controversial contemporary issues.

Normblog often laments the incivility of much writing on the Web and occasionally speculates as to its causes. Contemporary rudeness is not confined to the Web, but I think Norm and I agree that the anonymous and impersonal nature of the medium contributes to this phenomenon. Few of the worst offenders would address those they insult in the same way if they knew or could see them. *Normblog* is not anonymous. The blame for any offence caused by the site would fall to him, as would that for any falsehood or libel. This matters all the more because Norm has a real-world reputation worth protecting. Anonymous websites are not necessarily unreliable sites, but their creators lack an incentive to cultivate trust. So we have a sixth, and a linked seventh, indicator: good bloggers are often gracious bloggers, and knowing that there is a human face behind a digital

facade is all the more reassuring when that face belongs to an identifiable individual with face to lose.

I have briskly summarized qualities that often mark out worthwhile blogs and websites and that are shared by *normblog*:

(1)   They are updated often or regularly (by a human) for long
      periods of time.
(2)   Others consider their content to be worthwhile.
(3)   The content they present as original is original.
(4)   Their design is clear and simple.
(5)   Their use of language is correct.
(6)   Their use of language is respectful.
(7)   They are written by identifiable individuals with reputations
      worth protecting.

There are other, more subjective, reasons why I am, like so many
others, a regular reader of *normblog*. These reasons would be equally
applicable to other current paper publications. Norm knows what
strong and weak arguments look like. He takes the trouble to read
and take apart the contentions of media commentators whose logic
long ago fell beneath a level of reasoning for which I could muster
contempt. Further, he can be bothered to take their arguments apart
while they are still topical. His dissections testify over and over again
to the sorry state of certain recent debates and provide the rest of us
with a convenient searchable scrapbook of the derangement of a
public political class.

On *normblog*, Norm also writes about much more than politics in
a similarly thoughtful way. His outside interests overlap with several
of my own: the visual and performing arts, sport, literature, family
life, popular culture, and the Web itself. Of course there are
occasions when I disagree with what Norm says about these subjects
too, but, when I do, I take a moment to reflect upon my reasons for
doing so, something I could say of few other commentators, online
or off. This is central to *normblog*'s appeal. The best sites on the Web,
like *normblog* itself, are places I can go in the hope that my mind will
be changed. I thank Norm for the years of his blog to date and look
forward to reading *normblog* every day, I hope, for many more years
to come.

10

Geras on means and ends: the case for a prefigurative constraint

Jon Pike

I

The overall arc of Norman Geras's writings in the 1960s, 1970s, and 1980s shows a long-standing preoccupation with the ethics of socialism.[1] This was particularly clearly expressed in his seminal work on Rosa Luxemburg (Geras, 1976), in his authoritative account *Marx and Human Nature* (Geras, 1983), and in the work summarized in 'The Controversy over Marx and Justice' (in Geras, 1986). Geras persuaded many others to take seriously the ethics of social change and political agency, and his later political development, including his support for and advocacy of humanitarian interventionism, is perhaps only fully explicable in relation to his thinking about socialist morality in the 1970s and 1980s.

One of Norman Geras's most important pieces towards the end of this phase of his work is a characteristically lucid article in the *Socialist Register* for 1989 (Geras, 1989). It is, in many respects, a pivotal piece, representing both a conclusion drawn out from, and a shift away from, the more exegetical work on Marx and the classical Marxists such as Luxemburg. By 1989 Geras had clearly concluded that there was a significant lacuna in classical Marxism: it was blind to serious and detailed discussion of the ethics of radical social change. In 'Our Morals: The Ethics of Revolution' Geras argues that 'socialist discussion of revolutionary ethics ... and the discussion in particular of ends and means, tends to be framed in abstract generalities of a sort which yields neither specific rules or norms of conduct nor much practical guidance for concrete cases'. He goes on 'to suggest that there is a lot to be learned here, by way of trying to repair the deficiency, from another tradition of discourse altogether' (Geras, 1989: 185).

This tradition is the Just War tradition, a tradition that undergirds his political positions in the new millennium. According to Geras, socialists and others thinking about radical political change, and the morally proper ways to go about achieving it, ought to look to the tradition stretching from Aquinas to Michael Walzer, rather than the largely consequentialist formulations that were part of the classical Marxist canon – and the accompanying abstract generalities that fail to be action-guiding. It may be right to see this shift as part of a backlash against consequentialism in the later half of the twentieth century, along with Rawls, Nozick, Williams, Scanlon, and Macintyre; or, at least, to place Geras at the left pole of such a backlash, the part that took as its target audience the active left, and as its object, radical political action.

Such actions include the formation, policy, and internal regime of political parties, activist groups, and civil associations (especially trade unions), and the interventions that these groups make; the nature of participation in electoral processes; the structure of democratic citizens' forums; the formation of alliances, and the bases on which these are made; the organization of demonstrations, marches, meetings, and campaigns, together with their demands and slogans; strikes, pickets, and other industrial action; occupations, publicity campaigns, campaigns of consumer or other boycotts; methods of fundraising, recruiting, and organizing, including online; up to hostage taking, blackmail, and covert and violent political action, including social revolution.

When Geras writes about means and ends, he is generally concerned with *socialist* transformations and *socialist* revolution. But similar considerations to those brought to bear by Geras onto socialist transformations apply to other sorts of radical political change – actions designed to prevent or ameliorate global warming, and directed towards the establishment of a sustainable global economy; actions for the establishment of a society which is equal between the sexes; actions directed towards the reconciliation of communities which are in conflict on the basis of national antagonisms and competing narratives, land claims and the like. A more modest social-democratic objective – realizing Rawls's principles of distributive justice, for example – involves a similar framework. In each case we can consider a morally valuable outcome, or situation, or state of affairs – an end – and we can consider political actions aimed at securing the just outcome – transformative projects, or means.

Assume that these states of affairs are all of moral value, an assumption that I will return to, and we turn our attention to the political actions, decisions, and movements that might bring these about. We attend, then, to the moral theory of a *transformative politics* and confront Lenin's question: what is to be done? This is easily read as a tactical question, directing us to consider what is effective in bringing about a (more) just state of affairs. But, with Geras in 'Our Morals' (1989), we can consider also the reverse question – what is *not* to be done? What is proscribed for transformative politics? What does an ethically permissible transformative politics look like?

II

The first form of moral theory to be encountered in thinking about socialist ethics is consequentialism. By consequentialism, I mean the view that the rightness of an act, or more generally a policy, is entirely a matter of the goodness of its consequences. By crass consequentialism, I want to identify, outline, and be rude about a variant of this way of grounding moral judgements, whilst at the same time indicating the view that there are variants of this approach that are much more sophisticated and intellectually substantial. Crass consequentialism is consequentialism conceived of as both criterion of rightness (CR) *and* decision procedure (DP). The most notable proponents of this view are Ted Honderich, Noam Chomsky, and Peter Singer; and the view is common in leftist intellectuals. In the body of literature that I am concerned with this is primarily expressed in the little booklet of Trotsky, 'Their Morals and Ours' (1938) – to which Geras clearly nods in 'Our Morals: The Ethics of Revolution'. Much of the left is broadly consequentialist in this way. For this left, the actions to be undertaken are those which are, in the long term, effective in bringing about a more just society; the actions to be avoided, are those which fail to do so – hence the specifically limited nature of Trotsky's criticism of terrorism as *counterproductive*.[2]

On the other hand, the Just War tradition is, broadly speaking, rights based. As Walzer puts it in the preface to *Just and Unjust Wars*, 'the arguments we make about war are most fully understood . . . as

efforts to recognise and respect the rights of individual and associated men and women. The morality I shall expound is in its
philosophical form a doctrine of human rights' (Walzer, 1977: xxi–
xxii).[3] With these affiliations in mind, it looks as if Geras's paper 'Our
Morals' is a rights-based attack on consequentialist ethics. In
general, this is how much of the discussion of the problem of
political action looks – as an argument about what sort of moral
constraints ought to be placed on effective political action. The views
here can reach a high degree of sophistication, but are, I think, cate-
gorizable in terms of this dualism of effectiveness/permissibility.

But there is a third view. The third alternative can conveniently be
labelled 'prefigurative socialism'. Its central idea is that the movement for a state of affairs has the same shape or figure as the state of
affairs itself. Rather than effectiveness, or permissibility, the rela-
tional term here is representativeness, or exemplification. By using
the 'shape' or 'figure' metaphor here, I mean that the means possess
certain (moral) properties, moral properties that are replicated in the
sought-after end state. As Geras puts it (whilst criticizing this view),
'in the struggle for liberation the end must be prefigured or anticipated by, reflected or adumbrated in, the means to secure it'; 'The
burden of performing this simultaneous affirmation and denial is
carried by precisely that array of terms in which the means/end relationship is typically formulated: the end is prefigured, anticipated or
foreshadowed by, reflected, embodied or expressed in, the means
with which it is achieved' (Geras, 1976: 141, 147).

III

Taking this three-fold division we can situate possible political acts,
or means, in a Venn diagram (Figure 1), according to whether they
fit in the set of effective actions, rights-respecting actions, and prefigurative actions. We can look at the interrelations between these
different criteria. Three-fold divisions of moral theory are familiar.

Moreover, when the first two divisions are very generally aligned
with utilitarianism and rights, respectively, there is an almost irre-
sistible temptation to slot virtue ethics into the third hole. The
architectonic works here, too: prefigurative socialism has quite a lot
to do with Aristotle and virtue ethics, though that avenue cannot be
pursued here.

Before I outline the relations between the three approaches, and in

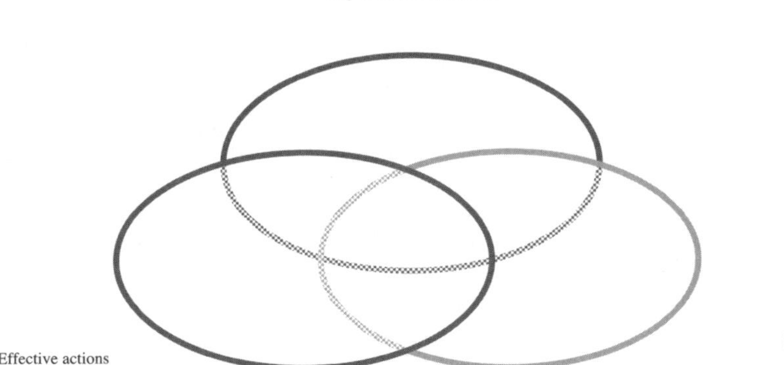

Figure 1 Three properties of political actions

order to get to grips with the argument, it might help to consider a particular policy option – carbon trading. Carbon trading allows relatively rich states to maintain high levels of carbon emissions by buying the carbon quota of relatively poor states. Consider such proposals against a series of criteria.

First, they look as if they may be effective in reducing, in the medium term, carbon emissions. At least it is not clear that they will be ineffective, though it depends on the policy to which carbon trading is compared. In comparison to the absence of international agreement on carbon emissions, it seems likely that carbon trading will reduce overall levels of carbon emissions; but against a comparison with a tightly enforced and restrictive policy that policed national and non-negotiable targets, a carbon trading policy would be less effective. But the efficiency of carbon trading is not the issue.

Second, it is not obvious that carbon trading is rights-violating, most obviously because it involves free market exchange. It may be said that the rights of future generations are violated by excessive carbon emissions, that carbon trading permits excessive carbon emissions and consequent rights violations. But this relies on a rather extended and controversial account of rights, and amounts to a rights-based objection to any moderate policy on carbon emissions now.

But third there is still something troubling about a policy of carbon trading even if its effectiveness and its rights-respecting character are both conceded. This concern on a third dimension points to a prefigurative account. On the basis of a prefigurative constraint, carbon trading would be ruled out, because it fails to prefigure international arrangements which are non-exploitative and egalitarian. If this is right, the policy is permissible from a consequentialist point of view, permissible from a rights-respecting point of view, but ruled out on the basis of a prefigurative conception of transformative politics.

However, it might be objected that that this is an issue which can be captured within the idea of deontological constraints; that the apparent need for a prefigurative conception arises because the contrast has been set up between consequentialism and rights, rather than between consequentialism and deontology (which can include a commitment to rights but isn't exhausted by it); and that a deontologist might object to the lack of non-exploitative and non-egalitarian relations *now*, rather than making any appeal to the idea of prefiguration.

I have two responses to this objection. First, in emphasizing the breadth of deontological commitments, the objection is in order, yet there are still morally relevant properties of sought-after states that are not easily captured by either crass consequentialist or deontological perspectives: the prefigurative constraint is neutral – indeed empty – between sought-after end states. It merely prescribes that the means used to reach a sought-after state of affairs prefigures that state of affairs. To object that the state of affairs could incorporate some other morally valuable property, which would then need to be prefigured or equally instantiated in a means, seems to concede this critical point. If it is the case that the sought-after end state is constituted (in part) by non-exploitative relations, then it either follows that the means to achieve this ought to be non-exploitative, or it does not follow. Prefigurative constrainers argue that it does follow.

Second, the objection seems to miss out on the means/end specificity of the prefigurative concern – the specific idea that something has gone wrong in utilizing means to an end which *rub up against* that end – and that this can only be captured with means/end talk. Now, it may be that those means have something wrong with them quite independently, but I want to argue that there is something awry in the bare lack of fit between means and end, over and above an independent evaluation of the means and the end.

I now turn to some relations between these approaches to transformative politics. As will be familiar, a common critique is that, whilst consequentialism rules out certain actions, it does not rule enough out, and even when it does rule actions out, it rules them out for the wrong reasons (Williams, 1985).

Prima facie, Just War theory is more restrictive than consequentialism: it imposes further obstacles on actions that would be effective, by ruling some of them out as unjust according to the rules of war.[4] For example, Just War theory prescribes that the rules of war are founded on rights, and endorses non-combatant immunity which consequentialism characteristically rejects. Suppose we simplify by thinking of Just War theory as essentially a rights-based theory (whilst acknowledging that there are substantial chunks of Just War theory, such as the issue of proportionality, which are heavily informed by consequentialist considerations). The constraints built into Just War theory prefigure a situation in which rights are protected and respected, and if such a situation were to obtain, then Just War theory would 'wither away' – it would be a set of empty categories of historical interest only. From this angle, Just War theory and prefigurative theory coincide.

At first sight, prefigurative strategies look yet more restrictive than Just War theory. It is possible that an action meets a rights-respecting constraint but not a prefigurative constraint, since the action does not resemble or prefigure the state of affairs to be achieved, as in the case of carbon trading. Applying a prefigurative constraint to the selection of political policies and actions will rule out actions that are rights-respecting but are not prefigurative, so it seems that a prefigurative constraint would be more restrictive than a rights-respecting constraint, ruling out a further subgroup of actions that was rights-respecting. In so far as the state of affairs that is sought after is one in which rights are respected, then it looks as if the prefigurative strategy must be one in which rights are respected.

However, this is not quite correct, for a prefigurative constraint, on its own, does not exclude all actions that fail to be rights-respecting. To see this, reflect that the content of the sought-after state of affairs is, thus far, unfixed. It could be that the sought-after state of affairs is one in which rights are respected, in which case prefigurative action to secure that state of affairs will also be rights-respecting action. But these are not the only states of affairs that one might aspire to achieve: the sought-after state of affairs may be one in which rights are not respected. States of affairs in which – to put it at the extreme – liberal rights are superseded by a society of universal friendliness are not prefigured by a movement in which those liberal rights form absolute – or even stringent – constraints. It is possible for the sought-after state of affairs to be one in which rights 'wither away' into a society of universal friendliness – as Aristotle puts it, 'when men are friends they have no need of justice, while when they are just they need friendship as well' (Aristotle, 1931: 142).

While it may be tempting – indeed, while it may be right – to dismiss this possibility as a hopelessly utopian and politically dangerous notion, its analytical significance is plain. Jeremy Waldron, for example, depicts the argument between those who seriously entertain the notion of the withering away of rights and those who do not, in the following way:

> The dispute here is between those who yearn for communal bonds so rigid that the question of what happens when they come apart will not arise or need to be faced, and on the other, those who are, first, realistic enough to notice the tragedy of the broken bond and ask, 'What happens next?'; and, second, optimistic enough to embrace the possibility of the construction of new bonds and new connections and ask 'How is that possible?' (Waldron, 1993: 391)

The yearning for communal bonds so strong that they cannot 'come apart' may be a sign of utopianism. Nonetheless it is conceptually quite in order to think of prefigurative actions that do not respect rights and that prefigure 'super-strength' communal bonds of the sort that Waldron has in mind. For present purposes, this is enough to show that prefigurative actions and rights-respecting actions do not necessarily coincide. Some of those who take seriously the idea of prefigurative politics have, at the same time, made clear their preference for super-strength bonds: the two often stand together.

Here, for example, is the eco-anarchist Murray Bookchin:

> subcultures begin to emerge which emphasise a natural diet against the society's synthetic diet, an extended family as against the monogamous family, sexual freedom as against sexual repression, tribalism as against atomisation, community as against urbanism, mutual aid as against competition, communism as against property and finally, anarchism as against hierarchy and the state. In the very act of refusing to live by bourgeois structures, the first seeds of the utopian lifestyle are planted. Negation passes into affirmation; the rejection of the present becomes the assertion of the future within the rotting guts of capitalism itself. (Bookchin, 2004: viii)

But those 'bourgeois structures' may be rights-based structures. It is clear how 'tribalism' (interestingly characterized by Bookchin in this positive way against atomism) can violate important rights. The further that the sought-after state of affairs diverges from a society in which rights are respected, the further prefigurative politics diverge from rights-respecting politics. The divergence in terms of the sought-after state of affairs from a rights-respecting state of affairs takes place in two dimensions – which we may stipulate as dimensions of *compliance* and of *relevance*. On the first dimension, compliance, a shift from rights-based means would follow from an explicit, if partial, denial of rights-respecting ends. Here, it is important that the sought-after state of affairs abandons various 'bourgeois' rights and, consequently, that the means to such a state of affairs actively negates or denies them. The other involves departures along a scale of relevance – that rights talk is not enshrined in the sought-after state of affairs, and is to that extent not involved, either by being acknowledged as a constraint, or negatively, as an active negation, in the movement to achieve the state of affairs. The specification of a relation of prefiguring depends on the sought-after state and the prefiguring act possessing the same, morally relevant properties. For some conceptions of sought-after states, rights-respecting is irrelevant. The compliance/relevance distinction provides a way of acknowledging some of the nuances of means/end relations. Theoretically informed sought-after states of affairs do not prescribe every property or feature of a state of affairs: they foreground one or another. Consequently, for a prefigurative act, some properties are more morally relevant than others.

In short, then:

(1) An action's being *effective* is neither necessary nor sufficient for its being rights-respecting or prefigurative.

(2) An action's being *prefigurative* is neither necessary nor sufficient for its being effective or rights-respecting.

(3) An action's being *rights-respecting* is neither necessary nor sufficient for its being effective or prefigurative.

Nevertheless, an act's moral value derives from its being effective, or rights-respecting, or prefigurative, or some combination.

Geras's criticism of the lacuna of the left, and in particular the Marxist left, on the moral basis of political acts is instructive, yet he is a strong critic of prefigurative politics. Geras's critique of prefiguration is most explicit in 'Our Morals: The Ethics of Revolution' and is worth quoting at length:

> I dispose in short order of one kind of answer to these questions. This is that in any such struggle the means must be prefigurative of the ends in view. Setting aside some problems about its precise meaning – for what does a quantity of timber prefigure: a scaffold or a barn? And what the laying down of weapons – a return of peace? Or impending massacre? One may concede a value to some such rough idea. If we can exemplify, can display, our good ends in the good ways and means we use to achieve them, so much the better. But in the present context, means cannot in general only reflect the ends in view, because they will also reflect their own beginning, so to put it. They are doubly determined: not only by what they are intended to achieve, the putative goal, but by that situation which is their starting point as well. It is in the nature of the problem under discussion – of revolution – that this starting point has ugly features, including the mobilisation of violence on its behalf. How could the means of opposing it not reflect some of that ugliness, how, even in trying to prefigure a better future, avoid being scarred by an awful past? Shooting at the direct agents of a hated tyranny is still killing people; it is a state of war and as such not prefigurative of human harmony or even of reasonably tolerable social order, though it may be necessary in order to achieve that. To point this out is just to insist on an indispensable minimum of realism. At the same time, it may then be said, revolutionary means must at least prefigure their intended ends to some, large, extent. But to what extent? Which non-prefigurative means, if one is going to speak in this way, may, and which may not be used in a just revolutionary struggle? The notion of prefiguration gives no determinate answer to our question, merely another language in which to formulate it. (Geras, 1989: 188–9)

There are three separate objections in this passage to the idea of a prefigurative constraint on action. The first is that the prefigurative requirement has no precise meaning. The second is that the prefigurative requirement necessarily ignores the fact that means 'reflect the ugliness of the starting point'. The third objection responds to a modification of the demand for a prefigurative constraint: the modification is that the means 'must reflect to some extent' and Geras rejects this as vague and not action guiding. On his account, the modified prefigurative requirement fails to discriminate between those actions that are permissible and those that are impermissible.

Here I essay a rejoinder to Geras's critique. First, I turn to the objection to the vagueness of the prefigurative constraint, illustrated by the questions about a quantity of timber, and the laying down of arms. Since a quantity of timber is not an act, let alone an act exhibiting specifiable moral properties, it does not seem to be in the right category for consideration as a prefigurative act. What about the laying down of arms? This is an act, and an act with specifiable moral properties. One moral property of the act is the setting aside of violent means for resolving conflict. It prefigures a more general state of affairs in which violent means for resolving conflict are set aside.

But the laying down of arms may not, of course, *bring about* a general state of affairs in which violent means for resolving conflict are set aside. It may bring about a massacre of the defenceless. It is no part of my argument that prefigurative acts ought to be recommended when such consequences arise: distinguishing the different constraints which an act ought to be measured against invites us to consider the extent to which an act meets *more than one* constraint. Distinguishing the relation of prefiguring a state of affairs from the relation of being effective in bringing about a state of affairs is helpful in understanding how acts might *both* prefigure and be causally efficacious in bringing about a state of affairs, *or* prefigure, but not be effective, *or* be effective but not prefigure, and so on.

Geras's second objection appears to recognize all this, and the response is straightforwardly concessive: the task here is to disentangle the significance of prefigurative politics from concern about an 'indispensable minimum of realism'. Realism cannot be dispensed with: the important questions here are answered only casuistically, on the basis of calculations of effective political strategy and so on. It seems reasonable here, though, to suggest that the overarching thesis that Geras advances in 'Our Morals' points towards an answer to this particular problem: the need to take seriously the Just War tradition as a guide to socialist action cannot be adequately rebutted by invoking 'an indispensable minimum of realism'. Why should not the same be said for prefiguration? Walzer's Just War theory takes realism seriously, as evidenced by his account of 'supreme emergency': conditions where, in the face of an imminent existential threat, the normal rules of war can rightfully be suspended. Under these circumstances, a minimum of realism entails the suspension of the ordinary rules of war: bombing the civilian population of a hated tyranny could also be permissible in conditions where a nation faces an existential threat, yet the rules of war are still normally operative. If, as Geras suggests, 'shooting at the direct agents of a hated tyranny' is necessary in order to achieve a reasonably tolerable social order, this may be considered analogous to the case of supreme emergency – whatever, the analytical work seems to start at this point, rather than end, with the citing of an 'indispensable minimum of realism'.

This leaves the third objection: about the indeterminateness of which prefigurative means ought to be employed to secure some desired state of affairs. Clearly, amongst the selection of means, criteria of effectiveness and rights-respecting need to be met: we ought to consider those means which are effective, rights-respecting and prefigurative. Amongst the prefigurative means to be selected are those prefigurative means which contain/reflect/exemplify/ instantiate those aspects of the end which give it – the end – moral value. Once again, it is important to tease apart the effectiveness of an act in bringing about a state of affairs from its prefigurative moral value. The value of a prefigurative act is a derivative value – not because it inevitably, or probably, *leads to* a state of moral value but because it contains *within itself* some moral value, by virtue of its resemblance to, or exemplification of, a state of affairs of moral value, even if that state of affairs does not come about. The moral value of a prefigurative act arises from its resemblance to – its prefiguring (in the relevant respect) of – a state of affairs that *itself* has moral value. This sort of deflationary response seems in order.

So we can set up a rough schema, asking the questions: does the act bring about the state of affairs? And does the act look like the state of affairs? In both ways, there are three different respects in which a precedent act can stand to a state of affairs – positive, negative, and neutral – and this applies to the figuring relation and the consequential relation. Each relation, therefore, has three different aspects (Figure 2). (Note, as stated, that the figuring relation between the act and the state of affairs is not causal: there is nothing implied about the consequences of the act for the state of affairs, although the respects in which the different relations stand map across to each other as in Figure 2.)

One result of this way of looking at things is that the source of moral value of a prefigurative act becomes clearer. Actions that are effective draw moral value from the state of affairs that they *bring*

Figuring relation	Prefigurative	Non-prefigurative	Counter-prefigurative
Consequential relation	Effective	Ineffective	Counterproductive

Figure 2 Some relations between actions and ends

about. Actions that are prefigurative draw moral value from the states of affairs that they *prefigure* – at least when they exemplify or instantiate the state of affairs, when the relation is that of a token to a type. Actions that are *counter-prefigurative* may, at the same time be *effective* in bringing about a state of affairs which, figuratively, they do not represent, exemplify or resemble – rather, they misrepresent, and counter-exemplify that state of affairs. A war to end all wars may succeed in ending all wars. Coercive intervention may establish democratic institutions. A strategy of organized ostracism may secure mutual respect and friendship. Violent revolution may usher in a society of universal friendliness. In each case, counter-prefigurative actions may be effective. But in each case something of moral value is lost.

The middle column of Figure 2 is important in the relation of actions to states of affairs in the following way. First, look at the consequential relation. An action may be effective in bringing about a state of affairs, or be counterproductive in bringing about that state of affairs. But it may also simply be *ineffective* – neither productive nor counterproductive. Here, empirical information drawn from the history of the left, especially that part of the left that Geras concerns himself with in this period, is germane. For political actors, particularly political actors on the left, this ought to be freely admitted as a very common category. Some sort of political action is tried, and it just fails. It does not bring substantial social change, but it does not make things altogether worse. The dominance of the category of the 'ineffective' as an empirical reality ought to be admitted. It is certainly possible to suggest that in the long run, and for reasons to do with the massive causal ramifications of quite trivial acts, there is always some net effect, in some way, on the course of events, and the bringing about of states of affairs from any action. But the recognition of such long-term ripples does not undermine the view that very many political acts – electoral interventions, demonstrations, conferences, marches, pickets, blogs, and so on are both trivial and of nugatory effect.

There is a similar category which applies to the figuring relation. We have seen various ways in which an action may prefigure a state of affairs, and ways in which it might be counter-prefigurative, but the middle ought not to be excluded. An action may look like the state of affairs it is designed to bring about, or it may resemble the photographic negative of the situation it is designed to bring about. But also it may simply not resemble such a state of affairs – it may be dissimilar, neither possessing the morally relevant properties, nor possessing corresponding morally relevant properties of disvalue. Whilst it is easy to argue for a constraint against action that is counterproductive, and – on the basis laid out above – to propose a constraint against actions that are counter-prefigurative *ceteris paribus*, the value of a concern with prefigurative acts comes about when we consider those acts in the middle column.

There are many political acts which are ineffective, though not counterproductive in bringing about the sought-after political change. Likewise, there are, in the panoply of political acts, many that neither prefigure nor counter-prefigure the sought-after state of affairs. Nevertheless, an action which is itself non-exploitative, or just, or egalitarian, or respects the dignity of persons prefigures the sought-after state of affairs which is non-exploitative, or just, or egalitarian, or respects the dignity of persons. *Acts* which respect the dignity of persons – just like large-scale social relations that respect the dignity of persons – have value. They have value in so far as respecting the dignity of persons has value. Egalitarian acts which are directed at an egalitarian state of affairs have value because egalitarian social relations have value. In so far as equality is a value, acts which respect an egalitarian ethos also have value. (Cohen, 2000; Wolff, 1998). In selecting those acts which are directed to some end, a bias towards prefigurative acts will itself generate moral value.

Why? Where do these values come from? Here I want only to gesture at a way of answering these questions with which Geras might be expected to have some sympathy. The sought-after state of affairs, and the actions that precede such a state of affairs, have value because of their coincidence with human needs. Geras clearly explicates the source of such moral value in his work on Marx's conception of human nature. He demonstrated both that Marx had a theory of human nature, and that he was right to do so. Geras argues thus:

an ethical position resting on a conception of human nature is a perfectly possible one, possible in the sense of being logically unobjectionable, coherent in principle. If one places a value on human life and human happiness and there exist universal needs that must be satisfied respectively to preserve and to promote these, then this furnishes, the value and the fact conjointly, a basis for normative judgment: such needs ought to be satisfied *ceteris paribus*. (Geras, 1983: 101)

Consequently, evaluating states of affairs according to the extent to which those human needs are met is entirely reasonable. With both the normative and the descriptive premise in place, we are in a position to deliver judgements on the possible states of affairs that are attainable or even merely imaginable. The point here is not to defend such a conception of the source of moral value against objections, though I have no serious doubt that it could be so defended. It is rather to say that such a conception of the source of moral value is obviously available to Geras, and there can be, in consequence, no serious problem in attributing moral value to sought- after states of affairs, by virtue of their possession of specific moral properties – such as being states of affairs of non-exploitation, or equality, or of respect for persons through a framework of rights, and so on. And it seems to me to be clear that acts designed to bring about such states of affairs of moral value, can themselves exhibit the same properties, and be for that reason, of moral value themselves.

IV

Any discussion of action directed towards deep social transformation must address the probabilities of success. A moral perspective on a push for *socialist* change needs to pay the utmost attention to the certain historical fact of its own disastrous failure. In his work in the 1970s and 1980s, Geras was writing about a project which, at least in appearance, was in the process of failing. In considering the moral responsibilities of those who continue to pursue similar or associated projects, there are multiple reasons for endorsing a conservative and prefigurative approach to moral means. The alternative is to say something like the following: we are aiming for a state of considerable moral value, one in which human capabilities will be liberated as never before, exploitation will be eradicated, persons will be respected, and so on. We acknowledge that, in the recent past, attempts to establish such states of affairs have gone disastrously wrong, and caused great harms. Nevertheless, in taking actions towards such a state of affairs, in risking this project again, there is (sadly) nothing we can do now that prefigures, or resembles, or gives you a taste of the state of affairs to be realized. Rather, you need to trust us that even counter-prefigurative actions will deliver the goods.

If the prefigurative set of actions is over-hastily closed off then we need to think with the utmost seriousness about the probabilities of securing whatever it is that we aim to produce but are unable to exemplify, or model, or prefigure. When we look at the history of attempted radical transformations it is clear that some of them justified, on consequentialist grounds, action that were rights-infringing and counter-prefigurative. What was not *pre*figured, never got figured.

In this chapter I have suggested that there are several independent criteria against which to measure any proposal for political action to secure some sought-after state of affairs. I argue that such action can be considered for its effectiveness, against a series of moral proscriptions and judgements drawn from the Just War tradition, and according to whether it prefigures the sought-after state of affairs. Matching each of these criteria is a mark of value against an action. For those seeking radical social transformation, the task of pursuing prefigurative means, side by side with these other considerations, has particular importance.

Notes

1 I wish to thank Carolyn Price, Derek Matravers, Timothy Chappell, Chris Belshaw, and the editors of this volume, Eve Garrard and Steve de Wijze, for their helpful comments on earlier drafts of this material.
2 '"Just the same," the moralist continues to insist, "does it mean that in the class struggle against capitalists all means are permissible: lying, frame-up, betrayal, murder, and so on?" Permissible and obligatory are those and only those means, we answer, which unite the revolutionary proletariat, fill their hearts with irreconcilable hostility to oppression, teach them contempt for official morality and its democratic echoers, imbue them with consciousness of their own historic mission, raise their courage and spirit of self-sacrifice in the struggle. Precisely from this it flows that not all means are permissible' (Trotsky, 1938: 172).
3 There is, of course, a considerable literature on the topic of Dirty Hands in politics (see de Wijze, this volume, pp. 150–74). This literature

examines the significance of constraints on political actions, but, to the best of my knowledge, it does not separately discuss a prefigurative constraint. See for example Coady, 1993; Walzer, 1973.

4 Consider the Venn diagram presentation (Figure 1), which indicates that there is no reason at this level of abstraction to consider Just War theory as more restrictive than consequentialist theory: Just War theory does not rule out ineffective actions in the way that consequentialist theory does. It's merely a waste of time to consider those actions that lie outside the set of effective actions.

11

Resistance beyond the moral boundary: some thoughts on the limits of dirty hands

Stephen de Wijze

In James Goldman's impressive play *The Lion in Winter*, Eleanor of Aquitaine, Henry II's wife, angrily responds to her husband's accusation of cruelty:

> One son is all I've got, and you can blot him out and call me cruel. For these ten years you've lived with everything I've lost and loved another woman through it all. And, I'm cruel? I could peel you like a pear, and God himself would call it justice. Nothing I could do to you is wanton: nothing is too much. (Goldman, 1964: 41)

Eleanor's sin in Henry's eyes is to refuse his request for an annulment of their marriage so that he can remarry and father another legitimate son and a new heir to the English throne. For Henry, the three adult sons he had with Eleanor are manifestly unsuitable heirs, hence his aim to have a new son with Alais Capet (his lover and the king of France's sister). Eleanor's last two sentences resonate with those who have resisted oppression and are themselves accused of immorality or unfairness because of their actions. It is especially galling and unjust to be accused of cruelty and immoral behaviour by one's oppressor or abuser. It rightly provokes a great sense of outrage since such accusations, among other things, serve to invert the moral order. Good becomes bad with immoral and evil persons perversely claiming the mantle of fairness. What further aggravates this injury is that such persons appeal to the moral goodness of those they oppress in order to continue their immoral or evil projects. As Eleanor points out, after years of Henry's cruelty and torment, to be accused of cruelty herself is more than hypocritical, it is particularly spiteful. Even if Eleanor's decisions and actions were indeed cruel, they were, nevertheless, still fitting and just. We understand and empathize with Eleanor's retort: 'Nothing I could do to you is wanton: nothing is too much.'

I doubt though whether 'peeling someone like a pear' could ever be morally justified, but when people are abused and treated unjustly a robust response is appropriate, even when it is cruel. Such a response is apt since it seeks to stop the abuse and restore justice, and, importantly, to disabuse the oppressor of his or her false and pernicious claims to fairness and justice. Inaction or silence in the face of injustice usually licenses and encourages more of the same. All this, it seems to me, is clear enough and for most people uncontroversial. But just how one ought to respond to injustice, and which moral limits one ought to respect, is certainly not. For millennia this issue has raised many pressing and complex normative questions for those who wish to act within ethical boundaries and not succumb to the actions, wishes, and world-view of their tormentors. This problem is a universal concern and has been long and widely discussed within all religious doctrines and by philosophers, historians, playwrights, and novelists,[1] all seeking to clarify what would constitute the appropriate means to achieve justice in a world where evil obtains. These discussions, to put it another way, seek to delineate the normative constraints that good and moral persons ought to respect when fighting injustice, cruelty, and other even more terrible crimes.

In his excellent paper 'Our Morals',[2] Norman Geras makes a considerable contribution to this debate by carefully examining what he calls 'the ethics of revolution' (21) from a socialist perspective. He seeks to uncover normative principles which might guide 'whether in judgment or in action' (21) social revolutions that in all likelihood will involve violent resistance. Geras's paper is a *tour de force*, one that carefully and methodically investigates the central issues with which any serious inquiry of this kind must get to grips. His primary concern in the paper is to address a particular problem within the socialist tradition; namely, that hitherto discussions on the means/ends problem have been 'wanting in specificity' (36). Hence the second, and major, part of his essay seeks to outline 'a precise code or moral limits and moral rules' (38) within which a socialist ethic of revolution could properly operate when fighting social injustices and other forms of oppression and abuse. My focus in this chapter is on an aspect of this discussion which I believe can usefully be expanded. These insights, it seems to me, apply to political action more widely construed and not only to the socialist tradition within which Geras was writing. Agents as politicians and/or leaders of resistance movements sometimes face intractable moral conflicts or dilemmas when they try to act effectively and, at the same time, respect moral boundaries. These situations are best described as the problem of 'dirty hands' (hereafter DH): situations where agents cannot avoid moral wrongdoing when doing what is the right thing to do. When fighting oppression or protecting citizens from danger, politicians or activists face situations within 'a complex of immorality',[3] where their actions are both morally justified yet nevertheless at the same time also morally wrong. Geras doesn't refer to the problem in this way but he has the DH scenario in mind when he asks whether individual rights – as very important agent-centred restrictions – are absolute in every circumstance.[4] He rightly concludes that tragically there will be cases where the moral horror of allowing certain consequences to obtain (such as the massacre of hundreds or the destruction of a city) has 'to be allowed to override the rights of the innocent'(49). The key focus of this chapter is to pursue the implications of accepting the reality of such cases by examining the limits of these difficult scenarios.

I begin this chapter by setting out the specific options and problems facing those who resist tyranny and injustice. I reject two well-known alternative approaches, namely a ruthless amoralism and an ineffective pacifism. Both of these options are seriously flawed for reasons I will briefly discuss. Consequently, I opt for the third approach, actions circumscribed by a carefully considered moral framework in line with the one argued for by Geras. Within this approach there are ragged edges, so to speak, where we have situations which throw up intractable moral conflicts, and this leads to a discussion of that set of cases that are best described as DH scenarios. These cases leave us with a moral position, as Kate Soper points out, which 'is not easy to formulate or render into a coherent whole, since it requires us to combine respect for the individual with an agreement to waive that respect in certain conditions' (Soper, 1987: 113). The very possibility of such DH scenarios is strongly resisted by many, but I shall assume that they are a pervasive and unavoidable aspect of our moral reality. The remainder of the chapter will then explore the boundaries and circumstances of DH situations in order to elucidate the limits of these difficult and ethically tangled situations. However, if we advocate resistance to oppression and injustice then, as Geras rightly points out, we have an important duty to try and bring a 'disciplined, scrupulous and discriminating ethical code into the dark history' (45) we seek to change.

Assumptions

This chapter rests on a number of simplifying assumptions. Firstly, it neither examines nor defends any particular historical example of resistance to injustice or tyranny. Secondly, it does not focus on any particular agent of action, be it a group, an individual, a revolutionary movement or a government. Thirdly, it does not champion any particular method of resistance which could be carried out by this myriad of different actors. The claims throughout the chapter are necessarily general and seek to identify moral limits on any action or project whoever carries it out. Resistance to injustices, tyranny and other abuses involves a triadic relationship between the *person or group* responsible for an action/project, the *method of resistance* used, and the nature of *particular acts* themselves. Consequently, resistance takes many forms and can be carried out by very different actors. For example, resistance to injustice might be exercised by the state responding to terrorist attacks, or by a minority group resisting the oppression of the majority.[5] Resistance can also sometimes be carried out by groups or by an individual resisting the predations of the state or something global such as the exploitative aspects of a particular economic system such as capitalism. Resistance can also be found, and often has been found, where a nation resists the imperial ambitions or the imposition of tyranny by a stronger nation. This resistance can take the form of a violent revolution, or an all-out war, or a more pacific approach that exerts pressure on the *status quo* by, for example, civil rights marches and legal challenges. The triadic relationship operates in all these instances and my concern here is to seek a better understanding of how one part of this triadic relationship – the nature of particular actions to end oppression and injustice – ought to be constrained in the face of intractable moral conflicts, specifically in the case of DH scenarios.

Furthermore, in order to simplify matters, I shall assume throughout this chapter that individuals resisting injustices are leaders – of a country or a group or a revolutionary movement. This simplifying assumption is useful to enable a focus on the particular normative difficulties – the *sui generis* moral responsibilities – facing individuals when they act on behalf of others in the face of terrible injustices. These difficulties are clearly not restricted to leaders, but typically they do arise more frequently for leaders in politics, widely construed. Those agents that represent organizations or nations or revolutionary movements are essentially politicians (or at least they are individuals engaged in political acts) and as a result they accept additional moral duties of care and protection for those under their care. What is more, as leaders they face more frequently, and more starkly, those moral dilemmas where, in order to achieve laudable ends, they may need to employ morally problematic means.

A final assumption is that the cases of resistance with which I am concerned are legitimate responses to genuine injustices of some kind. Actual cases are very often mired in controversy about the nature of the injustice and, consequently, whether the acts of resistance are legitimate. The vociferous debate that endures over whether to label a group as 'terrorists' or 'freedom fighters' is a case in point. The latter's actions are seen as morally acceptable (even laudable) since they are victims seeking to achieve their liberty, while the former are condemned as evil criminals who need to be caught and punished for their terrible deeds. Acknowledging this controversy is not to endorse a relativistic and false claim that 'one man's terrorist is another man's freedom fighter'. I have no sympathy for this relativistic stance concerning the nature of terrible actions. However, I shall sidestep these issues since resolving them here is well beyond the scope of this chapter.[6] My focus is solely on the question of the moral limits to legitimate and robust responses to injustice.

Responding to injustice: three approaches

Amoralism

We do not live in a just world. This is probably the least controversial claim that can be made in political theory.[7] However, another widely accepted, if not nearly universal, view is that injustice and oppression must be fought and resisted whenever possible. Here the difficulties begin: *how* ought we to resist injustice and tyranny? While there are many different responses, three in particular have been dominant in the literature. Firstly, what I call the 'amoralist view' (AV) argues that resistance must not be constrained by moral limits or boundaries. If there is a moral obligation at all, it is to fight the injustices and eradicate them as quickly as possible. How we do this depends on the hard realities of the particular situation. We need to choose the means that are most effective, and this requires that we use prudence, pragmatism, and efficacy as the criteria for assessing possible actions or plans. We do what is necessary to defeat injustice and tyranny, and the focus on normative constraints is both naive and counterproductive. The naivety is due to a misunderstanding of power and its exercise in the real world. It is counterproductive because normative constraints result in poor or bad decisions in the face of a determined and immoral adversary. This view has considerable currency among an influential group of political theorists who are often referred to as Political Realists.[8] Trotsky's dismissive quip about those who engage in 'Kantian-priestly and Vegetarian-Quaker prattle about the sacredness of human life' is apposite here.[9] If we are distracted by abstract moral concerns, we run the risk of allowing the injustices to continue and those who perpetrate them to grow stronger. Hans Morgenthau makes a similar claim when he lays out the principles of Political Realism. Successful and responsible political action understands

> prudence – the weighing of the consequences of alternative political actions – to be the supreme virtue in politics. Ethics in the abstract judges action by its conformity with the moral law; political ethics judges action by its political consequences. (Morgenthau, 1978: 12)[10]

Despite its initial intuitive appeal, the AV perspective is seriously flawed for at least three reasons. Firstly, there is the very great danger that when moral constraints are eschewed for pragmatic reasons, this leads to the perpetration of terrible abuses in the name of fighting injustice. Since serious conflicts almost always bring out the worst in some persons, weakening or removing moral constraints on our actions has serious deleterious effects, one of which is to effectively give licence to those who no longer care about what is done to individuals if this contributes to the desired goal. This leads, unsurprisingly, to the easy acceptance of terrible abuses in the name of liberation or fighting oppression. This acceptance is not merely the bad faith justifications of immoral persons (which it often is) but is also a trap into which good persons who genuinely seek an end to injustice fall. When driven, as Arendt points out, by a 'passion for compassion' (Arendt, 1990: 71), by the need to end the suffering of many, the sacrifice of individuals to this end seems right, natural, and easy.

Secondly, if we accept that autonomous human action is always constrained by moral concerns, then there is no good reason to think that, when engaged in conflict, ethical boundaries become irrelevant. Moral strictures are needed to protect individuals from the predations of others and this function is especially important when engaged in deadly conflict. This is not to reject the hard political realities faced by agents but, as Geras points out, even these constraints 'never fully close down the space of political choice and individual decision' (23). Consequently, moral concerns remain pertinent and are needed more than ever given the nature of conflict and the potential to do terrible harm to others.

The third reason that AV is seriously flawed is due to a lack of foresight concerning the long-term effect of our own immoral actions. The chances of establishing an enduring just society are seriously diminished if the methods for achieving this are brutal, bloody and unjust. The AV fails to give sufficient weight to the problem that the use of brutal and unjust methods used to remove injustices very often (perhaps always) backfires, resulting in a situation that is as bad as if not worse than what existed before.[11] This does not invariably preclude acting in a way that violates the rights of persons, but when this is done the full moral weight of such acts needs to be recognized, and the moral pollution for so acting acknowledged and appropriately felt. I return to this in my later discussion of DH.[12]

Pacifism

The second approach to fighting injustice is one that takes a pacifist perspective (PP).[13] This view argues that resistance to injustices is necessary but that this resistance must only take place through non-violent means. There is a moral and a pragmatic argument against the use of violence. The moral argument, one found among Quakers and others, is that there is an unbreakable prohibition on the use of violence. It is a matter of principle and, no matter the injustice, violent responses always remain morally unacceptable. The pragmatic argument often runs in conjunction with the moral one (but need not do so); it asserts that violence always has deleterious unintended consequences. Violence breeds more violence and hence its use is counterproductive.[14] Consequently resistance must be peaceful and take the form of demonstrations, civil disobedience, and the organization of change through the ballot box or by judicial challenges. Here we find the methods employed by Mahatma Gandhi and Martin Luther King, peaceful resistance which in time brought about the desired changes. However, while this approach undoubtedly has considerable appeal, it also contains at least one fatal flaw. It assumes that those who will do evil will themselves be constrained by some moral boundaries and limits such that, for example, they will not seek to exterminate their enemy to the last man, woman, and child. The barbarity of regimes such as Hitler's Nazi Germany, Stalin's Soviet Union, and Pol Pot's Cambodia, to mention just a few such cases, serves as a pertinent and horrifying reminder that non-violent resistance can be worse than useless – it can encourage those who do evil to feel further empowered to fulfil their perverse and evil ideological dreams. It leaves people defenceless against the worst kind of tyranny and cruelty.[15] What is more, to hold a pacifist position for ourselves as a personal individual decision may be justifiable but it is deeply problematic for leaders whose first duty is the protection of those under their care.

Resisting within moral constraints

The third approach when responding to injustice acknowledges the crucial importance of moral constraints and seeks to delineate legitimate actions within them. This approach has different paths that can be taken depending on whether we adopt a primarily consequentialist or deontological focus.[16] Most leaders (like moral agents generally) adopt some combination of the two as this best resonates with their moral intuitions. Most forms of deontology accept the relevance of consequences to the moral standing of an action. A deontological moral theory that refuses to take consequences into account no matter how grave they would be is a form of fanaticism and is strongly counter to our most basic moral intuitions tested under a rigorous method of wide reflective equilibrium.[17] Similarly, a consequentialist approach that rejects all deontological principles will fail to take the 'distinction between persons seriously'.[18] We would be rightly appalled by a society that enslaved a small percentage of its population even if so doing considerably increased the welfare of the rest.

However, despite, and within, this tension between deontic and telic moral obligations, much has been written to delineate limits on what is acceptable action in conflict situations, of which perhaps the most well known is Just War Theory (JWT).[19] The conditions to be met before starting a just war (*jus ad bellum*) and the conditions restricting what can be done when actually engaged in combat (*jus in bello*) are an elaborate and carefully constructed set of moral constraints which carefully delimit when and by what means we can legitimately engage in conflict.[20] As pointed out earlier, I am concerned only with justifiable resistance, so it is the *jus in bello* conditions which are of particular interest and the focus of the discussion here.[21] They provide a useful guide for establishing moral limits on actions that resist injustice and tyranny. There are three generally accepted conditions required for *jus in bello*, although there is much commentary on exactly what they entail and what they prohibit combatants from doing. The first concerns the question of who is a legitimate target (the condition of discrimination and non-combatant immunity), while the second considers the amount of force needed to achieve just aims (the issue of proportionality). These two conditions prohibit the deliberate targeting of non-combatants and limit the amount of force that can be used. Actions must be proportional to the goal sought so that the loss of life and damage caused does not exceed what is needed to achieve victory. By implication weapons that are considered unusually cruel or which cannot be used in a discriminating manner or which cause death and destruction in a disproportionate manner (such as nuclear or chemical weapons) are forbidden. Similarly, actions that are *mala in se* (evil in themselves) such as rape, torture, genocide, or ethnic cleansing are forbidden as breaching the *jus in bello* conditions. The third condition concerns the requirement to target the enemy in terms of military necessity alone and to eschew motives of revenge or punishment.[22]

A detailed discussion of these *jus in bello* conditions is beyond the scope of the chapter but it is worth noting that they offer a useful starting point for outlining the moral conditions which apply to those who resist injustices and tyranny. Indeed, Geras makes just this point and evokes the *jus in bello* doctrine to provide specificity to his idea of a socialistic ethic of revolution (38). He purposely deploys the criteria of discrimination and non-combatant immunity in combination with those of minimal force and proportionality. Geras is quite clear that targeting military and police personnel or military instalments is legitimate while bombing supermarkets, restaurants, hospitals, and other civilian locations is not. As he says, attacking civilians 'is not, or not only, a "mistake", tactically, politically. It is a moral wrong, a crime' (41).

Similarly, acting in a manner that causes gratuitous suffering by the use of especially cruel or destructive weapons, or by engaging in actions that are *mala in se*, constitutes a moral crime with no 'ifs' and 'buts'. For example, the practice of 'necklacing' during the 1980s in South Africa, the placing of a burning tyre around the neck of a person to cause a slow and painful death, is rightly condemned by Geras even for known informers and collaborators of the hated apartheid regime (36). This prohibition on *mala in se* acts remains in place no matter how brutal or vicious the enemy. The attempts to excuse brutality and cruelty perpetrated by those who are fighting against injustices simply don't stand up to scrutiny. Even if we can understand why, *in extremis*, those subject to terrible injustices will themselves act brutally, this does not make such actions morally right or exempt from condemnation (45). To fail to make this point explicit or to try and cover the moral crimes because they were acting in a good cause simply encourages future abuses which, apart from being morally reprehensible, will almost certainly have deleterious consequences for the kind of society that will emerge from the struggle to remove injustices.[23]

With all this I have no quarrel at all; it is undoubtedly a valuable addition to the socialist ethic of revolution in particular and our understanding of the moral limits of resistance more generally. It does need to be made explicit that acceptance of the above restrictions on resistance is predicated on a prior acceptance of a non-negotiable normative principle: namely, that all persons have inalienable rights of which the most important is the right to life. This is the right, all things being equal, not to be killed or violated (46). The 'all things being equal' clause is needed to cover the cases where this right can be properly abrogated such as when engaged in a just war or just resistance or in legitimate self-defence. And, as pointed out above, even in such specific circumstances, persons remain protected from cruel and unusual punishments such as torture or rape. If certain individuals deserve punishment, this must be done in a humane and just manner with the degree and length of punishment decided by a properly constituted and fair court of law. The recognition of such rights and prohibitions is not a weakness or aspect of vulnerability for those fighting against oppression. Rather, it is an integral part of what constitutes just behaviour and it is an essential normative basis for any future just and humane society with the appropriate and necessary focus on respect for human life and well-being. Without this focus it will be very difficult to fight against what Hampshire calls the 'great evils': those states of affairs 'which are to be avoided for reasons that are independent of any reflective thought'[24] such as physical suffering, starvation, destruction of family, and imprisonment.[25]

Tragically, and far too often, revolutions against tyranny and injustice have ended up with social conditions that were the same as or even worse than the evils they sought to overcome. The excesses of Stalin and Mao, among others, are cases in point. There is a tendency among Marxist thinkers to dismiss the liberal emphasis on fundamental rights informing constitutional essentials and issues of basic justice as masking exploitation in a capitalist society. Trotsky's dismissal of such talk as 'Kantian-priestly and Vegetarian-Quaker prattle' confuses the cynical way in which rights talk has been (and still often is) used by the unscrupulous politician to maintain injustices and prevent change with the importance of having such rights enshrined as the normative foundation of a political system. Their formal instantiation is crucial to the goal of eventually ensuring that all actions are constrained by such princi-ples. Seeking an end to oppression is necessary and laudable, but it is crucially important that a 'passion for compassion' does not lead to a view that the sacrifice of a few individuals or the use of *mala in se* methods are accepted as inevitable and justified. Marxists have been prone to this way of thinking about the ethics of revolution because they combine a distinctive ideology with a form of 'anti-utopian utopian' thinking.[26] The former is a type of consequentialism that dismisses the interests of individuals in the present or near future for the purpose of eventually attaining eman-cipation from oppressive social structures. The latter is the evocation of a utopian society in the distant future without elabo-rating on its specifics. As Lukes puts it:

> It [Marxism] has repeatedly presumed to foresee the future, in which that emancipation is somehow guaranteed, while forswearing the clar-ification of the long-term consequences by which alternative courses of action can be judged. In short, it has offered the unsubstantiated promise of a world 'without lies and violence', thereby rendering their

acceptance in this world easier than it might have been. (Lukes, 1991: 209–10)

These two tendencies result in an approach to moral questions that leaves Marxists without the moral resources to oppose terrible abuses. As Lukes rightly points out:

> Marxism has from the beginning exhibited a certain approach to moral questions that has disabled it from offering moral resistance to measures taken in its name; in particular, despite its rich view of freedom and compelling vision of human liberation, it has been unable to offer an adequate account of justice, rights and the means-ends problem and, thus, an adequate response to injustice, the violation of rights, and the resort to impermissible means in the present. (Lukes, 1991: 198)

Consequently, a crucial element of Geras' essay 'Our Morals' is its clear insistence that resistance against oppression must take place within the boundaries of universalist moral values. His work serves as a valuable and much needed corrective within the Marxist tradition.[27]

Exceeding the limits: necessary actions outside the moral boundaries

Resisting within moral limits is premised on the normative principle that individuals, both combatants and civilians, have non-negotiable rights, primary of which is that they may not be killed or violated. This principle is universal and absolute, or, as Geras points out, 'all but absolute' (49). And here lies the difficulty. In order to engage in *effective* resistance, circumstances arise where it is impossible to comply with this principle. There are unavoidable situations where the killing of innocent persons may be necessary to avert a far greater amount of death and suffering. The unenviable choice is between either violating the deontic prescription to respect individual rights, or failing to meet the consequentialist requirement to bring about the least possible death and suffering.[28] These are very difficult, often tragic, situations where politicians and leaders act knowing that they will get DH. They face moral condemnation no matter what they choose to do since they are caught in an unavoidable complex of immorality. They must do wrong in order to do right and there is no absolutist deontological or consequentialist interpretation of the dilemmatic moral situation that resolves this tension.[29]

Geras notes this problem and is at pains to stress that when we are forced to do wrong, even if such acts are justified in cases of 'supreme emergency'[30] or bring about the lesser evil, they remain morally wrong and must be acknowledged as such. As he succinctly points out, the necessary wrongdoing is 'produced out of the irresoluble conflict between two types of moral reasoning, the reckoning of consequences and the respect for individual rights' (49). When this happens we *override* individual rights, we do not negate or eradicate them. This leads to a very difficult ethical situation that is not easy to articulate in neat rules or formulate as a coherent whole, as Soper reminds us (Soper, 1987: 113). Nevertheless, it is an importunate part of our moral reality and more can and needs to be said about such morally difficult scenarios.

I should add here that certain kinds of conflict are more likely to generate DH situations than others. Many recent conflicts are characterized by an enormous asymmetry of power. This asymmetry poses problems for those who fight injustice whether they have overwhelming military power or are effectively defenceless.[31] For those powerful states combating terrorism, the enemy will hide behind civilians, making it very hard to attack them without causing significant collateral damage. For those resisting injustice without military resources, fighting a repressive state or group may require actions that place civilians in grave danger of reprisal and indiscriminate violence. The constraints outlined by the *jus in bello* conditions appear to be either unsuitable or impossible to fulfil in such circumstances. The reasons are that the practical task of distinguishing between combatants and civilians becomes very hard to fulfil, and such constraints also lack the necessary refinements to deal with an enemy that is fanatical and ruthless, and seeks to inflict maximum casualties on innocents.[32] Given this, DH scenarios may be more widespread in cases of resistance to oppression or in the fight against terrorism than is commonly thought. If this is true, we need as a matter of urgency to say something about the limits beyond the moral limits. We need to better understand both how to identify genuine cases of DH and assess the moral costs of such actions. Specious claims about having to get DH need to be identified to prevent abuse which in the heat of the moment, especially where politicians are uninterested in moral constraints, happens all too easily. When DH cases are genuine, the moral pollution needs to be acknowledged, restitution made, and the necessary remorse felt for so acting.[33] We can and must interrogate the limits of our actions even when justifiably violating deontic prohibitions. We need to ask, what motive ought to guide the actions of agents when they step outside of the boundaries of an ethic of resistance? What kind of leaders or politicians do we want and need to fight injustice? What kind of character and outlook would ensure that they are able to do what is necessary only when it is absolutely necessary? The remainder of this chapter seeks to offer some general guidelines on reasonable limits beyond the normal moral boundary.

Identifying DH scenarios

How can we distinguish DH acts from those which are simply immoral and without any justification? One way is to offer a set of necessary and sufficient conditions that must be met for an action to be properly described as a case of DH. However, developing such conditions is notoriously difficult as similar attempts in the past for concepts such as 'knowledge' have shown. Nevertheless, it is possible to offer some conditions which will provide the requisite guidance for weeding out spurious claims to DH. I lay out the conditions without arguing for them. I have done this elsewhere and I do not claim that these conditions are definitive or that they could not be challenged or improved.[34] It may turn out that looking for family resemblances rather than necessary and sufficient conditions is more productive. However, the point remains that finding a way to distinguish genuine DH acts from those which are merely self-serving justifications for immoral acts is of crucial importance. These conditions for getting DH provide some insights on where to look for the restraints on our actions when we transgress the moral boundary.

A DH scenario, then, is a special kind of moral conflict, one that involves committing 'dirty acts' due to the choices forced on a person within 'a complex of immorality'. When moral persons, especially responsible politicians or leaders, face an unavoidable clash between telic and deontic duties, their actions, whatever they decide to do, entail committing a moral crime.[35] Such leaders are motivated by laudable moral concerns which drive them to commit these moral violations. They fully accept responsibility for so acting and are also willing to pay a moral price and feel the appropriate remorse for having so to act. Despite this necessity to engage in unavoidable immorality, the acts are always constrained by the criteria of proportionality and 'reasonable success'. The latter refers to the required good faith assessment prior to acting to ascertain whether there is a reasonable chance of success in ensuring the lesser evil does obtain, given the relevant information available at the time. To countenance any violation without concern for its damaging effects, or to act knowing that there is a very good chance that all it will do is increase the evils we are seeking to avoid or minimize, is simply immoral – at best a form of savage and misguided revenge. Still more damaging, such acts are themselves a form of the immorality or evil that those who genuinely get DH are seeking to combat. So, in summary, there are four conditions that need to be met before we can claim to have a DH scenario. They are:

(1) An action or policy emanating from unavoidable moral conflict/dilemma must involve a justified betrayal of a person or an important value or principle.

(2) An agent must be moved by moral considerations, typically when they hold strong special obligations to particular individuals or groups, to commit moral violations.

(3) The action chosen in order to bring about the lesser evil was made necessary under 'a complex of immorality' forced upon the agent by the immoral/evil projects of individuals or organizations.

(4) All dirty hands actions must (i) be reasonably expected to succeed in bringing about the lesser evil (typically reducing the deleterious consequences of the immoral/evil project) and (ii) be proportional to the harm they will reduce or prevent.[36]

Compliance with these conditions cannot be easily ascertained by the observation of leaders who face such situations. This is due to a number of factors, among which are a lack of complete information and, most importantly, our inability to ascertain with certainty an agent's true motives. However, where the principles prove particularly useful is for a process of self-assessment. If a leader wants to behave in a morally justified way when facing terrible and irresolvable moral conflicts, these criteria can be used as a guide to whether the action considered is a case of DH or not.

Limits to DH actions: proportionality, reasonable success and motive

The four conditions that distinguish DH scenarios from straightforwardly immoral acts or projects reveal the limits and boundaries for dirty actions. While such actions violate fundamental moral prohibitions and commit a moral crime, they are nevertheless also the right thing to do. This justifiability, in part, rests on the fact that they are actions or projects in which the nature and extent of the violation is calibrated to minimize the moral violation and bring about the lesser evil. Specifically drawing on conditions 2 and 4 above, there are three factors that serve to limit the kind of actions that can be legitimately implemented under a DH rubric; namely, proportionality, reasonable success, and proper motive. None of these three constraints is easy to delineate with precision, yet taken together they do offer a rough framework for demarcating what are the limits of an acceptable DH action. Let us examine each in turn. Firstly, the notion of proportionality serves, as it does in JWT, to ensure that, even when engaged in terrible actions, there is a serious attempt to keep the violence and harm to a minimum – just enough to achieve the desired end and no more. Not only does adhering to the principle of proportionality make the conflict less vicious and bloody but it also makes a future peace and coexistence with the enemy more likely. As far as is possible, the dirty action needs to overcome (or form part of a series of actions to overcome) an unjust regime (or fight against terrorism) but also to avoid planting the seeds of deep bitterness and future conflict.[37] However, the proportionality condition is notoriously difficult to operationalize. Beyond the largely anodyne claim that all acts must not cause more harm than good, its application to specific situations is almost always strongly contested.[38] The difficulties arise for the following reasons. Firstly, there is no clear way to establish an independent and widely accepted set of values against which harm inflicted can be measured. Secondly, the task of determining proportionality requires empirical assessments which during conflicts are always hotly contested. Thirdly, the proportionality condition is open to different formulations, each with different implications for the legitimacy of certain actions even if there is the unlikely agreement on the appropriate values and the empirical assessments.[39] Even so, the proportionality criterion provides one important element in the assessment of what constitutes the boundary beyond which dirty acts are not justifiable.

The second factor for constraining DH actions is that of 'reasonable success'. This criterion aims to ensure that the violation which a dirty act involves is done only when there is a reasonable chance it will result in bringing about the lesser evil. Moral violations are always deleterious actions and it is important that the cost of so acting has a reasonable chance of bringing about an equal or greater compensating benefit. Dirty acts must not be used for revenge or convenience but in order to obtain a state of affairs that is the lesser of two evils. However, like proportionality, this criterion is hard to operationalize given the context of specific cases. The question of what constitutes 'reasonableness' and 'success' almost always remains contested.[40] Nevertheless, if a judgement is made in good faith and on the best information available at the time, in conjunction with a plausible assessment of the relevant past experience, then it can serve to constrain the kinds of dirty acts that can properly be carried out.

This leads to the third constraint that justifiable dirty acts must arise from the proper motivation. This involves doing wrong to do right *for a moral reason* and no other. The proper motivation is crucial since it safeguards the primacy of fundamental rights which trump other concerns such as those based on pragmatism or convenience. We identify DH actions in part by the motive for such acts, and this very motivation also serves as the boundary for the kinds and extent of dirty acts. The aim is always to bring about the lesser evil when faced by an unavoidable moral conflict or dilemma. So when we get DH by violating an absolute moral principle, such as the prohibition on torture or murder, the moral motivation for so acting requires that the violation on balance brings about a better state of affairs. This obligatory moral goal serves to limit even those actions beyond the moral boundaries. Of course, this constraint is general, and what it will allow or prohibit depends very much on the details of the moral dilemma facing the leader. The devil is very much in the detail here. If a leader is resisting genocide or facing a 'supreme emergency', the kind of dirty acts that could be justifiable will be far harsher and more harmful than situations where the oppression or threat is less deadly. Similarly, what kind of dirty acts could be justified under a DH rubric in the fight against terrorism depends on the nature and severity of the threat. If the terrorists manage to obtain a weapon with huge destructive power, such as a nuclear device, then measures taken to stop their actions could be justifiably very harsh indeed.[41]

Character and an ethic of responsibility

The previous section focused on specifying necessary constraints for DH acts by looking at their likely consequences and the specific moral motivation of each particular action. The hope is that these constraints together will ensure that justified wrongful actions will be done for the right moral reason, and will eliminate or reduce the oppression and injustice perpetrated by others. But, as already pointed out in the previous section, these constraints are difficult to operationalize, and consequently their successful application requires leaders or politicians who have the appropriate attitude and character to enable them to resist the powerful temptation to ignore such constraints when facing difficult situations.[42] To this end, we need to offer an account of the type of leader or politician we want to protect us and act on our behalf. To put it another way, we need to ascertain which leaders or politicians are most able to combat oppression and injustice within the constraints of morality and, when absolutely necessary, to employ justified dirty actions while remaining cognizant of the crime committed and the limits beyond the moral boundary. A possible answer to this question is to turn to insights from virtue ethics and look to the necessary character traits and dispositions of those in the role of leader or politician.

Let us first turn to the issue of character. One of the ways in which those who dirty their hands can establish the limits of such actions is to ask what a virtuous person would do in such circumstances. We learn from reading the ancient Greek playwrights, such as Aeschylus or Sophocles,[43] that when faced with a moral dilemma how we act is only one dimension of the problem (and perhaps not even the most important aspect to consider). What is of immense importance is recognizing what we will become when we commit a moral crime, even one that is also morally justified. A realization of this kind in a leader is evidence both that he is, in Walzer's words, 'not too good for politics and that he is good enough' (Walzer, 1973: 167–8). The good leader understands and accepts the burden of operating under an 'ethic of responsibility',[44] that in order to attain worthy and important goals it is sometimes necessary and morally justified to engage in moral crimes. It is important to note that the insight here is not that we need politicians and leaders who in the face of injustice are ruthless and efficient, but differ from immoral politicians in that they feel bad about having so to act. Rather, the insight here is that if the constraints on DH actions are to be effective, we need leaders who are constitutionally deeply hesitant and averse to committing moral crimes. These predispositions will ensure that such leaders will only get DH when it is really necessary and, very importantly, will seek to keep the moral crime to an absolute minimum.[45] What is more, this recognition that they are committing a moral crime for which they have become morally polluted and must pay a moral cost will act as a further restraint on DH actions unless absolutely necessary. In short, leaders who are in a position to harm others, even if for fully justified reasons, need to be strong moral persons who recognize and insist that it is always a moral crime to violate the fundamental rights of others. In recognition of this, their first and powerful instinct is to refuse to act in ways that will do such harm and violate fundamental rights if any reasonable alternative is available. As Walzer eloquently puts it:

> A morally strong leader is someone who understands why it is wrong to kill the innocent and refuses to do so, refuses again and again, until the heavens are about to fall. And then he becomes a moral criminal ... who knows that he can't do what he has to do – and finally does. (Walzer, 2004: 45)

Finally, what should such leaders who get DH feel about themselves? And how should we feel about those who commit moral crimes on our behalf? Leaders ought to feel the full weight of their actions, and when engaged in serious moral crimes the appropriate moral emotion is tragic remorse. Furthermore, when such moral violations are committed, there is a need where possible to make the appropriate restitution to those who have been wrongly harmed. Such leaders ought to strive for a situation where DH actions are kept to an absolute minimum so that they contribute to establishing a world where there is justice and peace and civility within conflict. Even when resistance to oppression or the fight against terrorism necessitates that leaders or politicians 'sink in filth and embrace the butcher' (Brecht, 2001: 25), they must never believe that the rightness of their goal gives them licence to engage in unconstrained violence and domination where no outrage is forbidden and no moral limits or costs are recognized.

Final comments

I began this chapter by setting out the specific options and problems facing politicians, and leaders more generally, who resist tyranny and injustice. I rejected two approaches as deeply flawed: namely, amoralism and pacifism. I then argued for the centrality of moral concerns, especially the assumption that all persons ought to be treated with respect, and that their right to not be harmed or killed needs to be taken as well-nigh absolute, even though we know that situations will arise where these rights will be justifiably violated. These constraints are fundamental and a necessary limit on the kind of legitimate actions which can be perpetrated in our battle against injustice and tyranny. However, within this framework I focused on situations where intractable moral conflicts leave us with the problem of DH, a pervasive and unavoidable part of our moral reality. Here we are caught in a complex of immorality not of our choosing where situations arise which force us to violate fundamental rights in order to bring about the lesser evil. This chapter has focused on bringing clarity to this problem by offering some minimal conditions that can serve as constraints even when doing wrong in order to do right. When we are morally obliged to commit moral violations, this does not leave us in a situation where anything goes. In short, I have tried to offer some minimal guidelines for what would constrain the extent and frequency of a justified moral crime; a set of limits beyond the moral boundary, so to speak. It is an aspect of our moral reality that is acknowledged by Geras (and others), but little is said beyond the claim that a justified moral crime is committed. I have tried to put some flesh on these bare bones. Although we may face situations where our choices are not between good and bad but between various kinds of evil, nevertheless we must and can strive to act within limits and boundaries. We can endeavour to minimize suffering and injustice even when we are committing justified moral violations in our resistance to the worst forms of tyranny and oppression.[46]

Notes

1 For a flavour of recent examples of such literature see Brecht, 2001; Camus, 1984; and Sartre, 1948.

2 Geras, 1990. All page numbers in brackets in the main text refer to this book unless otherwise stated.

3 By 'a complex of immorality' I mean situations which are brought about
   by the not insignificant immoral actions of others and which leave an
   agent in the unenviable position where whatever he or she chooses to do
   in response results in committing a moral wrong. I do not include situations in which natural events have brought about moral conflicts. This
   latter situation leads to tragic choices rather than DH scenarios (or
   some other form of inescapable moral wrongdoing). See de Wijze, 2007.

4 Geras does footnote Michael Walzer's seminal article 'Political Action:
   The Problem of Dirty Hands' (Walzer, 1973) on DH when raising the
   'all but absolute' aspect of certain individual rights such as the right not
   to be killed or violated (49 and footnote 35).

5 Or, conversely, it could be the majority resisting the oppression of the
   minority, as in South Africa during the apartheid era.

6 I understand terrorism to be a form of political violence that aims to
   randomly kill and maim defenceless civilians (typically women,
   children, and the elderly) in order to achieve certain political goals by
   spreading fear and panic among the population at large. For extended
   discussions on the definition of terrorism see Ganor, 2008. Also see
   Walzer, 2000: chapter 12; Coady, 2004; Waldron, 2004; and Meisels,
   2009.

7 See Nagel, 2005: 113, who begins his paper with this remark.

8 Machiavelli, Hobbes, and, recently, Morgenthau are the main proponents of the Realist doctrine. Machiavelli, for example, advised princes
   who wished to maintain their rule to 'learn how not to be virtuous, and
   to make use of this or not according to need' (Machiavelli, 1981: 91).

9 'As for us, we were never concerned with the Kantian-priestly and vegetarian-Quaker prattle about the "sacredness of human life." We were
   revolutionaries in opposition, and have remained revolutionaries in
   power. To make the individual sacred we must destroy the social order
   which crucifies him. And this problem can only be solved by blood and
   iron' (Trotsky, 1920).

10 Morgenthau quotes Abraham Lincoln to drive home his point: 'I do the
   very best I know how, the very best I can, and I mean to keep doing so
   until the end. If the end brings me out all right, what is said against me
   won't amount to anything. If the end brings me out wrong, ten angels
   swearing I was right would make no difference' (Morgenthau, 1978:
   12).

11 This realization may lead to the view that, in resisting injustice, the
   method for doing so must prefigure the end we seek to obtain. The
   prefiguration argument is advocated by Pike in chapter 10 of this
   volume.

12 For a detailed criticism of the Realist perspective see Walzer, 2000:
   chapter 1.

13 The PP can be understood in at least two ways, one of which is that we ought never to resist injustices since they are to be borne with fortitude and patience. We must always turn the other cheek as suffering now in this world brings rewards later in the afterlife. Clearly, this view is championed by particular religious doctrines that insist that our present existence is a vale of tears, a test for the world to come, and hence there is no need to resist injustice in this world. I reject this position and write from a secular perspective which has as its focus the physical and psychological welfare of individuals in the world as it is now. I hold a meliorist view of society, such that social institutions and political arrangements are both corrigible and improvable. We can and must set moral limits to what we do and we need to fight against those who violate rights and seek to dominate others. In short, suffering and injustice are not inevitable.

14 This pacifist argument appears similar to one used against the AV position but is significantly different in that it rejects the very *possibility of ever justifying the use of violence*. The non-pacifist argument against AV challenges the claim that there is *no need to offer a moral justification* for acts that violate fundamental rights.

15 Geras rightly gives the pacifist position short shrift. As he says, such a doctrine would 'deprive people of all weapons save passive resistance in the face of any oppression or threat, however terrible. If this is not a sufficient case against it, I am unsure what could be' (23).

16 A third normative approach which has recently had a revival among contemporary moral theorists is virtue ethics. While deontological and consequentialist approaches are concerned primarily with developing universal rules/principles for right/good conduct, virtue ethics focuses on the *character of the agent*. I return to some of the insights of virtue ethics later in my discussion of the moral limits beyond the boundaries. For more background on virtue ethics see Darwall, 2003: introduction and Part II.

17 Space prevents me from discussing this method at length. I follow Nielsen's account of wide reflective equilibrium (WRE), which 'seeks to produce, and perspicaciously display, coherence among (a) our considered moral convictions, (b) a consistent cluster of moral principles, (c) a consistent cluster of background theories (including moral theories) about our social world and how we function in it, and (d) an empirically based, broadly scientific, conception and account of human nature'. See Nielsen, 1994: 24. For extensive comment on WRE method see Scanlon, 2002; Nielsen, 1994; Daniels, 1979; Rawls, 1971. For opposition to and criticism of WRE see Brandt, 1990 and Hare, 1973.

18 Rawls, 1971: 27 makes this point when he critiques the utilitarian account of justice. Also see Rawls's comment that all ethical theories

(and here he is referring to deontic accounts) that are 'worth our attention take consequences into account when judging rightness' (1971: 30).

19 Other specific or focused attempts to offer moral constraints to our actions when engaged in conflict are the Doctrine of Double Effect and the variety of Arguments from Self Defence. See Leverick, 2006: chapter 3 and McIntyre, 2009.

20 Recently, there has been an attempt to outline the requirements for justice when the war is concluded (*jus post bellum*) so that the winning side can ensure the creation of a future peace and treat those vanquished in the correct moral way. See Bass, 2004 and Orend, 2002.

21 There are six *jus ad bellum* conditions which must be met before it is legitimate to go to war. They can be summarized as follows. 1. just cause 2. last resort 3. proper authority 4. right intention 5. proportionality and 6. reasonable success. Each of these conditions requires, and has been subject to, considerable criticism and commentary. For a taste of this, see Orend, 2006; Walzer, 2000; and Elshtain, 1992.

22 For a good overview of these conditions see Orend, 2005.

23 Geras also rightly points out that to claim that we cannot criticize those who face terrible injustices because we cannot make moral judgements from the outside, so to speak, leads to unacceptable silence in the face of terrible abuses (46).

24 Hampshire, 1989: 106.

25 One of the attractive aspects of Marxism in all of its variations is that it insists that political institutions and political actions must focus on counteracting the great evils. For example, the existence of poverty in society must not be accepted as a natural and inevitable evil but the result of particular unjust forms of economic organization which can be changed with the appropriate political action.

26 Lukes, 1991: 197–210.

27 Geras, in conversation with me, describes himself as a 'liberal socialist'. This description captures his criticism of capitalist society combined with his admiration of egalitarian liberal theories of justice that adhere to fundamental human rights as crucial components of a good society. Geras puts it this way in his *Imprints* interview: 'With regard to other versions of progressive hope, the most attractive one for me would have to be egalitarian liberalism. However, notwithstanding the common ground I recognize with this strand of the liberal tradition, the egalitarianism there seems to me to be always diluted or compromised by some large degree of indulgence towards the structures and relations of capitalism.' He then adds: 'I have occasionally found myself identified with analytical Marxism, and I do recognize a loose relationship to it, but it is no more than that. I have benefited from reading the work of some of

the leading figures of analytical Marxism, in particular Jerry Cohen's, and I share a general attachment to the "analytical" standards that members of this intellectual current have aspired to: standards of clarity, precision, consistency and so forth. I share with them, too, an interest in the appropriate normative foundations of a left-wing critique of capitalist societies, a belief in universalist values and an openness to the intellectual resources of liberal political thought.' See Geras, 2002.

28 The clash can also arise between purely deontic requirements such as the duty to protect and defend, and the prohibition on violating an individual's right to life. However, in politics the clash is usually most acute between deontic and telic obligations.

29 This, of course, is a controversial claim since many would argue that the very notion of DH is confused and that a proper understanding of moral theory, either deontological or consequentialist, dissolves this *prima facie* moral conflict or dilemma. I have defended the very possibility of DH elsewhere. See de Wijze, 2007.

30 This is a term employed by Michael Walzer which he attributes to Winston Churchill during the darkest times during the Second World War. See Walzer, 2004: 33–50. Michael Ignatieff also considers the issue of supreme emergencies. See Ignatieff, 2004: chapters 1 and 2.

31 See Ignatieff, 2004: chapters 3 and 4 on 'The Weakness of the Strong' and 'The Strength of the Weak' respectively.

32 The terrible events of 9/11 in New York and Washington (and other similar horrendous attacks) with the use of suicide bombers to cause maximum civilian casualties are illustrative of the form of fanatical terrorism. Should such groups obtain weapons of mass destruction, the consequences could be catastrophic.

33 I have argued elsewhere that the appropriate moral emotion for those who get DH is 'tragic-remorse', a species of remorse that both acknowledges wrongdoing and the moral pollution that accompanies it in tandem with understanding and admiration for those agents who did what was necessary to bring about the lesser evil. See de Wijze, 2005.

34 See de Wijze, 2007 and de Wijze and Goodwin, 2009: 532.

35 I assume for the purposes of this paper that the complex of immorality in which we find ourselves is a serious one and consequently DH acts involve serious moral crimes.

36 In setting out the four conditions, I am indebted to Stocker, 1990: especially chapters 1 and 2. This does not mean that Stocker would endorse my four conditions.

37 Here the insights of a *jus post bellum* are apt. The aim is to ensure a just and sustainable peace after bitter conflict.

38 For a careful discussion of the proportionality criterion in times of war see Hurka, 2005 and Walzer, 2000: 129–33.

39 For example, it is not clear how we should regard the cost of non-combatants' lives compared with those of soldiers. Could we justify the death of two civilians if this would save the lives of one hundred soldiers, or vice versa? These formulae will always remain arbitrary and open to contestation.

40 One way of assessing reasonable success in practice is to follow the similar methodology for defining 'reasonableness' in legal cases. For example, courts decide on whether there is 'a reasonable expectation of privacy' by taking into account the accepted notions of privacy within a society at a given time in conjunction with the reasons for wanting to violate this expectation by examining the persuasiveness of 'public interest' arguments (among other things).

41 One serious concern here is that claims of 'supreme emergency' or that terrorists have weapons of mass destruction could be used by dishonest governments or leaders to justify deeply immoral actions and further their own unjust ends. This is of course a grave danger, but it does not detract from the need to be clear on what would be legitimate DH acts and how we should circumscribe them.

42 The other side of this problem is that some leaders or politicians, even when able to act to reduce terrible oppression and injustice, may refuse to do so because it requires getting DH and they refuse to act immorally under any circumstances. For example, a politician who refuses to use immoral methods to protect citizens from a devastating terrorist attack could rightly be accused of moral dereliction or abrogation of his or her primary duty. Similarly a leader who refuses to resist horrendous abuses because it requires the use of violence or deceit would be guilty of not protecting those whose lives are under his or her care and protection.

43 See in particular Aeschylus's *Agamemnon* and Sophocles's *Antigone*.

44 I take this term from Weber, 1958: 120, who contrasts an 'ethic of responsibility' with an 'ethic of ultimate ends'.

45 Bernard Williams makes a similar point when he says: 'The point – and this is basic to my argument – is that only those [politicians] who are reluctant or disinclined to do the morally disagreeable when it is really necessary have much chance of not doing it when it is not necessary' (Williams, 1981: 62).

46 I am indebted to Eve Garrard and Norman Geras for their insightful comments on an earlier draft of this paper.

12

Democracy first

David Aaronovitch

Towards the end of 2009 the *Guardian* newspaper ran a feature on the lives of teenage boys (Irby, 2009). In a series of side-boxes a random assortment of boys gave brief answers to some questions about their lives. One was 14-year-old Baba Dalawarzada, a refugee from Afghanistan. 'Do you like where you live?' he was asked. 'My home here is brilliant. It's much better than in my country: the Taliban, they used to tell us not to listen to music, not to watch TV. They just didn't let us live our lives.'

The struggle against the most reactionary forces on the planet, exemplified by religious totalitarians, is frequently characterized as an attempt to 'impose' a Western style of thinking on societies that do not want it. Paradoxically – in the West itself – such positions are often occupied by those who are hyper-vigilant about even the smallest sign that the state might be encroaching on their privacy or their rights.

But the obvious problem with the relativist position on democracy is that, without democracy, without a free contest of ideas, it has no way of knowing what the people in other countries or societies really want. Is it the case that women in strictly misogynistic and patriarchal societies prefer the security of their miserable lot to the precariousness resulting from their having access to education and health care? How would we know? Is it the case that most young Afghan men in Taliban areas would rather be told whether or not they may listen to music or wear a beard, because this is what someone with a gun says is virtuous or what someone abroad says is their traditional way of life? Again, how would we know? If there were no threat of violence, or coercion from armed groups, what would people themselves freely choose?

This isn't a question about whether it is right to wander the globe mob-handed, forcibly converting every tyranny, theocracy, and failed nation into a state modelled on Canada. We don't even have the capacity yet to intervene with force to prevent or curtail genocide, let alone to engage in constitutional terra-forming. It is rather about what attitude someone who imagines themselves to be progressive should take to the lack of democracy, or the possibility of enhanced democracy, both at home and abroad.

Parts of the left – a 'side' in politics upon which I would place myself – have long had an ambivalent attitude towards democracy at best, and sometimes a purely instrumental view of it. It is an irony that the left could always understand the virtues of, say, the Chartist demands for widened suffrage, the Civil Rights marchers' quest for voter registration and the Suffragette campaign for women's votes, and yet resist the democratization of institutions that it, itself, controlled.

To take but one example, at the Labour Party conference in 1978 there was a motion calling for the mandatory reselection of Labour MPs, in an attempt to make them more accountable to local parties (imagined then to possess greater ideological commitment). The leadership of the Labour Party opposed such moves, but it was widely expected that it would lose the vote, since several large trade unions, including the transport workers' and the engineering workers' unions, were committed in its favour. In the event the motion was lost by 3.07 million to 2.7 million. Then it transpired that the General Secretary of the engineers' union, Hugh Scanlon, had – as he claimed – made a mistake and voted the wrong way. It was believed by many commentators that Scanlon's error had been deliberate.

Deprived of victory the left raised a hue and cry about the absence of democracy. But their objection was not to the block vote per se (they had, earlier in the conference, used it to defeat the leadership over pay policy) but to Scanlon's defying of the wishes of his delegation. The brute statistics, however, tell their own story. The block vote of any one of the major unions represented a figure greater than the entire membership of the party, with all affiliated union members deemed to be de facto Labour Party members, and with these massive votes deployed on their behalf, often without even the most rudimentary consultation. The left-wing historian Perry Anderson described the block vote as 'a Leviathan of dead members … the working class version of the Rotten Borough – Old Sarum inverted as it were, with inflation rather than a reduction of numbers.' (Anderson, 1992: 349)

At the factory level the left was to be found arguing for strike votes at workplace meetings on the basis that these non-secret ballots, taken in the heat of an 'informed' debate (usually only informed by one point of view) were superior to secret ballots. In the first place such votes were taken after 'listening to the arguments' and in the second they would be uncontaminated by 'interference' from the media. A logic of this kind was observable in the famous remarks of one of the most influential miners' leaders, Mick McGahey, at the beginning of the catastrophic strike of 1984/5. Arguing, in effect, against a national strike ballot of the whole union membership, technically necessary to call a national strike, McGahey insisted that miners would not be 'constitutionalised out of their jobs' (Simons, 1999). Instead it was decided that miners already on strike would picket those pits still working, and that this would gain the solidity of action that the ballot (were it successful) was designed to achieve. In other words the left and the union leaderships had little faith in what union members would do, left to themselves. It is also true that they may have intuited what the American writer and academic Cass R. Sunstein has more recently proved, that a group of like-minded people met together are more likely to go to extremes than if they deliberate on their own (see Sunstein, 2009).

So the left and centre-left view of democracy at home could be absolutely functional, rather than principled, in that it was the outcome that should determine the democratic form, and not the integrity of the process.

If this was the attitude at home, it was much more so when it came to foreign affairs. It was rightly a matter of violent criticism that, during the cold war, Western policy was guided by membership or affiliation of one camp or another, or else by a short-term calculation of domestic interest, and not by the inherent virtues, democratic or civic, of foreign states. It was appalling that America should tolerate Franco, should fete the Shah and subsidize the Somozas, all 'bastards' whose own peoples were left voteless and liberty-free. Kissingerian realpolitik seemed to be a licence to do deals with the dreadful, while averting one's eyes from the casualties.

Of course, sections of the left were as bad, if not worse. Loyalty to the Soviet Union led many doughty fighters of injustice at home to negate the presence of a far worse injustice over there. Well after the

Stalin era there could be found many on the left who would suggest that, though Russian democracy was imperfect, and mistakes had been made, nevertheless the ordinary Russian exercised a genuine form of power through factory meetings, and that – in any case – wasn't Western democracy characterized by a formal and empty ritual in which voters were invited to make a mark, once every five years, against the name of one of a number of almost identical parties?

Remarkably, even twenty years after the fall of the Berlin Wall, the release of the Stasi files, and the revelatory tsunami of material on life in Soviet Russia dispelled any possible last lingering illusions about the 'people's democracies', one may find the general secretary of the British Trades Union Congress travelling to Havana in early 2009 for the celebrations of the fiftieth anniversary of the revolution and making a speech in which there is not one single word about the complete absence of democratic freedoms in Cuba.

Indeed, Mr Barber's attenuated notion of democracy was present in the first line: 'I am proud to bring greetings from the British trade union movement and the 6.5 million workers we represent.' (Barber, 2009). A Martian might wonder how the greetings of these millions were collected and expressed; we don't have to wonder – we know they were never asked.

Barber was proud of his links with the Cuban trade unions (they are state appointed bodies), ecstatic over Cuban social and economic achievements 'that would shame many richer nations', proud of Cuba's record in 'international solidarity', condemnatory of the 'brutal and unnecessary' US embargo against Cuba, similarly condemnatory of the treatment of the Miami Five – a group of Cuban spies given overlong sentences in the US – citing Amnesty International's criticism of the American courts, and ended with this peroration: 'International solidarity is at the heart of trade unionism, and at this time of global crisis, it is more important than ever that we work together, in the interests of working people . . . Viva Cuba, Viva Revolution!'

If Barber was aware of Amnesty's work on the treatment of Cuban dissidents, their imprisonment for daring to raise a petition, and their dreadful treatment in prison, he didn't suggest it for a moment. His view seemed to be that the social advances in Cuba outweighed the problem of the complete lack of functional democracy and basic political liberty. It is an irony that Barber, who was almost certainly shielded from any real contact with ordinary Cubans (from whom he would have heard a very different tale) is now wrong about the compensating glories of the island's decrepit education and health systems.

However, a similar attitude has been displayed, for different reasons, towards China. There the glories of the command structure allied to capitalist economics have created a check-free environment for economic growth. If the authorities want to build an airport – or, indeed, to decree a greener economy – then it is so ordered, without the messy business of consultation or planning inquiries. I have heard several political businessmen express their admiration for the Chinese system and heard them speculate that, politically, this technocracy has much to teach the West. And if that's true of China, then it may also be true of developing countries, in which the issue of democracy should be a second (or third or fourth) order question. Sometimes this is wrapped up in a formula in which the construction of a civil society (however that is to be achieved) should precede any discussion of democratic forms.

A fairly typical, though blunt, assessment of this kind was provided by the British journalist Simon Jenkins, also in *The Guardian*, about a week after Baba Dalawarzada's brief interview. 'It does not matter to the British people', wrote Jenkins, 'how the Afghans choose to conduct an election. It does not matter how one of the poorest countries in the world chooses to govern itself under the UN charter of self-determination. Few elections outside western democracies bear much scrutiny. We still hold our noses and deal with Iran, Kenya, Zimbabwe and Russia.' (Jenkins, 2009)

There is, even in Jenkins's terms, a problem here. Obviously it does matter objectively, otherwise Baba might be in Kandahar and not in Leicester, and it is hard to imagine an Afghan parliament voting to allow that Mr Bin Laden to use their country as a springboard for attacks on faraway superpowers. Jenkins's first error is to confuse necessary and sufficient conditions. His second is to confuse what 'matters' with a policy of direct intervention.

It is certainly true that the existence of the formal underpinnings of democracy – freedom of speech, expression, organization and assembly, constitutional safeguards, and universal suffrage – are insufficient in themselves to guarantee a well-ordered and functional society. There is a need for education and information exchange, a requirement for rudimentary social justice and effective monitoring of the system. But without democracy – the system in which rulers are subject to challenge and removal and in which all people have the capacity (used or not) to exercise an opinion – everything else usually fails. That is why progressives should always find themselves on the side of democracy first.

13

Geras on context and indifference

Gideon Calder

A great deal of light is shed by Norman Geras's writing, whether about cricket or Marx's *Theses*, Laclau and Mouffe or *Life is Beautiful*. It is a very particular kind of light, the writing itself a particular kind of writing. Both are characterized by what might be called a meticulous *aboutness*. Rather than conjuring fresh frameworks, or neologizing, Geras's attentions have been to the richness of what is already there, in theoretical writing and in human experience. This is intricate labour, drawing out significances, contradictions, implications, while immersed in its application to different kinds of seam: an argument, a thinker's *oeuvre*, a moment in history. Yet, in an ambidextrous way, the work operates simultaneously amid these specifics and also at the level of theoretical generality. It is partisan, impassioned, literary, but at the same time arrestingly sober. Early in my own theoretical work, it seemed to me important to track down Geras's analyses of things. Uncannily, the 'things' in question – Marx, post-structuralism, socialist ethics, Ashes test series, the Holocaust – tended to chime with my own interests. And in each case that distinctive kind of light was shed whether or not I agreed with the specifics of the Geras line, although for the most part I tended to.

Marx and Human Nature (1983) provides one example of the particular kinds of illumination I mean. Encountered as part of the undergraduate reading list for a course on Marx, this book was billed as 'required reading', with all the connotations of burden that the phrase brings with it. It tackles an issue in *Marxisant* scholarship – whether or not Marx was committed to a view of human nature – which seemed to me at first a minor diversion. Less than that, in fact. More like a fleeting distraction in a lay-by off a bypass road itself some considerable distance from the questions about the political usefulness of Marxism which were *obviously* the main priority. Yet reading it reversed my original view of the map. What had seemed marginal now seemed central, and an arid terrain became vivid and dramatic. It helped establish a thought which I'd glimpsed already in a half-baked, shaky version: that ontological questions – so in the case of human nature, a generalized treatment of what we are like, and how we flourish – are unavoidable in emancipatory thought and practice, and in 'useable' considerations of what a better society would be like. As normative theorists it's not so much a matter of *whether* we dabble in such accounts, but *how*. That this thought has in various ways become regarded as unhelpful or jejune – on which, more below – does not diminish its purchase.

When later I read 'The Controversy about Marx and Justice' (1989), it struck me as doing a similar job with regard to the relationship between the normative impetus of Marx's writing and its wider descriptive and explanatory concerns. Thus, again, it's not *whether* Marx had a normative agenda, but *how* he did – its shape, its implications, and the contradictions between the lurking ethical content of his work and his coexisting 'impatience with the world of norms and values' (1989: 268). One didn't need to agree with every Geras point, scrupulous as the architecture of his arguments was, to get the resonance of these key, compelling products of his labour. Inconveniently, just as I was beginning my PhD research on Richard Rorty, Geras brought out his own study of his work (Geras, 1995). Here too was that familiar kind of meticulous aboutness, and sure eye for inconsistency and tension. Deeply demoralizing. But still it gave strong impetus, and food for thought that has endured long since that thesis was submitted.

So it is a great pleasure to be given this chance to mark debts owed for these and other illuminations of sticky problems to which Geras has turned his attention. In what follows, I address what, among them, is among the most adhesive: the relationship between individual moral agency and the unchosen social contexts in which, inevitably, that agency does its work. It seems to me that the social and ethical texture of this relationship – between agent and backdrop – is central to the architecture of all of Geras's theoretical work. It is one of the things which, implicitly or more loudly, that work is most importantly *about*, whatever other subject matter is at stake: Althusser; Luxemburg; ethics and the ends and means of revolution; crimes against humanity. My particular focus here will be on the normative accounting for collective moral failure – a key theme, of course, in *The Contract of Mutual Indifference* (Geras, 1998; hereafter, *CMI*). As Geras puts it elsewhere, reflecting on how we might convey the full moral horror of the Shoah: 'How in a world where there is care, love, any human value, can these things be done, and be allowed to be done, and continue to be done seemingly time without end?' (Geras, 2003: 62). Edmund Burke's famous dictum, cited there by Geras (1998: 20), provides a starting point: 'The one condition necessary for the triumph of evil is that good men do nothing.' It's a powerful aphorism of course, and highlights something to which ethical theorists have tended not to be very alert, if at all: the importance of the absence of the good – as well as the presence of the bad – in our understandings of situations of moral disaster (see on this Calder, 2005a). This particular kind of absence – people doing nothing – is crucial to the very possibility of anthropogenic calamity on the magnitude of the Nazi Holocaust, but on smaller scales too.

Even so, Burke's picture is incomplete: though the inaction of 'good' people is necessary for such calamities to ensue, it is not sufficient. My main focus in this chapter will be on what else might be needed to complete the picture. This question presses strongly on us, but also requires us to think beyond – or beneath – purely abstracted ethical theory. And a great strength of Geras's work is that it considers at the outset factors which, far too often in academic ethics, appear as afterthoughts or footnotes, or matters of otherwise subsequent detail. For here we find that the subject matter of ethics is – to use Raymond Geuss's phrase – 'constantly locat[ed] within the rest of human life' (Geuss, 2008: 7). This is, as I shall argue, exactly where it should be. 'Doing' ethics, as Geuss continues, requires 'unceasingly reflecting on the relations one's claims have with history, sociology, ethnology, psychology and economics'. My own view is that this reflection is done best under the auspices of a pluralist ethical naturalism. For such a position, values (rather than being 'subjective', or pure cultural constructions, or existing in a metaphysically separate realm) are in part claims about well-being – human or otherwise. Human well-being is itself a complex mixture – like humans themselves – of natural and social aspects, achievable in various ways but with, nonetheless, some crucial preconditions. This position emerges out of work done by those in a left-emancipatory tradition which resists both liberalism and postmodernism as adequate vehicles for progressive ethics, sympathetic though it may be with parts of those positions. It is best exemplified in the work of a string of recent Anglophone theorists – for example John O'Neill (1998; 2007), Andrew Sayer (2005), Russell Keat (2000). My job here is not to defend this view, but to compare it with Geras's. For the most part, on my interpretation, the momentum of his own work in ethics pushes in very similar directions. Yet when thinking through Burke's picture, it seems in some respects to shift course. Because I favour the kind of pluralist ethical naturalism just depicted, I don't think that shift is such a great idea – not just in general, but for the force of Geras's own arguments. It seems to me to create problematic ambiguities in his explanatory and normative agenda – and, in particular, to lead him to commit to 'thick', foundationalistic, claims about the inherent flawedness of human nature which are much more difficult to sustain. More on this in what follows.

People doing nothing: liberalism and indifference

A liberal culture underwrites moral indifference. It makes much room for the bystander to suffering. For the principal economic formation historically associated with liberalism, defended by liberals – whether confidently or apologetically – today as much as ever, is one in which it has been the norm for the wealth and comfort of some to be obtained through the hardship and poverty of others, and to stand right alongside these. It is a whole mode of collective existence. Not only an economy. A world, a culture, a set of everyday practices. (Geras, 1998: 59)

So, then, the spectator may settle in his seat on the ground, in the pavilion or – if he wants the best view, and without direct payment to the ground authority – in front of his television set. (Arlott, 1983: 35)

It's difficult to tell what deadpan John Arlott makes of his TV cricket spectator – a kind of model of consumerhood, at a distance from any threat of rain or the intrusion of fellow spectators, and with the capacity to switch channels at any time, should the action get dull, or the whim otherwise arise. Yet looking at these two quotes in juxtaposition, there is a parallel less facile than might first appear. Geras's depiction of the ethical landscape of liberal capitalism fits Arlott's cricket watcher neatly within it: in fact – self-contained, detached, risk-avoiding, unbeholden to others – he is an ideal inhabitant. That landscape is evoked regularly in *CMI*. In an account which echoes and complements other surveys of the moral climate of the modern, technologized society, Geras seeks in that climate an explanation of the kind of scale of indifference which might allow a moral calamity such as the Shoah to ensue. And liberalism – 'a paradigmatic liberalism of negative duties only, duties of non-interference', as Geras qualifies it for the purposes of his own account (1998: 58) – is identified as complicit in the maintenance of a social landscape in which living side by side with others who are suffering 'is not widely seen as a matter of moral depravity' (1998: 58). To make this claim is not to equate the evils of capitalism with those of fascism or Stalinism, nor to assume that liberal values are inextricable from capitalism itself. Rather, Geras's point is that a liberalism for which refraining from harm represents the extent of our moral obligations is inadequate as a response to the kinds of moral darkness which, in modern societies of deep structural inequality, abound. This is the world of the contract of mutual indifference. Stanley Cohen (2001: 68–75) has depicted this as the world of the 'everyday bystander' – the passive or unresponsive witness, the spectator who does not intervene. Cohen gives example after disturbing example of cases where this occurs as an aspect of the mundane, rather than in situations – such as that ensuing from the break-up of the former Yugoslavia, or in the Rwandan genocide of 1994 – of wider moral disaster.

But Geras's own focus is on the very widest such disaster: the Nazi genocide. How to account for 'bystanderism' on the scale required for such a catastrophe? His proposal: through the notion of a contract of mutual indifference, in which people accept as a quid pro quo that if they 'do not come to the aid of others who are under grave assault, in acute danger or crying need', then equally they 'cannot reasonably expect others to come to [their] aid in a similar emergency' (Geras, 1998: 28). This is not a contract in a formal sense, or the normative device familiar from contractarian political theory; it is rather, descriptively, presented as a 'model of the world which we really inhabit' (1998: 29). Arlott's spectator is, then, part of this way of life – and again, in caricature at least, he might indeed epitomize it, at least at its most mundane.[1]

In the first passage quoted above, the terms Geras uses about the culpability of liberalism for this kind of bystander culture – that it 'underwrites' and 'leaves room' – are carefully chosen. They are also ambiguous. They point, as I shall argue, to a wider ambiguity in Geras's work on ethics – not about liberalism or capitalism as such, but about their implications. This ambiguity is present too in the 'For...' with which the third sentence in the quoted passage above begins. Liberalism does not ensure bystanderism, but it allows for it. And it does this not by itself, but by association with capitalism. At the outset, this marks out Geras's account against the Weberian tones of alternative treatments of the sources of moral indifference, focusing as they do on the processes by which certain practices and orientations become 'rationalized', and so the norm. Thus Zygmunt Bauman locates these sources in the production of 'inter-human distance' symptomatic of modern industrial societies, where 'moral responsibility and moral inhibitions become inaudible' (Bauman, 1989: 192) as social institutions drive a wedge between good people and would-be objects of moral concern. And Alasdair MacIntyre identifies as typical of late modern societies a 'compartmentalization' of society and self, wherein the spheres of life become hermetically sealed from one another, in such a way that agents become incapable of judging their behaviour from any external standpoint (MacIntyre, 2006: 182, 196–9). On this point, whatever their social theoretical commitments elsewhere, Bauman and MacIntyre operate without much consideration of liberalism/capitalism per se. As does Jonathan Glover, in his *Humanity: A Moral History of the Twentieth Century* (1999), an impressive book nonetheless marked by a startling lack of engagement with that conjunction between moral climate and economic formation with which Geras starts his analysis.

Such sociological detail is crucial to the adequacy of ethical dealings with the Holocaust. Indeed, the force of Geuss's complaints about the mainstream idioms of normative theorizing might be summed up by considering just how bereft an account would be if it conducted those dealings in the manner of a series of abstract thought experiments, or neatly packaged-up dilemmas, as if the horrific example of Sophie's Choice might sum up the scale of the disaster in moral terms.[2] Accounting for the backdrop is crucial – and of course Geras's work is conducted with this in mind. Yet his account is not, in fact, as it might first seem. Although in *CMI* 'paradigmatic liberalism' and the material inequalities of capitalism are flagged up early as culprits for 'the loneliness of the doomed' (Geras, 1998: 8), and for the conjunction wherein 'disaster for some' is 'comfortably lived with by others', the ultimate momentum of the narrative points us in other explanatory directions. Indeed, the analysis is most at home, and richest, when dealing with existentialist and theological responses to the Holocaust, notions of radical evil, and the inherent flawedness of human nature – of 'bad conscience', 'guilt', 'lunatic beliefs', 'moral cowardice', 'failure to act against known wrongs'. As against Bauman's more exclusively sociological explanations, Geras, like MacIntyre, is more insistent on firming up a certain zone of individual culpability. 'You can spell out all the conditions, factors, contributory causes,' as he puts it: 'still, these were not bound to produce exactly *that*' (Geras, 1998: 157). And: 'There is something here that is not about modernity; something that is not about capitalism either. It is about humanity' (Geras, 1998: 164). In the end it is this essential human flawedness to which Geras devotes most attention. This means that the nature of liberalism's 'underwriting', its 'leaving room' – the contours of this space it makes, the extent of its complicity in atrocity – are not spelled out as they might be. In fact, hardly at all. Rather, they tend in *CMI* to be given periodic mention in the unfolding of an argument whose main action lies elsewhere.

Social structure and moral agency

This is curious. In the narrative of *CMI*, substantial elements of Geras's earlier meticulous analysis in social theory (see, for example, Geras 1977, for a finely calibrated delineation of structure/agency relations and other staple social-theoretical fare), and indeed the whole *flavour* of that kind of approach, drop out just at the moment when such things might seem most vital. For while one can certainly question Bauman's account of the Holocaust as a kind of effect of the technologically administered society, it seems that as part of so doing, and to provide an alternative, one needs to put forward another form of structural understanding in order just to arrive at the particular historical event that the Holocaust is. An obvious resource (though this in itself does not commend it, of course) would be the historical materialism for which, in a 2002 interview, Geras still registers clear and explicit support:

> [O]ne will understand an amount ranging between very little and next to nothing about the social and political world if one does not give central attention to the distribution of economic wealth and power and the class relations which flow from it. (Geras, 2002: 198)

Again: while *CMI* does give a bit of that kind of attention, it is certainly not central. Rather, the distribution of wealth and power under liberalism/capitalism features as a kind of unexplored motif amid the existential tenor of much of the discussion. At one point in the book the general drift of my point here is acknowledged straight up, in the form of an anticipated objection. What if,

> in the abstraction of mere 'individuals' and of the contract by which they are brought into relation, we have up to now overlooked (in a manner often thought to be characteristic of liberal political theory) those social factors, or structures, that result in different people being differently placed: in better positions or worse, with greater or lesser resources, with more and less available time, for coming to the aid of others. (Geras, 1998: 42–3)

Geras acknowledges questions hanging over the possibility of bringing such factors under the conception of the contract of mutual indifference. But he opts not to address those questions, except to say that he has no desire to risk 'belittling the extent to which anyone was restrained from helping behaviour by their own material hardships and conditions' (1998: 45). But that's it. At this stage it's worth pausing, and considering in juxtaposition the passages in the two previous block quotes. Similar moves are made to great effect in Geras's analyses of Laclau and Mouffe, and of Rorty: the highlighting of (at least apparent) incongruities amid the position at stake. Here, the messages of the two quoted passages are entirely congruent; they reinforce each other. But the incongruity comes in the respective textual role that each point plays. While the first is given as a reason *for* giving attention to inequality, the second comes as a precursor to the decision *not* to give such attention – or at least, not to let it interrupt the notion of the contract.

Is there a departure in Geras's work between his earlier, more extensive treatments of historical materialism and his later primary focus on ethics? Not explicitly. Meticulous throughout in his presentation of his own and others' ideas, he acknowledges no 'official' major changes of theoretical mind since his analyses of Luxemburg on the relationship between capitalism and democracy (1976: 198–200) – or indeed between stages of his own analysis of Marx on human nature (though see Soper, 1986: 49–50 for a note on an ostensibly key transition in this department). One way of reading this is that Geras is an erstwhile Marxist in denial about having lapsed, and made a transition to some other philosophical place. This kind of transition is common enough, of course – recent decades have seen stampedes in such directions. Still, I don't think it accounts for it. Geras, advertently, still has his Marxist head on, in this account of bystanderism: we hear there directly that modernity's cocktail of liberal norms and structural inequalities makes it pretty much ripe for the culture of indifference he depicts and condemns. The structure appealed to there is that of the liberalism/capitalism conjuncture. Yet structure, as the argument unfolds, becomes less central to our ultimate understanding of the Nazi genocide. The crucial explanatory ingredient is provided by flawed agency. So again: 'There is something here that is not about modernity; something that is not about capitalism either. It is about humanity' (Geras, 1998: 164).

Unpacking that 'something' leads to reference (ethical in register, rather than psychological) to 'radical evil': the individualized, agent-centred and definitively non-structural explanation of the human propensity for 'cruel desires', of the 'emotional charge produced – and maybe required – by the assault upon the innocent' (Geras, 1998: 163). This is an unexpected move. One way of looking at it is this: Geras shifts from an ethically naturalist, Aristotelian mode in which institutions are to be judged by (as Richard W. Miller puts it) 'the kinds of lives they promote' and proposed rights by 'assessing the consequences of embodying them in institutions' (Miller, 1981: 323), to a rather more numinous and individualized key, in which a normative appeal to radical evil – for Kant, of course, a kind of corruption of the will and an admission of the frailty of human nature (Kant, 1960: 21–39) – becomes the explanation to fill the gaps for which, it turns out, modernity and capitalism cannot themselves account. The ethical significance/inevitability of notions of human nature in the Marxist project is supplemented, now, by the acknowledgement of a vision of mixed, flawed, compromised human nature, to the extent of calamity. As a result, contextual understanding – the notion that we might understand human flaws better by situating individuals amid their relations, and the social structures they inhabit – is deemed itself a kind of moral failing.

And yet pushing such a contextual understanding further – considering how it might be that social relations allow such calamity to happen – seems crucial, as Enzo Traverso has argued (2001: 428), to figuring out the conditions of an ethic of solidarity, as against the contract of mutual indifference. We can expand on this point. It is one thing to argue that notions of what might count as human flourishing are crucial to the realization of any progressive political project. This observation...

> [S]ocialism has to justify itself as respecting certain constraints or limits that are laid down by our common human nature: that is to say, it must meet certain needs of human beings – from needs for basic nourishment to needs for free activity – better than these have so far been met historically; and it must afford certain basic protections to human beings, against violence, persecution, oppression and so forth. (Geras, 2007: 7)

... seems to me true for all egalitarianisms, liberal, socialist or otherwise. It is an aspect of Geras's basic ethical naturalism, as emerges from his earlier works, where the appeal to universal human needs and capacities carries strong normative force, always with an equally strong insistence that it is only under certain kinds of social relations that such needs will be met, and such capacities flourish. But to defend the significance/inevitability of accounts of human nature in this 'thin' sense – for example, to invoke a minimal substantivism, as I have called it elsewhere, against purely procedural accounts of justice (Ceva and Calder, 2009), and to insist that some appeal to shared human needs and capacities is inevitable in so doing – is one thing. To commit to a thick account of flawedness is another. For at this point one runs the risk of undermining the very force of one's original point about the importance of social relations to our flourishing, or not. This is a point which Geras himself extends elegantly, in *Marx and Human Nature*:

> [C]onservative and reactionary assumptions about what is inherent in human nature are pervasive. That they are owes a lot, probably, to the historical influence of the Christian doctrine of original sin, but there are other doctrinal sources aplenty, sceptical as well as religious, new beside old, for assumptions of innate human wickedness and belief, correspondingly, in the permanence of social malignancy of one kind or another. Such ideas close off the avenues of thought against the prospect of liberation from manifold social oppressions. (Geras, 1983: 15–16)

Quite. To this, the earlier Geras insists that the correct response is not to junk human nature altogether, but to think more carefully about the needs and capacities which might be said to be 'basic' to it (1983: 16).

Such accounts will be contested, of course. But they are more sustainable, I would suggest, than accounts of radical human flawedness. Prosaic human flawedness is another thing: we give in to temptation, we find hypocrisy alarmingly easy, we do not always treat others as we would have them treat us, we rarely meet the standards of our own better selves. But while it *does* follow from the 'basics' of human nature that we are vulnerable to harm in certain ways, that we have basic needs for sustenance, that we have the generalized capacity to direct our own lives which might be thwarted or encouraged by social circumstances such as our access to education and healthcare – it simply *doesn't* follow from the facts of the calamity, the sheer moral disaster, of the Nazi genocide that human nature is somehow intrinsically flawed in some inevitable, inexplicable way, any more than it follows that a wholesale sociological argument from bureaucratic administration, Bauman-style, might suffice. What *does* seem intrinsic to any account of that calamity is an understanding of the kinds of failure of social relations which are a necessary condition – as Burke admits, in his partial way – of any such unfolding. If the point about radical evil is granted, then the rest of the account – for example, the ways in which indifference might be underwritten by a 'liberal culture' – in fact becomes peripheral. 'Underwriting' will mean, rather than anything stronger, something like 'providing a ground on which the dark side of human nature will flourish'. The problem becomes not social relations, but human beings themselves.

Why should Geras – despite his own appeal to the culpability of liberalism/capitalism, and his own meticulous attention to this particular 'seam' among others – want to leave such space for a hypostatized vision of flawed humanity? Why, in *CMI*, should he add to his earlier appeal to shared needs and capacities as 'constraints of precondition', as Keith Graham calls them (2002: 152ff.), a third appeal, to shared 'impulses' and 'dispositions' (Geras, 1998: 106, 109), and then under those latter headings include a potential 'malignancy' and 'great evil' (Geras, 1998: 114) generalized, as a feature of human nature itself, from the extreme calamity of the Holocaust? Geras is entirely right to reject as simplistic (not to say unwarrantedly deterministic) the notion that human beings would be uniformly good, and incapable of being 'the authors of any evil choice' (1998: 112), if only we get the backdrop of conditions and institutions against which they act to be sufficiently benign. He is also convincing in insisting – echoing others offering other moral/sociological 'takes' on the Holocaust (Bauman, MacIntyre, Arendt) – that the calamity 'was the work of human beings we are acquainted with' (Geras, 1998: 98): psychologically normal, compromised, good in parts. He is also, I think, entirely justified in concluding both that capitalism 'systematically produc[es] for millions of people . . . conditions of extreme want and oppression, in which hatreds are the more likely to accumulate, fester, erupt', and 'contributes a massive share' to evil, but at the same time is 'not responsible for all of it' (Geras, 1998: 169). All of this seems to me nuanced, careful, and – in fact – a much fuller moral account of what might allow events such as the Holocaust to happen than those offered by Bauman and MacIntyre – or indeed, Arendt. And yet, there is a need in *CMI* to stake this place for human nature as inevitably flawed in such ways as make the Holocaust possible. Geras himself wants not to 'conjure up' evil as 'some kind of metaphysical force' (2002: 204) – but, still, presents as universal traits of human beings aspects of self-interest and aggression. As Traverso writes, this 'seems partly to bolster the view of the Jewish genocide as a sudden eruption of evil lying dormant in the depths of human nature' (Traverso, 2001: 428).

We end up with two alternative positions – one, I would suggest, present in the earlier Geras, the other emerging in his ethical treatments of the Holocaust. These don't come in a simple chronological sequence, but emerge in different examples of Geras's intricate analytical labours. I'll express both in the terms used in my own introductory section above. From a common starting-point (0), we reach two distinct destinations.

> 0. Accounts of human nature – generalised treatments of what we are like, and how we flourish – are unavoidable in emancipatory thought and practice, and in 'useable' considerations of what a better society would be like.

Then either

> 1. This does not mean 'postulating some single optimal model of the human good or of human self-realisation' (Geras, 2007: 6), or any foundational claims about human 'goodness', 'badness' or otherwise. But it does mean that our discussion of better and worse social conditions and institutions will be constrained by certain basic factors about human existence.

or

> 2. These include foundational claims about human 'goodness', 'badness' or otherwise. The latter have particular explanatory importance in accounting for events of moral calamity. The Holocaust cannot be understood without taking on board the possibility of deeply embedded human impulses towards behaviour which itself can take the form of evil.

Claim (1) I take to be emblematic of the pluralist ethical naturalism endorsed earlier. Claim (2) seems to me ambitious, and much more difficult to sustain: to posit self-interest and aggression as universal traits of human nature raises the stakes in terms of provability, but is also weak in terms of explanatory power. Self-interest in mundane terms is easy enough to find examples of (though this does of course not entail its universality as a trait). But self-interest, or indeed aggression – or indeed any other such isolated psychological trait – simply does not seem in itself to account for acts of collective moral calamity, any more than it does for the relative success of certain versions of the market economy. Witness the limitations of rational choice approaches, methodological individualism, and so on (see Calder, 2005a) – approaches from which Geras himself has kept a distance. By incorporating such flaws as universal, claim (2) seems also to take the resistance to contextualism about human nature a step beyond what is warranted by Geras's own arguments on that point. So why should Geras, in *CMI*, be tempted by (2)? I want to suggest that the answer lies in a sometime conflation, in his work, of (i) appeal to context with (ii) relativism. In the remainder of this chapter, I'd like to offer a brief hypothesis along these lines.

With Geras against Geras on contextualism and anti-realism

Key parts of Geras's arguments against the post-Marxism of Laclau and Mouffe (1990), and against Rorty's pragmatism (1995), rest upon an appeal to a realist ontology, and a normative anti-contextualism. Both are, partly, summed up in the doctrine that 'If there is no truth, there is no injustice' (1995: 128) – and in the commitment to realism which emerges here:

> There is not just one true image of a person or description of an event or state of affairs. Different angles of vision and personal beliefs, different political, cultural or other purposes, different linguistic and

conceptual frameworks, will shape and colour the content of any description or narrative, yielding a plurality of possible representations of whatever is the subject at hand. Yet there is, for all that, a *way things were down there*, a reality constraining the range of adequate description, interpretation and explanation. (1995: 108 – emphasis in the original)

What is significant in Geras's work is that this realist commitment to 'a way things were down there' is regarded as the corollary of his normative anti-contextualism. For integral to the rejection of the notion that there might be 'no way things were down there' is a case for the moral abdication inherent in such a position. Thus Geras's realism is itself couched as a kind of normative commitment, in a way which complicates the widely habitual presumption that the realms of fact and value are logically and ontologically distinct.[3] This position, as elaborated through the critical labour of *Discourses of Extremity* (1990) and *Solidarity in the Conversation of Humankind* (1995), seems to me largely persuasive. And its significance is indeed especially pressing when one considers events of moral extremity, and the ethical relation of survivors and others to such events (see Calder, 2005b and 2008b for further exploration of these issues). When Geras disputes the claim that 'there is no pre-discursive objectivity or reality' (1990: 97), he does this always with a discernible normative underpinning, even when that normativity is not explicit. And his argument is none the worse for this; indeed, it is reinforced by it. It is part of a consistent resistance, across his works, to tendencies towards relativism and idealism in progressive thought.

In this respect the position that emerges in Geras's critiques of Laclau and Mouffe and Rorty consists in three interrelated claims. First: a realist ontology is possible, in ways, and to an extent, which both post-Marxism and Rorty's pragmatism seek to deny. Second: each of those positions (notwithstanding the determination of their proponents to avoid this) make ontological commitments which themselves, perhaps because they are furtive or inadvertent, are flawed. Third, there is a better ontological account on offer – better both in the sense of (descriptive and explanatory) adequacy and coherence, but also in terms of 'fit' with the kinds of progressive values to which both post-Marxists and Rortian pragmatists will be committed.

To this, a fourth claim might be added, more fleeting in Geras's work, but especially prominent in his recent writings first about the

Holocaust, and then subsequently about 9/11 and the Iraq war. This is that contextual*izing* (identifying and exploring the backdrop to actions or events) commits the same kinds of sins of relativism – ethical and ontological – as contextual*ism* (the metaphysical claim that everything is contextual) does. To put it differently: to seek to explain acts of moral calamity through attention to the social and economic contexts which form their backdrop is to deny their truth, and thus their injustice. It is truer to condemn them 'for what they are', than to account for them in such a way. For any such accounting-for will be a relativization, and thus a softening, and perhaps to some degree an excusing, of the severity of the event. Thus speaking of 9/11, Geras decries the fact that in its aftermath,

> in no time at all there was a great chorus of left and liberal opinion … saying 'Yes, terrible, appalling, but…'; the 'but' following so close upon the 'yes' as to squeeze out any adequate registration of either the significance or the horror of what had occurred. (Geras, 2002: 206)

Here is where I get nervous. This is not because I wish in any way to dispute Geras's view that 'the attacks of September 11 were a moral crime without qualification or mitigation' (2002: 209) – though I did, and do, take a different line from his on the justifiability of the 2003 invasion of Iraq. It is because (the implied flippancy of tone aside) to say 'Yes, terrible, appalling, but…' seems to me *exactly* the way to respond to events such as the September 11 attacks. To imply that to understand their context is to forgive runs right against the wisdom of Geras's own work in closely relating 'how' and 'what' to 'should'; the intricate labour of exploring the complexity of events to the equally intricate labour of drawing complex moral positions in response. This is not to suggest that the world, our actions, any event, might be contextualized 'all the way down', or that there is beyond discourse no 'way things were down there'. Quite the opposite. It is being duly respectful of the 'way things were down there' to say that though we know an action is wrong, or an event is disastrous, we might not fully understand its conditions, and have good reasons not to jump to simplistic conclusions about these. Fallibilism is not the same as relativism; indeed, it is key to the kind of realism which Geras otherwise defends that we might, in all such judgements, be wrong – or at least, less right than we thought. It is to rebut, as the inanity it is, John Major's famous 1993 injunction that we should 'condemn a little more and understand a little less'.

Geras seems to me himself to be equally committed to that rebuttal. To be a 'yes-butter' of the kind that denies the horror of events in order to serve some ideological purpose is, indeed, morally indefensible. Yet 'yes-buttery', in principle, need not buy into full-on relativism, or the notion that to explain is to excuse. Nor is saying 'Yes, but...' to commit to any notion of moral equivalence between (in the case of 9/11) the values of those carrying out the attacks, and 'Western values' in a generalized sense, or the disastrous notion that the victims somehow 'deserved' their fate. But it is to make the case for a relation of ethical theory to the rest of life. In its pluralist ethical naturalist vein, the intricacy of Geras's labours is suffused with the importance of such relations. Exploring them runs with, not counter to, the non-idealist universalism the pursuit of which illuminates that work.

Notes

1 I use a cricket-related analogy in recognition of Geras's own affinities, though he himself is understandably hesitant to draw political-philosophical conclusions from his own interests in the game: 'as a spectator at sport,' as he has said elsewhere, 'I prefer to forget about politics, even if this is not always possible' (2002: 212). But even within apolitical spectatorhood there is still room for normative judgement. At one point during the fourth Ashes test at Headingley in 1997, Geras's 'view from the boundary' records a man in a neighbouring seat, growing increasingly restive. 'At one point he offered a semi-public reading from some tabloid, of bizarre and unlikely sexual facts. When I declined the beer he kindly offered me, he asked if I was "just here for the cricket"' (Geras and Holliday, 1997: 89). On reading this, I laughed out loud.

2 William Styron's *Sophie's Choice* (1976) tells the story of a woman given, at Auschwitz, and as a 'reward' for not being Jewish, a choice: one of her children will be spared the gas chamber, as long as she chooses which one. My point here is not to diminish the power or resonance of this case, but to point out that the intensely drastic nature of the dilemma, considered just as such, tells us relatively little about the particularity of the Holocaust as an affront to ethics, or the sources of culpability for it.

3 There is another kind of argument, in *Solidarity* (1995), for realism vis-à-vis the conditions in which we converse about the world, at pp. 118–20. This argument is a transcendental one, about the conditions of possibility of discourse itself: without a prior, 'structured, somewhat stable and differentiated world', 'language across a public space with shared symbols would be impossible'. For me, this argument is under-

played in the book, and too hasty. In any case it would be illuminating to know what Geras himself might think of the relation between this particular case and the wider normative terms upon which much of the rest of his argument for ontological realism is based.

14

Humanism and social hope

Shane O'Neill

One of the most significant and consistent strands in the work of Norman Geras has been the emphasis he has placed on the relation between normative or critical theory and a philosophical account of human nature (Geras, 1983, 1995, 1999a). Geras believes that some form of the latter is essential as an inescapable foundation for any convincing account of the former. Political theory is for Geras about the pursuit of truth, justice and human solidarity. By focusing on the essential features of human selfhood, on the nature of humanity as such, he believes that we can ground normative thinking and critical social theory on a rational, philosophical foundation that is both universally significant and morally substantive. He takes the universalism of human reason, and indeed of truth and justice, to be crucial to the articulation of a sound normative vision, and he views all forms of particularism, or relativism, to be exclusionary in morally arbitrary ways, and hence undermining of the bonds of human solidarity (Geras, 1995). Geras also believes that critical accounts of human reason should be substantive rather than merely procedural, since he takes any proposed procedure of reason to be only as rational as the substantive moral principles that it will inevitably presuppose (Geras, 1999b). It has, therefore, been a central aspect of Geras's work to argue that utopian thinking, of the right kind, needs philosophical foundations. Before we explore further this key issue for philosophically inspired social criticism, it will be useful to set the question in a relevant historical context.

Enlightenment hope

It was not uncommon among the intellectuals of late eighteenth-century Europe to engage in reflection on the connections between human nature and social hope. In that historical setting exhilarat-ingly optimistic visions were commonplace, accounts of how the world might be transformed for the better were it only to be ordered according to the dictates of human reason. Typically amongst these philosophers of the Enlightenment, the Marquis de Condorcet (1955) expresses, in his *Sketch for a Historical Picture of the Progress of the Human Mind* of 1795, what seems to us to be an outrageously impassioned hymn to the dawn of human reason and the imminent emancipation of human beings from all forms of oppression.

'The time will come therefore', Condorcet declares, 'when the sun will shine only on free men who know no other master but their reason' (1955: 179). Human reason, according to Condorcet, has been the driving force of history, and the development of our rational faculties has made possible ever more rapid progress towards a perfect form of human society. Condorcet and his fellow Enlightenment philosophers felt assured that nature had 'linked together in an unbreakable chain truth, happiness and virtue' (1955: 193). He was confident enough to predict in 1795 that the future would see 'the abolition of inequality between nations, the progress of equality within each nation, and the true perfection of mankind' (1955: 173), although he wisely did not commit himself to any particular time frame. All human beings would, he believed, have the opportunity, through education and the free use of their reason, to perfect themselves and to achieve happiness. As we acquired through rational, scientific inquiry greater knowledge of the truth of nature and society, we would each realize our true human selves and would work in cooperation and solidarity with one another to create the perfect human society. Here we have a commitment to truth, to authentic selfhood and to human solidarity, to emancipation grounded in human reason, to a utopian vision secured and anchored for us in its philosophical foundations. Reason sets humanity free.

With more than two hundred years' hindsight we can see that Condorcet seriously underestimated the risks as opposed to the opportunities associated with any attempt to rationalize the world. Our confidence in the emancipatory potential of the Enlightenment project has been shaken to its core by a catalogue of wars, genocides and tyrannical regimes, by the overwhelming risk of global warming and ecological degradation, by the deepening inequalities between the rich and the poor of the world, and by the onset in an era of global terror of an insecure world of mistrust, hostility and fear. In spite of the vast resources that have been expended in developing the natural and social sciences, we seem no closer to bringing to an end the misery and oppression that large sections of the world's population endure daily. It might be suggested, more harshly, that the actual rationalization process we have experienced has enabled the rich and powerful to protect their interests more effectively against those who are in greatest need of emancipation. Bearing all this in mind, it is tempting, in the face of such immense socio-political challenges and what appears to be an increasingly uphill struggle for justice, to despair of Enlightenment reasoning.

The legacy of the Enlightenment has, of course, been a subject of much heated debate in philosophical circles at least since the time of Nietzsche, but especially since the debates about postmodernism that began to rage in the 1980s (Geras and Wokler, 2000). And yet, wherever we stand on the question of that legacy, hope springs eternal. And if hope is to be nourished, then we need to have dreams of a better future, utopian visions that drive us on in the pursuit of emancipation. For progressive political thinkers, despair is not an option, but rather we need to articulate utopian aspirations as to where we should be going, what we should be seeking to achieve and what we might dare to hope for. Unlike Condorcet, however, we cannot be so confident about the emancipatory potential of a rationalized world. We have to take on board more than two hundred years of historical experience, much of it detrimental to hopes for justice, as we ask today where the dialectic of Enlightenment has left the connection between a vision of a world where human misery is minimized and a philosophical account of human reason.

Does the hope of greater solidarity among people who currently fear, mistrust or even despise one another, depend in any sense on our grasping the 'truth' about the human condition? Does a shared aspiration to justice require a philosophical foundation in an account of universal reason as an essential aspect of human nature? Influential theorists of neo-Nietzschean persuasion, such as Michel Foucault (1980), have concluded from their investigations into relations of power/knowledge in modern societies that progressive politics should be combined with radical critiques of reason. For Foucault and many others, the project of Enlightenment has itself been implicated in the perpetuation of much of the misery and oppression that we still see around us. Many of these theorists offer little hope for a better future, but those who do, such as Richard Rorty (1999), offer it without philosophical foundations.

As was noted earlier, Norman Geras has consistently expressed grave concerns about such anti-foundationalist thinking. Geras believes that such thinking inevitably undermines the aspirations that are most appropriate to progressive politics today. He has always urged us to recognize the essential connection between a philosophical account of humanity, its nature and its reason, and the hope that a more just world can be created, one in which human suffering is minimized. Geras confronted anti-foundational thinking most directly in the period between his major contributions to debates about Marx (1983) and his work on the implications of the Holocaust and other crimes against humanity for moral reasoning (1999a). The most important work of this period was his book from 1995 on Rorty, *Solidarity in the Conversation of Humankind*. In that book, Geras took very seriously the challenge Rorty (1989) had set for all philosophically minded progressive thinkers. Rorty's challenge, to those who resisted his invitation to give up on philosophy, was to ask why utopian hope should be built on philosophical foundations, and why such hope could not be supported effectively without unnecessary theoretical baggage. From Rorty's perspective, all philosophical frameworks that seek to ground notions of truth ('the way things really are in the world'), human nature (accounts of 'true selves' or 'humanity as such') or universal reason (whether substantive or procedural) are mere crutches that can and should be abandoned since they contribute nothing to our prospects of realizing our social hopes for a better world.

So the question we need to revisit here is whether or not the hope of a world in which human suffering is minimized requires philosophical foundations. If it does, we also need to know what sort of foundations this hope should have. I'm going to take three contrasting positions into consideration. First, there is Rorty's position, a post-philosophical version of pragmatism that insists that universal notions of 'humanity' or 'human reason' are neither necessary nor desirable as foundations for social hope. Then there is Geras's philosophical humanism, which offers substantive accounts of universal reason and human nature as philosophical grounds for hope. Third, there is a procedural form of universalism that is integral to the discourse ethics advocated by many contemporary critical theorists, most notably by Jürgen Habermas (1990). This third perspective offers critiques of both of the alternatives and it presents a different reading of the connection between philosophical theory and social hope. I will first outline the basis of Rorty's challenge and will then consider the relative merits of the two accounts of universal human reason that are on offer as responses to it. We will assess, in concluding, what lessons might be learned from Rorty's attempt to sever the connection between philosophy and social hope.

Hope in place of knowledge

In *Philosophy and Social Hope* (1999) Rorty suggests that what is distinctive about pragmatism is 'that it substitutes the notion of a better human future for the notions of "reality", "reason" and "nature"' (1999: 27). Rather than seek to acquire the kind of knowledge that philosophers have traditionally been after (knowledge of truth, human nature, reason and the like), Rorty thinks we should simply focus on providing a future-oriented hope for better things to come. But that hope does not depend on our grasping truth, if by that we mean something like 'the one way things really are in the world'. Instead of truth, all we need is better forms of justification. Practices of justification are always tied to particular contexts and so can be distinguished from any absolute notion of a truth that corresponds to some unchangeable reality – the reality of a human nature, for example. As is clear from the following passage, neither justification nor even inquiry itself has, for Rorty, anything to do with truth:

> Inquiry and justification have lots of mutual aims, but they do not have an overarching aim called truth. Inquiry and justification are activities we language-users cannot help engaging in; we do not need a goal called 'truth' to help us do so, any more than our digestive organs need a goal called health to set them to work … [T]he agenda for our justifying activity is provided for by the diverse beliefs and desires we encounter in our fellow language-users. There would only be a 'higher' aim of inquiry called 'truth' if there were such a thing as ultimate justification – justification before God, or before the tribunal of reason, as opposed to any merely finite human audience. (1999: 37–8)

Rorty does not believe that there can be, in Hilary Putnam's term, a 'God's eye view' and so we can never grasp truth, can never access the one way the world really is.

A 'God's eye view' would have to take in all possible perspectives that any human person could bring to bear on any particular subject. This is not possible, as the terms in which we understand all features of our lives and our societies will vary from one context to another, for historical and cultural reasons. We are always evolving culturally and looking for new ways of understanding that will help us to cope with the demands we find most pressing at any particular time. If philosophers are going to be useful, therefore, they should not be seeking to nail down the truth, but rather they should help to provide us with new vocabularies that might assist us in dealing with the challenges we face in our present contexts. They should also assist us in abandoning old vocabularies that were developed to tackle earlier historical challenges but that are no longer of any social or cultural use. Rorty believes that notions of truth, reality, human nature and universal reason are all aspects of a vocabulary that has now outlived its usefulness. None of these traditional philosophical notions will, in his estimation, help us to realize a better future.

Rorty's main hope for the future, one that is shared by Geras, is for a socialist utopia articulated in terms of 'a global, cosmopolitan, democratic, egalitarian, classless, casteless society' (1999: xii). Since he does not believe that philosophy will help us to achieve such a society, it is worth noting what he had to say about the intellectual tradition of 'critical theory', that way of thinking, inaugurated by Marx, that seeks to integrate philosophical reflection on reason and its limits, or 'critique', with the articulation of the human impulse for emancipation from unnecessary forms of suffering. Rorty considered contemporary critical theory as 'the attempt of philosophy professors to make the study of Kant, Hegel and various other books intelligible only to philosophy professors, relevant to the struggle for social justice' (Rorty, 2001a: 51). Rorty does not consider these efforts to have been very successful and he wonders what relevance philosophy actually has to the effective, critical investigation of those conditions that cause large sections of the world's population to live in misery and destitution. Indeed, he doubts its relevance to our capacity to tackle effectively any form of injustice or oppression.

According to Rorty the critical investigations we require are not best carried out by philosophers. One suspects that he believes that his fellow philosophers have an unrivalled knack for approaching the struggle for emancipation in a manner that is far more convoluted and boring than it should be. Nor, according to Rorty, do we need convoluted positivistic causal explanations of what's wrong with the world because that will probably prove to be equally inaccessible for most potential readers. Effective criticism of injustice is more likely to come from, in Rorty's own words, 'journalists who can report their findings to the rest of us without using either the jargon of the social sciences or that of philosophy' (2001a: 51). These critical journalists might certainly benefit from the work of academic allies who could be described as 'imaginative and well-read trend-spotters' (2001a: 51). Rorty thinks of Marx, Habermas and Foucault in these terms. Each of them noticed dangerous trends in their historical contexts and articulated important critical perspectives on them. It was their contributions to our new vocabularies for dealing with significant trends in modern societies, rather than their efforts to seek truth, not that Foucault was 'guilty' of this, that make their work valuable. In other words, they were not helped much in the most important aspects of their work by their familiarity with the philosophical canon.

Defending universalism: competing strategies

Although most of Rorty's post-philosophical thoughts on social hope were published after *Solidarity in the Conversation of Humankind*, the argumentative strategy Geras adopted in that book retains its relevance. Rorty's main aim in this context, which is to sever the connection between philosophy and social hope, had been consistently present in his work even before the clear statement he gave of the position in *Contingency, Irony and Solidarity* (1989). Geras's principal criticism of Rorty's approach is that while he frequently rejects as grounds for greater human solidarity a universalist philosophical account of human nature, he relies on and presupposes such an account himself in much of what he has to say in support of his own social hopes (1995: 47–70). Geras refers to numerous passages from Rorty's work in defending his view that the latter is consistently inconsistent in denying explicitly a set of ideas that he implicitly affirms (Geras, 1995: 60–1). The ideas in question concern certain characteristics that are universally shared by all persons, characteristics that are distinctively human. These are, for Geras, true features of human nature, 'things like pain and humiliation, cherishing one's loved ones and grieving for them' (Geras 2001: 169). Geras argues that, on the basis of these shared characteristics, each of us has the potential to identify with all other human beings or with humanity as such. This common humanity provides an appropriate foundation for the hope that a just, classless, egalitarian, global society can be achieved.

Geras (2001) argues that Rorty cannot do without this universalist underpinning to the hopes they share. Rorty (2001b) suggests in response that hope always springs from some particular human context, from a sense of solidarity one has with one's own moral community, and not typically from any identification with humanity as such. But he has to acknowledge that the parameters of this moral community always have the potential to expand through interaction with others beyond the immediate circle of loyalty. The only way to block the expansion of this potentially ever widening circle of greater solidarity is through morally arbitrary exclusions that could not form any part of the kind of progressive political programme that Rorty subscribes to. So if the circle of solidarity can include all human beings, and cultural and political aspects of the globalization process would seem to provide more rather than fewer opportunities for this to happen, then the idea of a common humanity would seem to be an important element of the commitment to greater human solidarity.

Geras's critique of Rorty is based on a substantive account of universal human reason. Human reason for Geras is a faculty that each member of the human species shares regardless of their particular attachments or identities. It is a vital aspect of our human nature and is thus connected to the full range of distinctively human characterics, our shared needs, capacities, experiences and values. It allows us to reach mutual understanding with other human beings no matter what identity-based differences there may be between us. Human reason permits us to reflect together on the material and psychological needs we share, or the potential each of us has to suffer, or the experience we have of 'mortality, illness, grief, pain … well-being, love, dignity, integrity or flourishing' (Geras, 1999b: 162). This shared humanity motivates us to reach agreements with one another as to how best to deal with the threats we face or the opportunities that lie before us. This is why Geras thinks that this substantive account of human reason is necessary in order to ground our hopes for greater solidarity and for justice.

Before we return to Rorty's possible responses to these arguments, we need to introduce our third perspective. Discourse ethics offers an alternative way of defending universalism against Rorty's post-philosophical arguments. Its advocates claim that it can mediate effectively between the kind of substantive humanism that Geras proposes and the death of truth as heralded by Rorty (Habermas, 2000). According to the discourse ethicist, Rorty is right to suggest that our substantive ethical commitments derive from our being embedded within particular identity-forming contexts and that there is a plurality of such contexts in the contemporary world. Under conditions of modernity there is no substantive account of reason – grounded, say, in a philosophically derived view of human nature or of the goals of humanity as such – that can command universal assent. We must not, therefore, assume any substantive view as to the way the world really is, or the truth of human nature, in seeking to justify any particular utopian vision. In fact philosophers should *qua* philosophers refrain from advocating substantive visions at all, of justice, true human nature, an emancipated society or whatever. In a pluralist world any such commitment stands in need of justification. The appropriate context of justification is that of an inclusive and uncoerced dialogue where all human beings who may be affected by the outcome will have a chance to engage as effective participants. We have to test our claims in real exchanges with others, not in isolated philosophical reflection on the substance of human reason (Habermas, 1990).

According to the discourse ethicist, therefore, Geras is right to admonish Rorty for rejecting the use of philosophical reflection on reason as grounds for social hope. Without any philosophical criteria of reason, Rorty leaves himself bereft of any critical standards according to which we might adjudicate between competing substantive commitments to our possible futures. The main problem with Rorty's abandonment of philosophy is that he has collapsed the distinction between justification to a particular audience and truth as a critical ideal.

Habermas (1984/87), who is by some distance the most original and significant advocate of discourse ethics, argues that a critical theory of society can be developed from a reconstructive analysis of our most fundamental capacity as human beings, and that is the know-how each of us has to use language communicatively in an effort to reach mutual understanding with other people. Whenever we use language in this way, in contrast with a strategic use of language to get something we want, then we are engaging in what he calls communicative action. This practice involves us making certain idealizing presuppositions. As we seek to reach an understanding with others we presuppose not only that the views we are articulating or the claims we make, implicitly or explicitly, as to the truth of some state of affairs or the normative rightness of some perspective or other, are valid in the particular context in which our utterances are made but also that they represent our best guess as to what conclusions might be drawn on the matter in hand under ideal conditions. These idealizing presuppositions, therefore, have context-transcending power in that they signify that the validity of our actual claims is underpinned not by the immediate context alone but by the force of the better argument.

Habermas (1990) outlines a number of idealizing presuppositions in his reconstruction of our capacity to use language for communicative, as opposed to merely strategic, purposes. Two are particularly significant and they concern, first, the inclusion of all affected and, second, the neutralization of power. We could not be engaging in communicative action if we were seeking to exclude arbitrarily from the discussion some of the people who are affected by the subject under consideration. Nor could we be engaging in communicative action were we to impose our views on others through the use of force, or by threatening some harm to them. Of course, some people, Rorty for one, use language communicatively, and eloquently, by trying to persuade audiences that the very idea of the 'force of the better argument' as a critical criterion of adjudication relies on the kind of 'God's eye view' that is unavailable to us. People won't agree which argument has more rational force behind it because no amount of talk about idealizations and the like is likely to bring people together to share one perspective (Rorty, 2000).

But Habermas (2000) argues in response that what he is defending is a procedure of justification that points towards truth. This is not the same as a substantive philosophical foundation for truth that represents the kind of 'God's eye view' that Rorty rightly thinks of as being unavailable to us. In this sense, Habermas shares Rorty's anti-foundationalism. He also maintains that Rorty gets caught in a performative contradiction when he tries to dismiss the significance of the notion of validity that can be grounded in the idealizing presuppositions of communicative action. Rorty affirms in his practice of argumentation those very idealizations that he seeks to deny in the content of what he is saying. The validity of the claims we make is underpinned by critical principles that are internal to the practice of communication itself. In this sense these idealizing presuppositions are unavoidable for those who use language communicatively, and that includes all but the most damaged of human beings. For the discourse ethicist, utopian aspirations can have no substantive foundation but they must rather submit themselves to the procedural test of an inclusive and uncoerced dialogue in order to ground and justify their claim to rational acceptability.

Reason and Utopia

So we have considered two forms of universalist argument that might be pressed against Rorty's claims. Both seek to expose contradictions in Rorty's abandonment of philosophical commitments. Geras argues that Rorty affirms yet denies a commitment to a substantive form of humanism, while discourse ethicists like Habermas argue that Rorty makes the same idealizing presuppositions as all communicative actors even when he is seeking to deny them. Discourse ethicists believe that philosophical humanists like Geras help themselves to a more substantive set of philosophical assumptions than would be warranted under conditions of modern pluralism. Geras, on the other hand, suggests that discourse ethics is itself vulnerable to the kind of argument that he has pressed against Rorty, that it both presupposes and denies certain substantive assumptions concerning human nature. I suggest now two moves that will narrow the gap between Geras's position and the perspective of discourse ethics so that we can take the best of the two versions of universalism as a response to Rorty.

There is nothing in Geras's work to suggest that he would not agree with Habermas and Rorty that there can be no philosophical certainty, no Archimedean point, no pure reason. He seems to accept, in other words, that all substantive claims that might be made through philosophical argument stand in need of justification, and that all are corrigible. Geras is in other words a fallibilist and so not a strict foundationalist at all, if by the latter term we mean somebody who seeks to build arguments from a starting point of philosophical certainty. So Geras's account of human nature, the substantive ideas about our reason that he claims to be presupposed by Rorty in spite of his denials, are all presented in a fallible manner. They may be justifiable but they may yet prove not to be. We can never know for certain but we can continue to test these assumptions by engaging in dialogue with people, and the more diverse the range of people we engage with the better. So emphasizing the fallibilism that underlies Geras's position is the first of two moves in narrowing the gap between our two versions of universalism.

The second move is to get the discourse ethicist to admit that there is no such thing as a pure, stand-alone rational procedure without some normative substance behind it. It seems appropriate, out of sensitivity to the plurality of substantive commitments that are out there in the modern world, for us to strip away all but the bare philosophical necessities for grounding a critical perspective on the claims we make on one another. There is clearly some virtue in this commitment to a thin theoretical base, or to a kind of philosophical parsimony. Yet thinness does not imply nothingness. There is always some substance to such bases and the account Habermas gives of human beings as creatures who are capable of language use, in communicative and strategic forms, is no exception. The more we think about what kind of beings these communicative actors are, however, the more we have to acknowledge that an adequately comprehensive account of what is involved in the critical evaluation of competing claims will involve pretty substantive philosophical commitments. But what we are doing in making such claims is reconstructing, in a fallible way, the presuppositions of communicative action. Our reconstructions stand themselves in need of justification and can only be tested in dialogue with others, and the more diverse those others are the better.

We need to be explicit about the corrigibility of the claims we make when trying to provide the best possible reading of the practices of justification we should be seeking to institutionalize in society. Reconstructive arguments of this kind must also be difference-sensitive in that they invite others to consider whether or not things look the same way from wherever they are standing. The philosophical task of the moral universalist today is to provide substantive, difference-sensitive, fallible accounts of the practices of justification that are most appropriate to the critical assessment of competing utopian visions in modern societies.

If this is a viable task for philosophers, is there any sting left in Rorty's challenge? There is clearly a case for arguing that Rorty's utopian hopes would best be sustained by a substantive yet fallible form of universalism that is focused on practices of justification.

Rorty himself acknowledges that language use is a vital and distinctive feature of being human and he has no problem with the idea that there are appropriate criteria of justification available to us in assessing competing claims as to the kind of future we should aspire to. Among these criteria he includes virtues of argumentation such as coherence, reasonableness, tolerance and more generally the attempt to convince others with persuasion rather than force, cruelty or brutality. Nor does Rorty question the importance of getting as many people involved as possible in the dialogue (Rorty, 1999: 82). So his position on justification is not that far removed from that of Habermas. There is, however, one crucial remaining difference.

Rorty seems to wonder why Habermas would want to decorate himself with philosophical prizes, ones that seem to tell the world that he has secured grounds for the universal validity of our arguments. Why would any utopian socialist want to wear a T-shirt declaring that he or she has discovered the 'truth' or the secrets of 'human nature' or the essence of 'human reason'? Can't defenders of inequality claim that they have similar T-shirts at home? For Rorty, the more we try to nail these things down the more irrelevant our work becomes in the struggle for justice and the less inspiring our arguments are going to be for those many non-philosophers who could potentially share our utopian vision. We end up scrapping for philosophical prizes that are worthless in the context of our realizing a better future. This distracts us from the important work of persuading others as to what political goals we should be striving for, and then trying to secure those goals.

So while there are many argumentative merits in the critiques of Rorty that one finds in the work of his universalist critics, there does seem to be something important in what Rorty has had to say on this point. If philosophical reflection is to be of real use, then it needs to inspire and to motivate people to engage in emancipatory practices. Rorty thinks that arguing endlessly about truth, reason, reality, human nature and the like just doesn't get the job done. It is difficult to dismiss this charge out of hand, troubling though it may be for us philosophers to admit it.

15

Evaluation and the quantification of freedom

Hillel Steiner

Although the subject of freedom is not one which has figured prominently in Norm's extensive works, he and I have now been intermittently discussing philosophical aspects of it for over forty years.[1] And, given his characteristically acute analytical ear, it's been a source of some satisfaction – indeed, relief – to me that those discussions have hardly, if ever, been marked by any serious disagreement. I don't, of course, know how much longer my luck will hold out in this respect, but I believe there's a good chance that he will find little that is exceptionable in the argument that follows.

Those conversations on freedom, like so many other people's discussions of that concept, have often taken Isaiah Berlin's seminal 1958 lecture, 'Two Concepts of Liberty', as their point of departure. Quoting an epigram of Tawney's, Berlin there remarks that

> 'Freedom for the pike is death for the minnows'; the liberty of some must depend on the restraint of others. (Berlin, 1969: 124)

This comment is offered in the course of a plea for the drawing of a frontier between the respective domains of private life and public authority. But the exact location of this frontier, Berlin suggests, must be a matter for negotiation since 'no man's activity is so completely private as never to obstruct the lives of others in any way' (Berlin, 1969: 124).

I suppose that one question underlying the issue to which this chapter is ultimately addressed is whether this latter claim of Berlin's is best understood as registering a broad empirical generalization or some other sort of truth. Is he merely reporting a general fact about the kinds of activity that everyone actually engages in and/or the kinds of private lives that others actually lead? If so, we might well wonder *why* he thinks that public authority may intervene in – obstruct – some of those activities to prevent their obstruction of others' lives. For if, like Berlin, we're looking to reduce humanly created obstructions, why not have that authority intervene, instead, in those lives – or, at least, treat it as an open question as to whether it's the pike, rather than the minnows, whose liberty depends on the restraint of the other? We don't, after all, need to tax either our memories or our imaginations very severely to discover that some people lead lives that are pretty obstructive of others. Your freedom to pursue your chosen path through life, for instance, would probably not be enhanced by having a bunch of minnows swimming across it.

My own view is that Berlin's claim, whatever he may have thought it to be, is *not* one registering a broad empirical generalization. Rather, it (imprecisely) reflects an implication of his favoured negative concept of freedom itself. That implication, stated explicitly, is that any action we engage in – any way we lead our lives – obstructs others: *anything* we do renders impossible some conceivable action of others.[2] We cannot do anything without closing down some action-possibility for others. This is true regardless of whether or not, in doing something, it's part of our purpose to close down that action-possibility. And it's also true regardless of whether those others would actually have exploited that possibility, whether it was an action which they would have had any interest in doing. Our intentions and theirs have no bearing whatsoever on whether that action-possibility has been closed down. My inadvertently locking you up for three hours in a closet from which there is no escape closes down the possibility of your participating in a particular (concurrent) political demonstration with which you may be utterly unsympathetic.

Furthermore, my locking you up in that closet opens up some action-possibilities for others (including, perhaps, myself) that would otherwise have been closed. Had you not been locked up there, you would have gone to the cinema. As it is, someone else is now, and thereby, unprevented from occupying the cinema seat that you would have occupied. His or her freedom to occupy it has been purchased at the cost of your unfreedom to do so. Liberating slaves from the control of their owners reduces the freedom of those owners. Residents of the Hobbesian state of nature, though at liberty

– permitted – to do whatever they might wish to do, are not thereby free to do so, for they are extensively prevented from doing so by one another. And the creation of a legal system among them, though it may redistribute the freedoms they have, does not obviously thereby increase (or diminish) their overall magnitude.

It was thinking along these lines that led me, elsewhere, to the inference that there is a *Law of Conservation of Liberty* (hereafter, LCL).[3] The core of this inference is expressed in the claim that the magnitude of each person's overall freedom is inversely related to that of others. And I take this to imply that negative liberty is such that it makes no sense to speak of it as being aggregately increased or diminished – much less maximized, minimized, maximinned, and so forth – but only as being dispersed or concentrated to some particular extent (Steiner, 1994: 54).

I shall not here attempt to mount a full defence of LCL since, as you might imagine, it has met with far too many diverse objections to allow for the accomplishment of such a large project in a single chapter.[4] Instead, I propose to consider only one argument which, if correct, would certainly suffice to consign it to the dustbin of mistaken ideas. This argument, I hasten to add, is not one which has been directed exclusively against LCL and, indeed, its targets include several other accounts of negative liberty that decline to draw the LCL inference I advance in my own account of it.[5]

The argument in question is one which advances the claim that, in order to assess the *extent* of a person's overall freedom, we must take into account the *value* of that freedom. That is, our computation of the amount of freedom that each person has must reflect – by mathematically integrating – the amount of value attached to each of his or her particular freedoms. Let's call this the *Value Integration Claim* or VIC.

That VIC would, if correct, prove fatal for LCL is reasonably evident, for the values of the particular freedoms that severally compose our overall freedom can obviously vary enormously. If, as that claim suggests, the magnitude of a particular freedom is some partial function of its value, there is no reason why one person's loss of it – and others' consequent gain in freedom – would preserve that amount of value and, hence, according to VIC, the overall magnitude of the freedom enjoyed by all of them. Thus, let's suppose that you are a discerning film critic and one widely recognized as such. Then it seems plausible to believe that your freedom to sit in that cinema seat – a freedom which you lose by virtue of being locked up in the closet – may well be of considerably greater value than the thereby acquired freedom of someone else to occupy that seat. Indeed, the total value of all the freedoms you thereby lose may exceed the total value of all the freedoms thereby gained by others. In such circumstances, VIC would logically compel us to conclude that LCL has been falsified inasmuch as the total amount of freedom, jointly possessed by all, has been diminished. Or, conversely, *LCL* would equally be falsified if the value of your lost freedoms were to be *less* than the value of the freedoms thereby gained by others. For, in either case, the overall magnitude of the freedom possessed by all would not remain the same.

As those familiar with the analytical literature on the concept of freedom will immediately recognize, that claim about the relation between evaluation and measurement has been advanced by many different writers in several different forms.[6] However, the most recent argument for VIC, and one that certainly takes much closer account of the objections levelled against many of its predecessors, is to be found in Matthew Kramer's excellent book, *The Quality of Freedom* (2003), which presents one of the most searching and comprehensive discussions of the concept of freedom yet written. Accordingly, it is to Kramer's argument that what follows is primarily addressed.

Like Ian Carter and myself, Kramer advances a conception of freedom whereby questions of *whether* a person is free to do a specific act are to be construed as purely empirical questions about human prevention – ones to be answered on the basis of physical evidence alone. But he diverges from our view in contending that questions of *how much* freedom a person has must be answered by reference not only to physical magnitudes but also to evaluative ones. We have to know the values of the particular freedoms and unfreedoms we have, as well as their physical dimensions, in order to calculate their total magnitude. We must apply what Kramer calls *evaluative multipliers* to those physical dimensions, in order to discover how much freedom they each amount to and, hence, what their overall magnitude is.

Now, on the face of it, this seems odd. It's certainly *not* true of most things and properties. If we identify a set of things as grains of sand, we can calculate how much sand that set amounts to without any reference at all to the value of each of those grains. And the same is true of properties. Take weight: if I know the weight of each person and thing in an elevator, I can know the total amount of weight borne by that elevator without having the slightest idea of those components' respective values. Even in the case of freedom itself, doctors, scientists and engineers measure the freedom of diverse things – persons' limbs, non-human animals, clock pendulums – to move or remain stationary, without having recourse to evaluative multipliers. Yet Kramer wants to say that the case of human freedom is different. Why?

I think he's undoubtedly correct in finding support for this claim in many aspects of ordinary usage. The problem, however, is that ordinary usage is notoriously promiscuous in its disclosures of the conceptual properties of freedom: it licenses us to employ the word 'freedom' and its cognates in many ways that are – and are generally acknowledged to be – mutually inconsistent. For instance, many people would say – and many theories maintain – that those preventions to which others subject me are not curtailments of my freedom if they are preventions to which I've given my consent: Ulysses, they would say, is not made unfree when his sailors bind him to the mast as they approach the island of the Sirens. Whereas, on the conception of freedom expounded by Kramer, Carter and myself, such preventions would indeed count as freedom curtailments, though possibly well-justified ones. The general point here is that the existence of differences like these, and many others, tends to make ordinary usage a singularly unreliable oracle to consult on several seriously contested issues surrounding the concept of freedom. So the best we can aspire to do – and I say this not a little despondently – is to delineate, as precisely as possible, a variety of internally consistent conceptions of freedom, in the hope that one of these will recommend itself as being burdened with fewer counter-intuitive implications than the rest.[7]

Perhaps the most strongly counter-intuitive implication burdening earlier evaluative conceptions of overall freedom is what I've called the *negative numbers paradox*. This paradox is easily described. Suppose there are three actions, A, B and C. And suppose that I'm unprevented from doing – am free to do – A and B, and that the evaluative multipliers used in measuring those two freedoms are 20 and 10, respectively. I am, however, prevented from doing C, but that's a *good* thing because the freedom to do C is not valuable at all: in fact, it's a disvaluable freedom whose evaluative multiplier is therefore negative, say –5. What then happens to my overall freedom if or when the prevention of my doing C is removed – that is, if I become free to do C? The strongly counter-intuitive implication of earlier evaluative conceptions of overall freedom is that this liberation actually *reduces* my overall freedom from some product of 30 to some product of 25.

It is, I think, very much to his credit that Kramer's evaluative account of overall freedom acknowledges the absurdity of this paradoxical result, and commendably seeks to avoid it (Kramer, 2003: 443). So while rejecting Carter's claim and mine – that the purely physical dimensions of the particular freedoms composing a set of freedoms *alone* determine the extent of the overall freedom in that set – he is nonetheless at pains to sustain the 'primacy' of these physical dimensions by circumscribing the mathematical power of those freedoms' evaluative multipliers. And he does this by stipulating that they not be less than 1: the valency of all evaluative multipliers must be positive.

> The primacy of the purely physical dimensions of a person's overall freedom lies in the fact that the lowest value for any qualitatively-oriented multiplier is 1 ... Even when the possession of a particular freedom of some anomalous type is typically of disvalue for a human being, the qualitatively-oriented multiplier associated with any freedom of that type is not negative or zero ... If it does not make an augmentative difference to the weight of some particular freedom, then it makes no difference at all; it never makes a diminutional difference. (Kramer, 2003: 428–9)

Thus, Kramer's analysis of my foregoing schematic example would treat the evaluative multiplier of the freedom to do C as 1, rather than –5, with the consequence that liberation from the imposed physical restriction on my doing C would indeed increase (rather than paradoxically reduce) my overall freedom, but only slightly – from some product of 30 to some product of 31.

Now, the question I think we need to ask ourselves here is whether this stipulation circumscribing the valency of evaluative multipliers makes any sense. For whatever evaluative metric we might employ, it would seem clear that – symmetrically with valuable freedoms – the multipliers of non-valuable freedoms must be able to vary in their respective magnitudes, often considerably. If there are reasons why the freedom to do A can be twice as valuable as its counterpart for B, what possible reason is there to imagine that there can be no freedom to do an action, D, that is two – or two hundred – times less valuable than its counterpart for C? Why should the freedoms to do

C and D both be valued equally, as no more nor less than 1? If there can be degrees of valuableness, why can't there be degrees of non-valuableness?

In this connection, Kramer invokes an earlier argument which begins by maintaining that we must distinguish between the value of the *freedom* to do X and the value of *doing* X and, hence, that we cannot infer that the former value is negative from the fact that the latter is negative. Endorsing a view advanced by Ian Carter, he observes:

> Carter has argued lengthily and persuasively in favour of the view that freedom partakes of content-independent valuableness. That is, not only are many of P's particular freedoms valuable for P because of their specific contents, but in addition her overall liberty is valuable for her independently of any of those specific contents. (Kramer, 2003: 429)

But, even if this were true, that would not suffice to entail Kramer's circumscribing stipulation: namely, that no freedom can be negatively valued. Whatever evaluative metric it is that assigns a multiplier of no more than 1 to the freedom to scrape my hand slightly, it must surely assign a multiplier other than 1 to the freedom to scrape my hand badly, let alone the freedom to cut my hand right off. If that metric is to be, as he suggests, based on the objective interests of typical human beings, it's hard to see why the freedoms to do an enormous range of actions, variously damaging to those interests, should all be assigned one and the same evaluative multiplier – namely 1 – when the multipliers of freedoms to do interest-serving actions can vary as widely as the values of those services themselves and are, indeed, some function of them. In short, why the asymmetry?

Kramer's response is that my freedom to do even a negatively valued action can itself be positively valued, because my not being prevented by others from doing that action is 'an integral constituent of something else that is intrinsically good'.

> Specifically, it is a key ingredient of individual autonomy. An autonomous person gains and retains her status as such not only by arriving at most of her decisions in a reasonably reflective manner that bespeaks her self-determination, but also by having been free to behave in any number of ways that are contrary to the ways in which she actually behaves. In so far as the options open to a person have

been tightly constricted, she has lacked the room necessary for achieving and exhibiting full-fledged autonomy. (Kramer, 2003: 431)

I must confess that I'm a little unclear as to whether a person's being autonomous does depend in any way at all on her being free. Persons who, through reasonable reflection, arrive at the decision that of three options (A, B and C) A is best, seem to possess the same degree of autonomy regardless of whether they are unprevented from pursuing all of those options or only some of them. In any event though, and even if all non-preventions – all freedoms – *were* autonomy-enhancing, that would still be insufficient to imply that no freedoms can have negative evaluative multipliers – and this for one very salient reason. A person's autonomy is presumably only one amongst several dimensions of what is in her objective interests. And some of her conceivable actions may be at once so tempting *and* so damaging to her objective interests that these negative aspects quite overwhelm the positiveness of autonomy-enhancement in determining the valency of the evaluative multipliers for the freedoms to do those actions: that is, they make those multipliers *net* negative numbers.

This, for instance, seems to be exactly what happens in the previously mentioned case of Ulysses and the Sirens, where the freedom in question is that of steering his ship. Ulysses wants to be *rid* of that freedom: his valuation of it is undeniably negative. And so would be some of the evaluative multipliers generated by any freedom metric based upon the objective interests of typical human beings. More generally, this is what seems to be involved in many cases where persons choose to enter into enforceable agreements or contracts not to do certain actions which they would otherwise be unprevented from doing. In so choosing, they are clearly assigning negative multipliers, not only to those actions themselves, but also to the freedoms to do those actions.[8] Accordingly, if such multipliers *were* to be employed in estimating their overall freedom, we'd again incur the aforementioned paradoxical result: namely, that their retaining those freedoms would actually make their overall freedom less than it would be if they were to lose them. A freedom metric's incorporation of an autonomy sub-metric which is always positive is insufficient to guarantee that freedom metric's yielding a positive magnitude.

By way of conclusion, then, let me just say that to show, as I hope I've done, that the use of evaluative multipliers in assessing overall freedom must generate the *negative numbers paradox* is evidently still very far from providing a full defence of LCL. All that it achieves, in that regard, is the removal of one (not utterly insignificant) nail from its coffin!

Notes

1 The last such discussion, if memory serves, being a 2005 telephone conversation between myself in my study and Norm on a platform at Leeds railway station. Some philosophical issues are just a lot more urgent than is commonly appreciated! (For the paper that emerged from that discussion, see Geras, 2004)

2 By 'action' and 'ways of leading lives' – whether our own or others' – I mean to include forbearances as well as performances.

3 See Steiner, 1994: 52–4; 1983 and 1975: 49–50.

4 Included amongst such objections are: that negative freedom is *not* a bivalent concept (i.e. that it is not true that, with respect to any particular action, we are either free or unfree to do it); that the set of actions to which freedom-judgements apply consists of *only* actually desired actions and *not* conceivably desired ones; that each person's overall freedom is a function of *only* the particular freedoms – and *not* the particular unfreedoms – he or she enjoys; and that the amount of overall freedom in human society is *not* the simple sum of all individuals' amounts of overall freedom.

5 Most prominent among those accounts is that offered by Ian Carter. See Carter 1999.

6 The several different forms consist of different favoured bases for evaluation. Writers advancing such claims include: Sen, 1990: 451–85; Arneson, 1985: 425–48; Taylor, 1979; Feinberg, 1978: 18–19; Berlin, 1969: 130. For a representative sample of writings supporting one or another version of VIC, see Carter, Kramer and Steiner, 2007.

7 On the variety of conceptions of freedom sustained by ordinary usage, see Carter, Kramer and Steiner, 2007.

8 Indeed, we might accurately describe such relinquishments of personal freedom as exercises of something like *second-order autonomy*, respect for which is shown precisely by the relinquisher's co-contractors observing the terms of their contract and thereby sustaining his or her contracted unfreedom.

16

This green and pleasant land: Britain and the Jews[1]

Shalom Lappin

I will not cease from mental fight,
Nor shall my sword sleep in my hand,
Till we have built Jerusalem
In England's green and pleasant land.

(William Blake, *Jerusalem*, 1804)

Introduction

In 2006 the UK celebrated the 350th anniversary of Cromwell's readmission of Jews to England. This concluded a four-hundred-year absence of organized Jewish life in the country following the expulsion in 1290 under Edward I. According to a widely accepted view, held by many British Jews and non-Jews alike, Britain has provided generous sanctuary to waves of Jewish refugees fleeing European anti-Semitism. It has given them a tolerant, accepting environment in which they have progressed steadily from poverty and exclusion to full integration into British society. Britain is also frequently credited with leading the fight to save European Jews from the onslaught of Nazism and assisting the survivors to rebuild their lives after the Second World War.

Jonathan Sacks, the Chief Rabbi of the United Synagogue of the UK, expresses this attitude in his reflections on the anniversary of the readmission.

The Jews who came here loved Britain. They owed it their freedom to live as Jews without fear. In many cases they owed it their lives. Perhaps it takes an outsider fully to appreciate how remarkable Britain is. Jews loved its tolerance, its courtesy, its understated yet resolute commitment to liberty and civility. They loved Britain because it was British. It knew who and what it was: the leader of freedom in the modern world, the home of Shakespeare, Newton, the Industrial Revolution and the mother of parliaments. It had confidence in itself, and because it did so, it did not feel threatened by newcomers. Without that confidence, bad things happen. (Sacks, 2006)

In fact, there are good grounds for regarding this view of Britain's traditional relations with Jews as largely inaccurate. Recent events have seen the emergence of a distinctly uncomfortable environment for Anglo-Jewry. It might be suggested that this is a relatively new phenomenon conditioned entirely by current demographic and political factors. However, when one consults the historical record it becomes clear that much of what is now taking place bears a clear connection to a well-established pattern of widespread hostility to Jews as members of a cultural and ethnic collectivity that has existed in Britain over many centuries.

Since the start of the second Palestinian Intifada in September 2000, the press and public discussion in Britain have been dominated by strident and obsessive attacks on Israel. A part of this comment constitutes legitimate and, in some cases, well-motivated criticism of Israel's policies and conduct towards the Palestinians living under a repressive occupation in the territories beyond its 1967 borders. Vigorous critique is a feature of normal political debate to which any country involved in a bloody and long-standing conflict must expect to be subjected. However, much of this discourse goes well beyond objections to the policies of a government. It paints Israel as a demonic entity whose people are collectively guilty of unprecedented criminality. The country is portrayed as the instrument of an international conspiracy headed by a 'Zionist lobby' that dictates American, British, and, in some versions, all of the West's foreign policy.

These claims are no longer the preserve of extremists operating on the fringes of the political spectrum. They have seeped into mainstream discussion, where they are increasingly accepted as unexceptional. Several recent examples give an indication of how far this process has progressed.[2]

Lobbies and boycotts

Clare Short, Secretary of State for International Development in Tony Blair's government from 1997 until May 2003, posted the following statement on the *Skies are Weeping* website (http://weepingskies. blogspot.com), set up to promote a cantata written in memory of Rachel Corrie, the peace activist killed by an Israeli army bulldozer in Gaza in 2003:

> I am supporting the World Premiere of the Cantata for Rachel Corrie because there has been the usual campaign to silence even a cantata to commemorate a young woman who gave her life in order to stand for justice. I also believe that US backing for Israeli policies of expansion of the Israeli state and oppression of the Palestinian people is the major cause of bitter division and violence in the world. Best wishes. Clare Short MP.

In September 2006 the All Party Parliamentary Inquiry on Anti-Semitism released its report, in which it pointed to a disturbing increase in anti-Semitism in Britain in recent years.[3] It identified the frenzied demonization of Israel, to the exclusion of other countries involved in human rights abuses, in the press and on university campuses as a case of a political debate spilling over into group defamation. It also pointed out that this phenomenon was generating alarming levels of hostility towards Jews in Britain, some of it realized in increased violence directed at Jewish targets. In fact, the threat of attacks is such that the Jewish community is the only major ethnic or religious group in Britain that is forced to provide a permanent system of guards and surveillance for its schools, religious centres, and communal institutions, which it maintains largely at its own expense.

The report was greeted with widespread indifference. Many on what currently passes for the liberal left in Britain dismissed it as a deliberate attempt to reduce all criticism of Israel to anti-Semitism. David Clark, writing on the report in the *Guardian*, said:

> Real anti-semitism is a serious and growing problem, and there is a need for political consensus about how to tackle it. But debate is poisoned and consensus becomes difficult when allegations of anti-semitism are bandied about for reasons that have nothing to do with fighting racism. An inquiry that wants to confront anti-semitism should also confront those who cheapen the term through reckless misuse. (Clark, 2006)[4]

This response stands in marked contrast to the near universal expressions of concern and support for the victims of prejudice that have attended other government inquiries into racism, such as the Macpherson report, published in February 1999, on the racist murder of teenager Stephen Lawrence in 1993.

Richard Dawkins, who holds the Charles Simyoni Chair for the Public Understanding of Science at Oxford, is well known for his writings on genetics and evolution. He presents himself as a militant defender of scientific humanism, and he has achieved considerable notoriety for his polemics against religion, which he identifies as the major cause of war and repression (Dawkins, 2006). In the course of a recent interview in the *Guardian* on his campaign to promote atheism in America, Dawkins is quoted as saying:

> When you think about how fantastically successful the Jewish lobby has been, though, in fact, they are less numerous I am told – religious Jews anyway – than atheists and [yet they] more or less monopolise American foreign policy as far as many people can see. So if atheists could achieve a small fraction of that influence, the world would be a better place. (MacAskill, 2007)

Unlike Short, Dawkins has not made the Middle East one of his major public interests. His comment is (if accurately presented in the article) all the more revealing for being an offhand remark tangential to his primary concerns. No less significant is the fact that it provoked very little critical reaction. These sorts of remarks carry minimal (if any) cost to the career or public credibility of the people who make them, and they are now generally regarded as unexceptional in public discourse here.

Britain is unique among Western countries in hosting a large, high-profile campaign to boycott Israel. In 2007 four British unions passed boycott motions of one kind or another. These include the National Union of Journalists, UNISON (the public service union), the Transport and General Workers Union (TGWU), and the Universities and Colleges Union (UCU). The latter three are major organizations representing hundreds of thousands of members. The campaign for an academic boycott of Israel within the UCU (and its predecessor unions the AUT and NATFHE) has generated intense controversy both in the UK and abroad.

Organized labour in the USA and North American academic institutions have, for the most part, strongly rejected the British campaign, particularly the academic boycott.[5] Active hostility to Israel has increased markedly across Western Europe over the past seven years in a manner comparable to the emergence of extreme anti-Israel sentiment in the UK, and often surpassing it. However, the boycott has gained little if any traction on the Continent. In fact, the Confederation of German Trade Unions has recently spoken out against it.[6]

On 28 September 2007 the UCU announced that it had cancelled its planned year-long debate of the boycott (called for by a resolution passed at its annual conference in May 2007) in the light of legal advice stating that the proposed academic boycott of Israel would violate the UK's anti-discrimination laws.[7] Many boycott supporters greeted this decision with a volley of protest, charging that pressure from external lobby groups had suppressed free speech in the union through legal manoeuvres.

Six members of the UCU's Strategy and Finance Committee (the body that took the decision), who are affiliated with the UCU Left group, issued a statement explaining the Committee's reasons for accepting its lawyer's advice. In the course of this clarification they say, 'We do not doubt that well-funded groups are ready to engage in legal action against the Union, but even before that stage was reached, the Trustees made it clear that they would feel obliged to fulfil their legal duty to ensure that union funds were only spent on lawful purposes.'[8] The hint at the dark workings of an illicit lobby waiting in the wings to bankrupt the union with expensive legal action is unmistakable here.

Interestingly, Anthony Lester, the head of the legal team that advised the UCU to drop the campaign, is a leading human rights lawyer who has been helping to pioneer anti-racism and equal opportunity legislation since the early 1980s. The revelation of this fact seems to have had little impact on those boycott advocates who are describing the union's withdrawal from the motion as another instance of the effectiveness of a powerful international 'Zionist' operation to suppress all criticism of Israel.

At its May 2008 conference the UCU Executive introduced a slightly modified version of the 2007 resolution, and it was passed without opponents of the motion being permitted a significant opportunity to speak against it.[9]

While the influence of the 'Israel/Zionist lobby' is an increasingly prominent theme of public discussion in Britain, other cases of lobbying which affect both British government policy and academic freedom cause little, if any, concern, even when they are widely reported in the press. On 14 December 2006 the Attorney General, Lord Goldsmith, acting on Tony Blair's instructions, cancelled a major criminal investigation by the Serious Fraud Office into allegations that the British arms manufacturer BAE was paying large bribes to Saudi government officials in order to secure military contracts. The inquiry was halted to avoid losing Saudi business and to prevent possible damage to Britain's relations with the Saudi regime. In his statement announcing the decision Lord Goldsmith said:

> It has been necessary to balance the need to maintain the rule of law against the wider public interest. No weight has been given to commercial interests or to the national economic interest.
>
> The prime minister and the foreign and defence secretaries have expressed the clear view that continuation of the investigation would cause serious damage to UK/Saudi security, intelligence and diplomatic cooperation, which is likely to have seriously negative consequences for the UK public interest in terms of both national security and our highest priority foreign policy objectives in the Middle East. (Leigh and Evans, 2007)

The Organization for Economic Cooperation and Development (OECD) issued a sharp criticism of Britain's action, which, it said, may have violated the country's treaty obligations on the elimination of bribery and corruption in the awarding of international contracts (Evans, 2007). This affair represents a clear interference in domestic British legal processes by Saudi economic and political interests. It has also damaged Britain's international standing within the OECD. While it was widely covered in the media, it has had little impact on mainstream political debate on the influence of foreign lobbies in British public policy.

In 2006 Cambridge University Press (CUP) published *Alms for Jihad* by J. Millard Burr and Robert O. Collins, both of the University of California at Santa Barbara. The book studies several Islamic charities which, the authors claim, have provided funds to terrorist groups. In the spring of 2007 Sheikh Khalid bin Mahfouz, a Saudi businessman and banker, brought a libel suit in the British courts against CUP over assertions made in the book concerning members of his family. Libel laws in the UK strongly favour the plaintiff. To avoid a costly court case CUP withdrew the book from publication, destroyed the remaining unsold copies, and asked libraries to remove it from circulation. It also paid an undisclosed amount in a settlement. Bin Mahfouz has brought previous libel suits in Britain against several other authors and publishers who attempted to link him to financial support for al-Qaeda. All of them were settled without a trial, through the payment of damages. He has not been required to appear in court to provide evidence that the assertions which he has challenged are false (Donadio, 2007).

These suits would seem to constitute an obvious instance of a wealthy businessman using his financial resources, and the skewed British libel laws, to suppress the publication of material that he disapproves of. They have attracted little, if any, attention in the British media, and no reaction from people who express deep anxiety over the role of pro-Israel pressure groups in Britain and America in restricting discussion on the Middle East.

Given the intensity of this discussion and the deep animosity to Israel on display in much of the British media, the 'lobby' does not appear to be enjoying much success in controlling public debate. Its inability to constrain this debate is further indicated by the best-seller status of Mearsheimer and Walt's *The Israel Lobby and US Foreign Policy* (Mearsheimer and Walt, 2007), and the massive publicity generated by their article "The Israel Lobby" in the *London Review of Books* (Mearsheimer and Walt, 2006). The widespread protests over the putative suppression of criticism at the hands of the 'lobby' are strikingly selective in their concerns and bear little relation to the facts.

Arab and Islamic governments provide substantial funding for Middle East and Islamic studies programmes throughout UK and American universities without attracting the stigma of illicit lobbying. Saudi Arabia supports mosques and Islamic religious institutions in Britain and throughout Europe, sometimes with acutely problematic consequences, but this phenomenon does not seem to provoke the same sort of intense anxiety as the 'Israel lobby' does among most representatives of what is now packaged as 'progressive' opinion in Britain.

Israel's three-week military operation in Gaza in December 2008–January 2009 was accompanied by a significant intensification of anti-Israel comment in the British media, as well as an unprecedented increase in violence directed at the Jewish community in the UK (see Townsend, 2009).

The theme of collective Jewish malevolence driving a powerful international conspiracy that subverts the workings of government, the press, the economy, and foreign affairs is a staple of classic anti-Jewish mythology. Its rapid permeation of British public discourse requires explanation. If the popular view of Britain as historically benign in its view of Jews is accurate, then the rise of Jewish conspiracy obsessions in the context of Israel demonology constitutes a new phenomenon in which traditional European attitudes have been imported into a society where they have previously been denied a firm hold. One might seek to explain this event by pointing to the emergence of a multicultural ethic in Britain that, in legitimizing alternative cultural norms, seeks to appease radical Islamist ideas concerning Israel and Jews.

Rabbi Sacks seems to suggest something along these lines when he says:

> The paradox of our time is that multiculturalism, designed to make minorities feel more at home, has had the opposite effect. Britain is a less tolerant society today than it was fifty years ago when I was at school. Never once in those years did I experience anti-Semitism. Many of our children and grandchildren do experience it. Our postmodern culture with its moral relativism and its emphasis on rights rather than responsibilities has, by the law of unintended consequences, made things worse, not better. (Sacks, 2006)

In fact, this explanation is not convincing. While the growth of Islamist ideology in Britain has, as in the rest of Europe, played a significant role in promoting anti-Israel and anti-Jewish attitudes, Islamists do not occupy the positions of influence required to account for the current onslaught. The journalists of the British press, the politicians, the academics, and the leaders of the unions who are conducting this campaign and importing it into the political mainstream are, for the most part, neither Islamists nor Muslims. Moreover, 'liberal' apologists for radical Islamism do not, in general, embrace its hostility to feminism, gay rights, or Hindus. If they are sympathetic to its deep hatred of Israel and its anti-Semitism, then it is, apparently, because these resonate with their own beliefs.

In this chapter I will argue that the popular notion of Britain as a society tolerant of Jews seriously misrepresents the history of the country's relations with its Jewish population. This history reveals a widespread and deeply rooted view of Jews as fundamentally alien to

British life and illicit as a collectivity. Within the confines of this view Jews are acceptable to the extent that they can be rendered invisible through Anglicization, and they are problematic in proportion to the explicitness of their Jewish cultural identity. The social entry that Jews have been granted is, in general, conditional upon suppression of one's Jewish associations and cultural properties in the public domain, with those who distance themselves from these associations completely enjoying the highest level of acceptance.

These attitudes have shaped British conduct over many centuries on a wide range of issues, from Jewish immigration to Jewish political rights. That Jews are now fully enfranchised and protected by anti-discrimination laws has not eradicated many of the social views that have stigmatized and excluded them in the past. Moreover, the leadership of the British Jewish community has, over many generations, evolved strategies for surviving in this environment that involve accommodating and cooperating with many of the demands imposed by the non-Jewish framework in which they live.

When considered from this perspective, the current outburst of anti-Israel demonology and Zionist conspiracy-mongering is not an entirely novel phenomenon foreign to traditional British political behaviour. Instead it appears as a new version of a long-standing hostility to Jewish collectivity, a hostility to which Israel is the greatest challenge in modern history. The current reaction to Israel, then, mixes legitimate political criticism with deeply held social attitudes towards Jews. It is frequently difficult to disentangle these elements in the debate now occupying such a prominent place in British public discourse. To exhibit these attitudes more clearly and to trace their sources, it is necessary to briefly outline some of the defining events of British Jewish history from the time of the re-admission.

Cromwell and the readmission

According to a popular account of the readmission, the Puritan revolution produced a more favourable attitude towards Jews, and in 1656 Cromwell extended an invitation to Dutch Jews to settle in England. In fact, no such invitation was issued, and the recognition of the right of Jews to live in the country was not achieved through legislation or executive decree.[10]

In 1655 Rabbi Menashe ben Israel, an influential religious leader of the Amsterdam community, arrived in London to submit a request to Cromwell for readmission of Jews. He had written a pamphlet describing his proposed conditions for their residence. These included freedom of religious practice, the right to trade and engage in commerce, repeal of the medieval laws enacted against Jews, and communal autonomy for internal issues. The plan also specified the appointment of a special government officer to control the influx of Jewish immigrants, an oath of allegiance to the government, and strict surveillance of the newcomers.

Cromwell was interested in improving Britain's trade and commercial position, and he saw considerable advantage in attracting well-connected Jewish merchants from Amsterdam to relocate their business activities to London. He presented the proposal to the Council of State on 12 November 1655, but the Council was unable to agree on it. It referred the request to an external consultative conference, which met on 4 December and again on 18 December of that year. Various religious figures, and business interests in the City of London, expressed considerable opposition at these sessions, and noisy popular resentment was also very much in evidence. In the end, the conference did not reach a decision, and Cromwell adjourned it.

At the time of this controversy a community of Spanish Converso merchants existed in London. England and Spain had been at war since the autumn of 1655, and, as a result, this community was in a vulnerable position. Government officials seized the property of a wealthy member of the group, Antonio Rodriguez Robles, when he was denounced as a Spanish national by one of his rivals. He petitioned Cromwell for restoration of his interests on the grounds that he was not Spanish, but a Portuguese Jew who had fled the Inquisition. After some delay the Council of State appears to have approved the petition, and Robles's property was returned to him on 16 May 1656. This action created the informal basis for legalizing the Conversos' status as Jews, and they established a Synagogue on Cree Church Lane in London. It was through this individual precedent, then, that the existing Jewish presence in England, previously concealed by forced conversion, was recognized. Immigration of small numbers of Jews from the Spanish and Portuguese community in Amsterdam followed.

The precedent on the basis of which the Jewish presence in London was accepted did not provide legal recognition of a Jewish right to live in England. With the restoration of the monarchy under Charles II in 1660 (in fact, immediately after Cromwell's death in 1658), a significant movement of reaction agitated to reverse the readmission policy. Charles had no sympathy for this movement, and he deflected its demands, effectively placing the Jews under royal protection.

In the years following the restoration the Jewish community in London was able to prosper and slowly expand. They were left largely in peace, and several of the wealthier members achieved a high degree of social acceptance. However, they were subject to numerous economic and political restrictions (so, for example, they were not permitted to trade in retail as freemen of the City, nor could they occupy major political or judicial positions), and their collective position remained precarious. When attempts were made to rescind the legal constraints imposed on them, widespread popular opposition emerged in which the traditional hostility was on full display.

The Jewish Naturalization Bill (the Jew Bill) of 1753 provided a particularly clear instance of this pattern.[11] Alien residents were subject to a variety of disadvantages, such as prohibitions against owning or inheriting land, owning ships, or trading with overseas plantations. Jews could escape some of these limitations through a costly procedure of partial naturalization known as 'endenization', which still did not remove the ban on land inheritance. They were not, however, eligible for full naturalization, as this was open only to Christians. In the spring of 1753 both houses of parliament passed a bill permitting naturalization of foreign-born Jews who had been resident in Britain or Ireland for at least three years, and it became law with royal approval. During the following six months a massive popular campaign against the law was waged in the press, public meeting places, churches, and the streets. It featured traditional anti-Jewish prejudice, and played on the spectre of foreign Jews taking control of the country. This campaign was so vociferous that it forced repeal of the law on 20 December 1753.

Pogroms in Poland and the Ukraine in 1768 brought a wave of impoverished East European Jewish immigrants to London, where they were supported by the Jewish community. This influx created social problems and resentments that resulted in the government imposing restrictions on Jewish immigration in 1771 and 1774. The Jewish community itself supported these restrictions because of the negative reaction that the immigrants were attracting, and the strain on its charitable resources. The Lord Mayor of London offered free passage to Jewish immigrants willing to return to their countries of origin (see Roth, 1964: 235–6). Variations on this response to Jewish immigration were to be repeated throughout the first half of the twentieth century.

Popular notions of Cromwell inviting the Jews to return to England, and their arriving to a generous welcome, have no basis in fact. The opposition that Cromwell encountered in his attempt to secure legislative approval for Rabbi ben Manashe's proposal for readmission led him to abandon it. He succeeded in achieving limited recognition of the legitimacy of an already existing Jewish presence in London through an indirect precedent. This ruling was made in the context of a war with Spain in which Converso Jews fleeing the Inquisition were acknowledged as less problematic than agents of the Spanish monarchy. Once permitted to live openly in the country, the Jews were able to increase their numbers and gradually secure their positions through a series of informal arrangements and incremental improvements. Their willingness to sustain a low public profile was a perennially necessary condition of this process. Their position as a collectivity remained tenuous, and when efforts were made to address this position through progressive legislative changes that would have granted them recognition as a community with guaranteed rights, strong popular opposition and deep prejudice quickly emerged into full view.

Political emancipation

Another popular misconception concerning Anglo-Jewish history is the idea that Jews were granted full political rights by an act of Parliament in 1858. This is by no means the case. Until this date Jews were excluded from sitting as members of the House of Commons by the requirement that all newly elected MPs take a Christian oath in order to take their seats. Many Jews converted in order to overcome the legal and social obstacles that barred them from a wide variety of professions and many public offices.

Four bills for Jewish emancipation were introduced into Parliament between 1830 and 1836, but none of them passed. The first two were defeated in the House of Commons, while the latter two were overturned in the House of Lords. A Jewish Disabilities Bill was blocked in the House of Lords twice in 1848, and again in 1849,

1851, and each year from 1853 to 1857. Between 1830 and 1858 thirteen bills designed to permit Jewish membership in the House of Commons were rejected because of strong opposition, most of it in the House of Lords.[12]

Between 1847 and 1852 Lionel Rothschild was elected to the Commons three times, and on each occasion he was prevented from taking his seat. In 1858 Disraeli introduced a bill that permitted each chamber to determine its own conditions for membership independently. It encountered significant opposition in the Lords, but it was eventually passed by both houses. This law resulted in the Commons suspending the required Christian oath for MPs, and Rothschild was finally allowed to enter the House with an alternative pledge, eleven years after first being elected.

Contrary to a widespread impression, no general act of Jewish political emancipation was adopted. Rothschild established an individual precedent that permitted Jews to enter the House of Commons. This precedent applied only to the parliament in which it was passed, and it would have lapsed with its dissolution. To prevent this from happening, the provisions of the bill modifying the oath for the Commons were converted to a Standing Order, not bounded in time, in 1860. It was only with the passage of the Parliamentary Oaths Act in 1866 that Jews gained the right to sit in the Lords.

There is a clear analogy between the way in which Jews were readmitted to England in 1656 and the process of their political enfranchisement in the latter half of the nineteenth century. In both cases (as with the Jewish Naturalization Bill of 1753) attempts to extend rights to Jews through legislation failed, due to strong political opposition with a significant popular base. Eventually an individual precedent was created that was gradually expanded to open the way for incremental Jewish entry into British public life. It might be thought that this pattern is not unique to Jewish issues, but simply constitutes the way in which major social change is achieved in Britain. It is a country without a written constitution or a charter of rights, and it has historically relied on case law for its progress to more liberal and democratic institutions. Such a view would miss the sharp contrast that exists between the history of Jewish rights and that of other social causes in this country.

Broadly based movements for progressive reforms launched large-scale public campaigns from the end of the eighteenth century throughout the nineteenth and twentieth centuries. These were responsible for major changes in British institutions and attitudes. So, for example, seven years of protest and agitation throughout Britain by the Catholic Association produced the Catholic Emancipation Act of 1829. A large abolitionist movement with strong support from churches and liberal opinion brought about the Abolition of the Slave Trade Act in 1807, and the Slavery Abolition Act of 1833. A militant, well-organized suffragette campaign achieved the right to vote for women over 30 in 1918, and for women over 21 in 1928. Beginning with the Chartists in 1838 the British labour movement waged a continuing struggle for the economic and social rights of workers which eventually brought about acceptance of collective bargaining, extensive employee protection legislation, and the creation of the welfare state.

It is important to note that there were prominent supporters of Jewish political rights among liberals, dissenting Protestants, and evangelicals.[13] Thomas Babington Macaulay's speech 'Jewish Disabilities', delivered to the House of Commons on 17 April 1833, provides one of the more compelling statements of liberal principle in the nineteenth century. However, no genuine political movement supporting Jewish emancipation, of the kind that generated the great reforms of British public life, ever emerged in Britain. This matter remained a marginal concern to progressive circles, as well as to other political constituencies in the country.

Moreover, the Jews themselves were deeply ambivalent about the emancipation debate in Parliament, with a significant number not wanting to see it turned into a high-profile public issue for fear of attracting a negative response. Here, as in previous (and subsequent) cases the Anglo-Jewish leadership preferred to pursue a traditional strategy of protecting Jewish concerns through quiet diplomatic engagement. They relied on a few prominent members of the community to bring influence to bear on sympathetic figures in the British political elite. This strategy led them to shun public political activism in favour of discreet appeals to authority.

Immigration and anti-alien restrictions

A large wave of East European Jewish immigrants came to Britain in the twenty-five-year period from 1880 until 1905, escaping pogroms in Russia and anti-Jewish government actions in other East European countries. Many of them settled in the East End of

London, where they established a major centre of Jewish communal life. This influx increased the Jewish population in Britain from 65,000 in 1880 to 300,000 in 1914, with 200,000 concentrated in London.[14]

The arrival of large numbers of generally impoverished East European Jews gave rise to a strong anti-alien response that manifested itself in hostile press comment and popular campaigns demanding that the government restrict immigration. The Conservative government introduced the Aliens Act in April 1905, which was approved by Parliament and passed into law on 11 August of that year. The Act specified a number of criteria by which immigration officials could exclude aliens from entering the country. It was the first of a series of measures adopted in the early years of the twentieth century in order to severely limit entry of newcomers into the country.

These restrictions were, in large part, motivated by widespread animosity to the presence of Jewish immigrants. Arthur Balfour, the Conservative Prime Minister under whom the Aliens Act was passed (the same Balfour who, as Foreign Secretary, later issued the Balfour Declaration of 1917 for the establishment of a Jewish national home in Palestine) gave clear expression to this current of public opinion in his speech during the debate on the bill in the House of Commons, in July 1905:

> it would not be to the advantage of the civilisation of the country that there should be an immense body of persons who, however patriotic, able, and industrious, however much they threw themselves into the national life, still by their own action, remained a people apart and not merely held a religion differing from the vast majority of their fellow country-men, but only inter-married among themselves. (quoted in Defries, 2002: 28)

The First World War greatly intensified anti-alien sentiment, with hostility to Jewish immigrants prominent in this movement. There was strong pressure for the mass internment of all people from enemy countries, which would have affected large numbers of German and Austrian Jews. In 1914 the government passed the Aliens Restriction Act, which granted it special emergency powers allowing it to deport aliens, and requiring them to register with the police. In 1918 it imposed additional administrative restrictions that included a review of naturalization certificates issued during the war, a ban on civil service positions for people who were not citizens of Britain or an allied country (Russia ceased to be an ally after the Bolshevik revolution of 1917), and the requirement of identity cards for aliens. These restrictions and the conditions of the 1914 Act were extended under the Aliens Restriction Act amendment of 1919. Additional regulatory procedures were specified in the Aliens Order of 1920. As a result of these bills and administrative provisions, Jewish immigration to Britain was virtually cut off by the end of the First World War.

Agitation against aliens in general, and Jewish immigrants in particular, continued throughout the 1920s. David Cesarani (1989) cites a series of articles published in *The Times* at the end of November 1924 on 'Alien London' as expressing the tenor of this campaign. One of the articles contains the following statement:

> They stand aloof – not always without a touch of oriental arrogance – from their fellow citizens. They look upon us with suspicion and a certain contempt. Mixed marriages between orthodox Jews and Gentiles are forbidden. These people remain an alien element in our land.[15]

Throughout this period William Joynson-Hicks, a leading Conservative politician, promoted anti-Jewish attitudes within the government. In stark contrast to Balfour, he was also a strong opponent of Jewish settlement in Palestine, and he played a leading role in supporting the Palestinian Arab lobby in Britain.[16] He became Foreign Secretary in 1924 in Stanley Baldwin's government. During his tenure (1924–29) he reinforced the discriminatory practices that the Home Office had been implementing against East European Jewish immigrants prior to his assuming his position.

Although the Aliens Act was passed by a Conservative government, it was applied by its Liberal successor. Moreover, significant sections of the Labour movement, particularly the Trades Union Congress (TUC) and the left, supported the exclusion of Jewish immigrants and participated in the agitation against them that provided public support for anti-alien legislation.[17]

While anti-alien agitators and politicians frequently avoided explicit reference to Jews, they used the rhetoric of xenophobia to press for the curtailment of Jewish immigration, and to support the imposition of severe restrictions on Jewish immigrants who had succeeded in entering the country. This form of anti-alien discourse anticipated later campaigns in which anti-Semitism and other types of racism have been encoded in more indirect and politically palatable terms.

When large numbers of desperate Jewish refugees fleeing the Nazis sought sanctuary in Britain in the 1930s there was no need for new immigration controls to exclude them. The necessary restrictions had already been installed over the previous two decades to stem the flow from previous anti-Jewish violence in Eastern Europe.

Refugees from Nazism and survivors of the Holocaust

After the Nazis took power in Germany in 1933 Britain, like other Western countries, was besieged by requests from German Jews seeking to escape the escalating violence of the regime. Their numbers were greatly increased in 1938 with Germany's annexation of Austria and the Sudetenland in Czechoslovakia, followed by the *Kristallnacht* pogrom. Austrian, Czech, Slovak, and Polish Jews joined German refugees in their flight from the Nazi onslaught.

Throughout the pre-war period Britain maintained its system of rigorous controls on immigration, treating Jewish refugees as aliens subject to the existing restrictions.[18] These limited entry to people who were of benefit to the British economy. As the 1930s was a time of economic depression, the prospects for refugees obtaining visas under these conditions were minimal. The German Jewish refugees who did come to Britain were financially supported by the British Jewish community under the terms of a commitment that it made to the government. The community did not extend this commitment to Austrian and Czech refugees after the *Anschluss* of Austria, as it could no longer afford to absorb the expanding numbers of visa applicants.

The labour movement, as represented by the TUC, supported the government's policy of drastically limiting the flow of Jewish refugees. While strongly opposing the Nazi government and its persecution of Jews, it did not feel that it could accommodate an influx of cheap labour at a time of economic hardship.[19]

There were notable exceptions to the TUC endorsement of government policy. Eleanor Rathbone, a social activist, feminist, and independent MP, campaigned tirelessly throughout the 1930s and the war for government action to save European Jewry. Roy Harrod, an Oxford economist and a member of the Labour Party, argued that immigration promoted growth, and urged the labour movement to support a liberalized approach to refugees. However they, as well as other critics, had little if any impact on either government policy or organized labour's restrictionist position.[20]

Throughout the 1930s and the war years the British policy on Jewish refugees was driven by the view that only small numbers of individuals who came from cultural and professional backgrounds that facilitated assimilation into British society could be accepted. In general, a programme of temporary refuge and resettlement abroad was the strongly preferred option, with most refugees granted only transitional status. Government officials argued that if large numbers of the 'wrong' kind of refugee were admitted, it would create anti-Semitism in the country. Hence a West to East hierarchy was applied in which Germans were considered more desirable than Austrians, who in turn, were ranked above Czechs, followed by Poles and other East Europeans. The Home Secretary Samuel Hoare expressed this attitude in his comments to an Anglo-Jewish delegation on 1 April 1938:

> It would be necessary for the Home Office to discriminate very carefully as to the type of refugee who could be admitted to this country. If a flood of the wrong type of immigrants were allowed in there might be a serious danger of anti-semitic feeling being aroused in this country. The last thing which we wanted here was the creation of a Jewish problem.[21]

Although the Jewish Community invested vast efforts and resources in refugee relief, its leadership, for the most part, accepted the government restrictions and the rationale behind them. Otto Schiff, a leading figure in Anglo-Jewish refugee work, responded to Hoare's remark in the following terms:

> It was very difficult to get rid of a refugee … once he had entered and spent a few months in this country. The imposition of a visa was especially necessary in the case of Austrians who were largely of the shopkeeper and small trader class, and would therefore prove much more difficult to emigrate than the average German who had come to the United Kingdom.[22]

The extent to which the leadership of Anglo-Jewry had internalized the government policy on refugees is indicated by the reservations that a Jewish immigrant liaison officer expressed to the Chief Rabbi, J.H. Hertz, over the hostel for German Yeshiva students that the Chief Rabbi was sponsoring:

> How can this loyalty be demanded of any body of young men who are
> taught nothing about English ways, English history, or the English
> outlook? If they are not to be trained in this loyalty from the very first
> week of their arrival, what chance have they of merely comprehending,
> let alone feeling, that love of England which is the veritable fountain-
> head of these traditions of Anglo-Jewry of which we English Jews are
> so proud and which is itself the strongest bulwark against antisemitism
> in our midst.[23]

This correspondence took place in the context of an effort by the
community to resist a government move to intern all refugees from
Axis countries after the outbreak of war in 1939.

The *Kindertransports* of 1938 brought approximately 10,000
Jewish children from Germany and Austria to Britain. They are
frequently cited as an instance of British generosity towards Jews
escaping the Nazis, and indeed they stand as an important act of
decency in a dark time. A point that is not generally addressed in
discussions of this operation is the fact that the children were forced
to come alone because British immigration regulations, rather than
German exit controls, prevented their parents from accompanying
them. These regulations ensured that most became orphans in the
course of the war that followed their arrival.

A significant feature of government refugee policy was an insistence on not recognizing Jews as a distinct entity in any official rules
or procedures. This was ostensibly motivated by the desire to avoid
discrimination among different groups of refugees. In fact, it
seriously disadvantaged Jews and created a bizarre paradox. The
Jews were a primary target of Nazi racial persecution and genocide,
but Britain, as well as other allied countries, refused to acknowledge
them as such in their refugee programmes. In fact, political refugees,
Jewish or non-Jewish, who were pursued for their resistance activities
were given strong preference for asylum over economic or 'racial'
refugees, a class that included most Jewish victims of the Nazis.

During the war the government continued to enforce its highly
restrictive immigration procedures, even for small numbers of Jews
who were able to escape Nazi-controlled territory to neutral
countries like Portugal or Turkey, which accepted them on condition
that they be transferred to other venues. At the end of the war
approximately 60,000 Jewish refugees remained in Britain, with
another 10,000–20,000 having entered and then re-emigrated or
been deported. Therefore, from 1933 to 1945 a total of 70,000–

80,000 received refuge in the UK (London, 2000: 11–12). In addition, a net total of 216,000 moved to mandatory Palestine in the 1930s, until the government White Paper of 1939 curtailed Jewish immigration there.

The British response to the refugee crisis before and during the war was not different in kind from that of other Western democracies. The USA also imposed severe limitations on immigration in 1924, which remained in effect throughout the 1930s and the war years. Canada had perhaps the worst record, accepting fewer than 5,000 Jewish refugees between 1933 and 1945 (Abella and Troper, 1983).

Britain and the USA co-managed the Evian Conference of July 1938, which was designed to give the appearance of an international effort to assist the refugees while avoiding any substantive measures to accommodate them. Britain was particularly concerned that the conference not create a situation in which East European countries like Poland and Romania could use liberalized immigration policies in the West to unload their large and unwanted Jewish populations. Similarly, the Anglo-American Bermuda Conference in April 1943 was called in response to growing public pressure in both countries to rescue victims of the Nazi genocide, with both governments making certain that it yielded no tangible results.

Significant differences between British and American policy on assistance to victims of the Holocaust began to emerge when President Roosevelt established the War Refugees Board (WRB) in January 1944 at the urging of Henry Morgenthau, the Secretary of the Treasury. The WRB began to pursue a proactive programme of aid, primarily in the form of US government currency licences through which the American Joint Distribution Committee was able to use cash to fund Jewish resistance and escape from concentration camps. The British government opposed these efforts on the grounds that they undermined its economic blockade of Axis territory (London, 2000: 230–45).

In July 1944 Admiral Horthy, the regent of Hungary, offered to permit large numbers of the remaining Hungarian Jewish population to leave if Allied countries would grant them entry. Both the British and American governments were, in principle, prepared to accept the offer. But while the Americans urged immediate action, the British Cabinet delayed a formal commitment over a period of several weeks for fear that it would produce a large flood of refugees.

In the end, despite a joint Anglo-American statement in August indicating a willingness to assist Hungarian Jewry, the Germans resumed the deportation of Jews to the death camps (Kushner, 1994: 194–5).

The shift in the US government attitude that occurred at the beginning of 1944 was, in no small part, due to public pressure exerted by American Jewish groups and their supporters. They held a well-publicized mass rally in Madison Square Gardens in New York on 1 March 1943 to highlight the absence of government support for rescue operations, and they lobbied politicians and government officials. By contrast, the British Jewish community consistently refrained from publicly challenging the British government on its handling of refugees, and worked within the restrictions that it imposed. In effect the British government was able to use the Anglo-Jewish refugee aid committees and their resources as instruments of its policies.

A chasm opened up between British and American responses to Jewish refugees in the post-war period. In the years immediately following the war the restrictions on Jewish immigration to America remained in place. However, President Truman intervened in 1948 to ensure that the Displaced Persons Act of that year was not used to disadvantage Jewish refugees from the displaced persons (DP) camps of Europe. As a result, they were permitted to enter the USA in proportion to their numbers in the camps, and over 100,000 immigrated between 1945 and 1950.

In the period immediately following the war the British government maintained the legal restrictions on the 60,000 Jewish refugees still in the country. This included people who had served in the British army or worked for the war effort in other ways. They remained aliens without full rights to seek employment, and their presence in the UK was still officially temporary. In fact, there was no solid legal basis for these restrictions after the war, but the refugees were not informed of this fact. They were also frequently not told when some of these constraints were quietly lifted. The government retained hopes of encouraging as many refugees as possible to emigrate. It was not until the end of 1948 that their position in Britain was regularized, and they were granted the status of permanent residents.[24]

The post-war Labour government was unwilling to accept survivors in anything but token numbers. The Foreign Secretary Ernest Bevin insisted that Jews were not easily assimilated into

British life, and he argued that allowing in a substantial group would intensify the already considerable anti-Jewish sentiment that had arisen as a result of Britain's conflict with the Yishuv in mandatory Palestine. As a result, fewer than 5,000 survivors were granted entry from 1945 to 1950, under a family reunification programme (the Distressed Relatives scheme). During this period Britain was experiencing a severe labour shortage and recruited foreign workers. It absorbed approximately 365,000 non-Jewish immigrants, most from Eastern Europe and many from the same DP camps that housed Jewish refugees. The government issued over 600,000 alien work permits. The East European immigrants were not carefully screened, and, as a result, a number of war criminals and Nazi collaborators were permitted entry. It seems that for the British government the non-Jewish foreign workers did not pose the same problems of cultural incompatibility that the Jewish survivors did (Kushner, 1994: 229–37).

Bevin was committed to repatriating Jewish refugees to the countries that they had come from. Not only was he unwilling to allow them into Palestine, but he also wanted them excluded from Britain. Although post-war pogroms were taking place in Poland in 1946–47 and most refugees were desperate not to return to hostile environments in eastern and central Europe, the Nazi genocide had made little if any impact on Bevin's pre-war hostility to Jewish refugees.[25]

Britain's record on Jewish refugees has been meticulously documented and published in well-known work by mainstream British historians. Oddly, this record remains largely invisible in public discussion of the war. In fact, a self-congratulatory attitude is common in much of this discussion.

The TGWU recently provided a particularly striking example of how this attitude can be recruited into the service of the anti-Israel boycott campaign. When the TGWU passed its resolution calling for the boycott of Israeli products in July 2007, Barry Camfield, the deputy general-secretary of the union, was quoted in the *Jewish Chronicle* as seeking to deflect criticism of the motion by commenting that Britain had stood alone against Hitler and liberated Jewish victims of the Holocaust, 'So we will not have the Israeli state telling us that the boycott is anti-Semitic' (Josephs, 2007). Camfield's remarks (if accurately reported) are rich in unintended irony. Bevin was general secretary of the TGWU from 1922 until 1940, and a member of the General Council of the TUC from 1925 to 1940. During this period he played an important role in shaping organized labour's support for the Conservative government's restrictions on the entry of Jewish refugees. After the war, as Foreign Secretary in the Labour government, he took the lead in excluding survivors from the country. The current leadership of the TGWU, like many other boycott supporters, appear to be either unaware of their historical antecedents or simply indifferent to their significance in the context of the current discussion.

Many of the most vociferous anti-Zionists on the contemporary British 'left' insist that a solution to the Jewish refugee problem in the period of the Holocaust should have been found in the diaspora rather than in Palestine. They remain impressively obtuse to the fact that their own political precursors were instrumental in ruling out such a solution by helping to block Jewish immigration to Britain.

During a debate with the right-wing American commentator Daniel Pipes at the Clash of Civilizations conference in London on 20 January 2007 Ken Livingstone, London's former 'radical' mayor, claimed that the creation of Israel was a mistake which could have been avoided if the United States and Britain had accepted Jewish refugees from Nazism. In an earlier statement concerning his clash with a reporter from the *Evening Standard* Livingstone observed that the paper's sister publication, the *Daily Mail*, had campaigned against Jewish immigration in the early part of the twentieth century and expressed sympathies for Nazism in the 1930s.[26] He has carefully avoided acknowledging the part played by the British labour movement and large segments of the British left in keeping Jewish refugees out of the country during this period.

In fact the successful effort to restrict the entry of Jewish refugees was not the work of a specific political group, but a broadly based enterprise that spanned ideological differences. It was the result of a consensus that ran across the political and social spectrum, from upper-class Conservative politicians to working-class Labour activists and the unions.

Post-colonialism and Israel

Since the early 1970s Britain has developed into a post-colonial society in which it has (in large part) come to recognize the injustices of the empire that it imposed on large portions of the world's population in previous centuries. It has accepted historical responsibility for its role in colonialism and the slave trade, and this process has transformed its understanding of its past. It has also significantly changed the standards of political acceptability determining at least its official relationship to the large post-war immigrant communities that have come from the Indian subcontinent, the Caribbean, Africa, and other parts of its former overseas territories. Mainstream attitudes towards the British colonial presence in Ireland prior to the emergence of the Irish Free State and the establishment of the Irish Republic have been similarly, if less completely, affected by this evolution of historical and social attitudes.

Interestingly, the history of Britain's relationship with its Jewish population has not been subject to a comparable revision. Although the hostility to Jews that figured prominently throughout this history is closely related to the prejudices and the mindset that fuelled colonialism and its attendant racism, it has not been subsumed under the European practices that have formed the main targets of post-colonialist criticism and historiography.

In fact, the Jews have been quickly shuffled away from the status of victims of European racism into the role of the new colonialists. In the 1970s and 1980s the anti-Zionist left portrayed Israel and its supporters as instruments of Western imperialism in the Middle East. In recent years, they have been promoted to the primary agents of an international imperial project of which the West is increasingly seen as a hapless dupe.

This view is anticipated by Arnold Toynbee in the 1960s, who describes Israel in the following terms:

> Israeli colonialism since the establishment of the state of Israel is one of the two blackest cases in the whole history of colonialism in the modern age; and its blackness is thrown into relief by its date. The East European Zionists have been practising colonialism in Palestine in the extreme form of evicting and robbing the native Arab inhabitants at the very time when the West European peoples have been renouncing their temporary rule over non-European peoples. The other outstanding black case is the eviction of five agricultural Amerindian peoples – the Chickasaw, Choctaw, Creeks, Cherokees, and Seminoles – from their ancestral homes in what are now the states of Georgia, Alabama, Mississippi, and Tennessee to 'reservations' in what is now the state of Oklahoma. ... This nineteenth-century American colonialism was a crime; the Israeli colonialism, which was

being carried out at the time when I was writing, was a crime that was also a moral anachronism. (Toynbee, 1969: 266–7)

It is important to recognize that the basis of Toynbee's objection to Zionism is not, in the end, Israel's behaviour towards the Palestinians, but his view of the Jews as an illicit people who have no right to be a nation. Writing of Jewish religious culture he says:

> This is a great spiritual treasure which the Jews have to give to all peoples. But one cannot give a treasure and at the same time keep it to oneself. If the giving of this treasure is the Jews' mission, as it surely is, then this mission requires them, now at last, to make that their paramount aim in place of the incompatible aim that they have always put first, so far, ever since their experience of the Babylonish Captivity. They will have to give up the national form of the Jewish community's distinctive identity in order to become, without reservations, the missionaries of a universal church that will be open, on an equal footing, to anyone, Jew or Gentile, who gives his allegiance to Deutero-Isaiah's God and seeks to do His will. In our time the Zionist movement has been travelling in just the opposite direction to this. It has not only clung to, and accentuated, the national form of Jewish communal life. It has also put it back on to a territorial basis. (Toynbee, 1961: 515–16)

> The Jewish religion is meant for all mankind. So far from its being 'unthinkable' without the 'Chosen People', it cannot fulfil its destiny of becoming a universal religion unless and until the Jews renounce the national form of their distinctive communal identity for the sake of their universal religious mission. (Toynbee, 1961: 517)

Toynbee is expressing a classic Christian European notion of Jews as a community that ought not to exist as a collectivity. As we have seen, it has been at the core of deep-rooted mainstream attitudes towards Jews in Britain throughout the centuries. It is also a vintage case of what Edward Said has identified as 'Orientalism' (Said, 1978). Jews are not to be entrusted with the stewardship of their own culture, nor are they entitled to understand themselves in their own terms. The significance of their culture and their place in history is a matter to be determined by those who exercise power over them and have a true understanding of their significance and their needs.

Most proponents of Said's critique of Orientalism (like Said himself) have adopted a variant of Toynbee's view of Jews. Unlike other objects of European (and Middle Eastern) racism they are not entitled to liberation from external colonial coercion as a national group. They are in no position to decide who they are or where they belong in a properly constituted social order. Political independence and cultural autonomy are inappropriate concessions to a backward-looking particularism for a people that ought not to exist. Instead, they are to achieve 'freedom' through dissolution into other peoples' societies, so that their 'talents' can be responsibly harnessed. As in the past, their degree of acceptability is to be measured by their willingness to conform to an externally imposed notion of 'universalism' that excludes their collective existence in all but the most diffidently unobtrusive and compliant mode.

As in the case of Toynbee, the root objection that contemporary 'anti-colonialists', who are now defining mainstream discussion of the Middle East in Britain, bring against Israel is not what it has done (or is doing) but the irredeemable sin of its existence. Australia's ethnic cleansing of its aboriginal population does not undermine its integrity as a country, and America's history of internal colonialism, slavery, and military adventurism abroad has no bearing on the right of its people to constitute a nation. Pakistan's religiously motivated partition of the Indian subcontinent and the associated mass flight of Hindu refugees from its territory is irrelevant to its standing as a state.

By contrast Jews ought not to have a country, even if it is reformed into a model of secular liberal democracy. To allow them one is to grant legitimacy to a people that has none. The fact that the host societies in Europe, the Middle East, and North Africa, through which they were driven for centuries, were not able to provide for their basic physical survival is not taken to be a relevant factor in assessing the historical processes that created Israel and populated it with refugees from these societies. Nor is it admitted into consideration when framing the current Israeli-Palestinian conflict in anti-colonialist terms.

Toynbee's approach to Jews was, in turn, anticipated by a small group of militant anti-Zionists within the British Jewish community in the 1940s. The Jewish Fellowship was established in 1942 to combat Zionism and to promote the idea that Jews are a religious group rather than a national community. Their leaders came from the highest economic and social echelons of Anglo-Jewry, and they were heavily influenced by members of the Progressive Movement.[27] The Fellowship compared Zionism to Nazism as early as 1944, just as the nature of the Nazi genocide was becoming fully known in the

West. One of the Fellowship's leaders, Colonel Louis Gluckstein, said in testimony to the Anglo-American Committee on Palestine that 'to believe this [Jewish suffering] is a justification for Jewish separatism and Jewish nationalism seems to me the adoption of the Hitler doctrine' (quoted in Miller, 2000: 49).

The Jewish Fellowship was the antithesis of a radical organization. It represented a largely conservative elite of Jews who were concerned to protect their precarious position as recognized, if sponsored, members of the British power structure. They saw in Zionism and the creation of Israel a threat to their own position. They also seem to have been more than a little embarrassed by the Holocaust and its implications for their idea of a comfortable de-national Jewish life in Europe. In this they followed a long-standing pattern in Anglo-Jewry of accommodating themselves to the demand for invisibility as a condition for social acceptance. The idea that failure to conform to this demand will generate anti-Semitism was shared with British policy-makers who invoked it to exclude refugees from the country. The attitudes of the Jewish Fellowship have been echoed by a small but vocal minority of contemporary Jewish anti-Zionists who see Israel as an embarrassment that threatens them with a resurgence of anti-Semitism.

Conclusion

In the second half of the twentieth century explicit expression of hostility to Jews was rare in Britain. The emerging recognition of the full dimensions of the Holocaust created an environment where even coded anti-Jewish expressions were heavily stigmatized, and the traditional imagery of anti-Semitism was almost entirely banished from public discourse. In recent years, particularly since the end of 2000, increasing animosity towards Israel has been attended with a precipitous decline in the constraints against the language of group defamation, generally formulated in terms of 'Zionists' rather than 'Jews'.

Israel is a country like any other, and, as such, it should be held accountable to the same standards and norms that are applied to other nations. To criticize it on this basis is entirely legitimate, and when the criticisms are accurate they should be vigorously pursued. But the view of Israel that has emerged recently within the mainstream of British public discourse holds it to be not a normal country at all, but a criminal aberration that is sustained by a malicious conspiratorial lobby of international dimensions. At the foundation of this view is a perception of Jews as an illicit collectivity with no claim to legitimacy or recognition.

This idea is a central element of traditional European (and Middle Eastern) attitudes towards Jews. In this respect, Britain shares its cultural history with the rest of Europe. However, unlike most of continental Europe, Britain continues to promote a largely sanitized and self-laudatory understanding of its past relations with Jews in its own popular imagination, and this has served to misrepresent a history whose details are fully accessible as a matter of public record. The leadership of the British Jewish community has, for the most part, actively cooperated with this exercise in misrepresentation over the years as part of a strategy for surviving in an environment in which Jews enjoy an acutely conditional acceptance.

While current hostility to Jews in the UK is frequently packaged as 'progressive' political comment, its origins are in traditional social attitudes that have been integral to Britain's history for centuries. To recognize these origins requires a frank and realistic encounter with an aspect of the country's past that mainstream British opinion has so far managed to avoid.

Notes

1 An earlier and longer version of this chapter appeared in the Yale Initiative for the Interdisciplinary Study of Anti-Semitism Working Papers Series in 2008. The ideas contained in this chapter were presented in talks in the seminar series of the Yale Initiative for the Interdisciplinary study of Anti-Semitism in November 2007, and in the Oxford Hebrew and Jewish Studies Centre Israel Lecture Series in February 2008. I am grateful to the audiences of these forums for thoughtful feedback. I am indebted to Anthony Julius, Rory Miller, and Colin Shindler for invaluable discussion of many of the issues addressed here, and for generous assistance with historical research material. I would also like to thank Mitchell Cohen, Lori Coulter, Eve Garrard, Norman Geras, Jonathan Ginzburg, Ariel Hessayon, Edward Kaplan, Yaakov Lappin, Joe Rothstein, Charles Small, and Mort Weinfeld for very useful comments on earlier drafts of this chapter. I bear sole responsibility for the content of the chapter and any mistakes that it may contain.

2 For additional cases and a detailed discussion of the rise of a demoniz-

ing mythology in mainstream British discourse see Lappin 2003 and 2006.

3 The report is available from the Committee's website at www.thepcaa.org/Report.pdf.

4 The article carries the subtitle text 'Attempts to brand the left as anti-Jewish because of its support of Palestinian rights only make it harder to tackle genuine racism'.

5 See the statement of American Labour Unions of 18 July condemning the boycott at www.spme.net/cgi-bin/articles.cgi?ID=2647, and Traubmann (2007) on the statement by 300 US university presidents against the boycott.

6 The Deutsche Gewerkschaftsbund's anti-boycott resolution of 6 September 2007 is reported on the Jewish Labor Committee website at www.jewishlaborcommittee.org/2007/09/german_unions_follow_us_la bor.html.

7 The UCU press release on this decision appears on its website at www.ucu.org.uk/index.cfm?articleid=2829.

8 The full statement is available at www.engageonline.org.uk/blog /article.php?id=1456.

9 See Eve Garrard's account of the process through which this motion was adopted, at http://normblog.typepad.com/normblog/2008/05 /passing-motion-25–by-eve-garrard.html.

10 For descriptions of the readmission and Jewish life in the time of the Restoration see Hessayon, 2006; Katz, 1994; and Roth, 1964: chapters 7–8.

11 See Roth, 1964: 212–23 for the details of the Jew Bill controversy.

12 For an account of the struggle for Jewish political rights in the House of Commons see Enriques, 1968: and Roth, 1964: chapter 11 and Epilogue.

13 This period also saw the emergence of a small but prominent philo-Semitic element in English literature, as illustrated in some of the work of George Eliot, particularly *Daniel Deronda*, published in 1873. This positive view of Jews co-existed with the persistence of virulently negative images, like Dickens's Fagin in *Oliver Twist* (1838), within British literary culture of the nineteenth century.

14 For a discussion of turn-of-the-century East European Jewish immigration to Britain and the sequence of alien restriction acts which it provoked see Defries, 2002: chapters 2 and 5: and London, 2000: chapter 2.

15 *The Times*, 27 November 1924, cited in Cesarani, 1989.

16 See Cesarani, 1989 for an account of Joynson-Hicks's activities as an anti-Jewish politician.

17 See Cohen, 1985. Cohen also documents government policies designed

to exclude aliens, particularly Jews, from some of the key benefits of the welfare state that emerged in the early years of the last century.

18 For detailed accounts of Britain's response to Jewish refugees from Nazism see London, 2000; Kushner, 1994: and Wasserstein, 1979.

19 For the attitude of the British labour movement to the refugee crisis see Kushner, 1994: chapter 2.

20 See Kushner, 1994: 74–6 on Harrod, and chapter 6 on Rathbone.

21 Home Office minutes of the meeting with the Jewish delegation, 1 April 1938, PRO HO 213/42. Quoted in London, 2000: 61.

22 Home Office minutes of the meeting with the Jewish delegation, 1 April 1938, PRO HO 213/42. Quoted in London, 2000: 61.

23 Rothschild archives, London RAL 000/315C. Quoted in Kushner, 1994: 154.

24 See London, 2000: 260–6 on the post-war status of Jewish refugees in Britain.

25 See Borowicz, 1986 on the post-war pogroms in Poland.

26 'Ken Livingstone statement in full', CNN, 22 February 2005, http://edition.cnn.com/2005/WORLD/europe/02/22/livingstone. statement/index.html.

27 For a detailed and informative history of the Jewish Fellowship see Miller, 2000.

17

Cricket: the best-loved game

Ian Holliday

Norman Geras takes an enthusiastic interest in several of the world's great team sports, and no more than a passing acquaintance with the man or his blog will reveal where his major passions lie. Set above everything else, more elevated even than football and Manchester United, is cricket, the game best loved by Geras as both spectator and, latterly, writer. Many themes structure two books, a handful of articles and a multitude of online posts. In this chapter, three topics that surface repeatedly in his writings are addressed: the devotion of a lifetime fan to Test match cricket, long the paramount form of the game; unstinting support for Australia, by some distance the top Test team of recent decades; and combative analysis of Test match cricket as a contemporary spectator sport.

Love of the game

The most visible feature of Geras's cricket writings is simple yet profound: an abiding love of the game. The game in question here is not cricket in the many forms assumed during a lengthy history. Geras takes no interest in amateur strivings on dusty lots, sun-drenched beaches and village greens, no interest in county and provincial matches played in all major cricketing nations, and scarcely any greater interest in fashionable short forms of the game. Indeed, his stance on rapid-fire cricket completed within a matter of hours is dismissive. One-day internationals, watched by millions annually, are 'intrinsically unmemorable'.[1] Twenty20 internationals, hugely popular from the outset a few years ago, are the 'wreckage' of cricket's great tradition, or maybe 'just another game entirely'. The game Geras loves, the form that resides alone in his affection, is Test match cricket, played by a small number of nations linked to Britain by imperialism.

Distinguished from other types above all by the five days now allocated to each contest, Test match cricket is eulogized. Blogging at the start of an England–New Zealand series in which he had no particular stake, Geras wrote of 'The rhythms, the subtleties, the beauties, the sheer wonderful *duration* of Test match cricket'. Only partly tongue in cheek, he went on to say 'I think God made it to give people a glimpse of utopia'. Time and again in his writings, cricket in this guise is described in rapturous tones. Test match cricket 'encompasses an infinity of nuance and subtlety, of drama and movement, of passion and character, of quiet – sometimes even boredom – and excitement'. It is 'a game created by mere mortals, but providing a window on eternity'. It 'verges on the sublime'.

By extension, those who have scaled the loftiest peaks of performance are also accorded lavish praise. High in the pantheon are titans forming the backbone of legendary Australian teams: Donald Bradman with a batting average that still awaits serious challenge; Allan Border, giving no quarter and building the foundation for the finest run of success known to Test cricket; Ian Healy, 'one of the greatest of the wicket-keeping greats'; Steve Waugh, 'tough-as-nails, no bloody nonsense'; Mark Waugh, languid and brilliant fielding at slip; Shane Warne, 'possibly the greatest bowler who has ever played the game'; Glenn McGrath, 'the most chillingly efficient fast bowler of the past decade'; Adam Gilchrist, 'a force of nature'. But excellent players from other nations, notably West Indies, are also given their due: Garfield Sobers for 'the ease and grace with which he moved'; Gordon Greenidge, 'one of the most ruthlessly effective destroyers of a bowling attack'; Vivian Richards for 'menace ... as he walked out to begin an innings'; Michael Holding running in to bowl, 'one of the most beautiful sights in cricket'; Brian Lara, owner of the record Test match score not once, but twice. And, as is the case for many fans, the team in which Geras invested all hope as a boy growing up in Rhodesia remains special today: 'For *this* South African team, the South Africa of the mid-1950s, is *my* team. It is the team of my life, the one lodged in the deepest recesses of my consciousness.'

Away from the field of play, love of Test match cricket also generates profound respect for leading chroniclers of the game. Among first responders to action unfolding in the arena, one stands out: 'His Great Cricketing Holiness' Richie Benaud, 'commentator nonpareil, wise old guy, never using two words where one, or even none, will do'. In the larger sphere of cricket writers, known intimately by Geras through a personal library of 2,500 volumes put together since the late 1970s, two are placed above all others: C.L.R. James for *Beyond a Boundary*, 'the best book on cricket ever written'; and Gideon Haigh, 'cricket writer supreme'. Furthermore, alongside celebration of the masters, Geras provides on his blog a venue for fresh reports of cricketing moments that remain indelibly etched in the mind. To inaugurate the series, he recounted his own memory of Peter May, bowled by Neil Adcock for 61, at the first Test he attended: South Africa versus England in Johannesburg, 1957. 'Pessimist then, as I am still, with regard to all sporting matters, I was expecting May's innings to go on and on. But Adcock bowled him. Whoopee!'

A further feature of Geras's love for Test match cricket is the endless opportunity for analysis, debate, fun, and mischief generated by a vibrant tradition. Among teams constructed both at and away from cricket grounds are best Australian, English, South African, West Indian, and world XIs; best jazz, philosopher, and writer XIs; best cricketing As, Bs, Cs, and so on; and a surreal Feuerbach XI presented online in October 2005. In addition, there are musings on the decline and fall of great cricketing empires, West Indies in the 1990s, Australia just possibly today. And always when following cricket mainly in England, there is sky-watching. 'Many's the day I've sat at Old Trafford . . . scanning the heavens to try and judge the prospect.'

You beauty!

An early loyalty to South Africa notwithstanding, Geras throughout his cricketing life has barracked for Australia against England, and since the boycott of apartheid shut South Africa out of international sport in 1970 has supported them against all comers. Unsurprisingly, the long dominant streak on which Australia embarked in the late 1980s, the Australian Supremacy that stretched unbroken for a full two decades to the late 2000s, is another key theme in his writings. Here the central motif is not celebration of cricketing excellence wherever and whenever found, but rather forceful and raucous promotion of some of the most formidable teams known to the game.

At the core of this commitment is an absorption in the tradition of Ashes cricket played by Australia and England on a broadly two-year cycle. Watched three times in their entirety by Geras and chronicled twice in book form, Ashes series assume a peerless importance in his writings. 'This is Test cricket, and it is Ashes cricket – than which there is nothing more serious in sport.' Flowing from this are exacting standards to which successive generations of Australians, at once extremely vulnerable and massively superior, are held. No greater disappointment is expressed than with players who fail to live up to the responsibility placed on them. A Ricky Ponting declaration at Perth in 2006, setting England 557 to win, is 'idiotic' but ultimately inconsequential. An Adam Gilchrist declaration at Leeds in 2001, setting England 315 to win, is a 'sorry ... misjudgement' resulting in defeat. No matter that the series victory, 4–1, was still handsome; the chance of a rare clean sweep had gone begging. 'For these Australians of 2001, what a waste!'

Nonetheless, there remains plenty to celebrate in the supremacy, and in Geras's work even the sharpest chance is taken. In 1997, fewer than ten years into the streak, he recalls 'Border, Boon, Steve Waugh, Mark Taylor and more, rolling out the hundreds, batting to eternity', Terry Alderman's corridor of uncertainty and Warne's ball from hell. In 2001, looking now across more than a decade, he presents multiple indices of Australian superiority (all of which are updated after further series triumphs). In 2006–07, making his first trip to the country in which he has long invested so much emotional energy, he finally relishes the whitewash so needlessly passed up at the start of the decade. 'And Australia – my team – won 5–0.'

Cricket matters

It is only natural that this extended appreciation of Test match cricket and its great protagonists should prompt analysis of cricket as a spectator sport. Devoted solely to the five-day Test, Geras sets high standards not simply for players donning Australia's baggy green, but also for fans flocking to matches. Here too, in an experience chiefly of English venues, there is disappointment and censure. The sensibilities of some sitting in the stands on the third day of The Oval Test in 2001 are 'of the pond-life variety'. Being in Stand B on day three of the Old Trafford Test in 2006 is 'like watching cricket from a shithole'. The Western Terrace at Headingley is 'the dung-heap of cricket spectating'. All too often, English grounds are turned into 'a sea of baying supporters and endlessly cavorting louts'. The chants of 'Stand up if you hate Shane Warne', and much else besides, that ring from their stadiums are evidence of an 'impoverished and brutalising' sporting culture. England's Barmy Army, typically at the heart of all this, is 'an infestation'.

Never, however, is this the defining feature of Geras's cricket writings. Indeed, emerging far more strongly from them is a very different theme: sturdy defence of the place of cricket, and of all competitive sport, in human affairs. The argument is made most fully in response to Germaine Greer. For those who love it, sport offers 'something they get nowhere else – a combination of drama, spectacle, great skill, the observation of individual character under pressure, a contest that seems at the time to matter even if (when all is said and done) it matters only in a limited way, and moments of thrilling beauty'. Similarly, Noam Chomsky is taken to task for a 'snooty attitude' that paints spectator sport as an opiate. A linked point about the stories we tell about ourselves is made in concert with Frank Keating. Can a rounded social history really be written without regard to sport?

Moreover, the necessary concomitant of this line of thinking is also present. Cricket, like other major sports, cannot be bracketed off from the moral and political challenges posed by brutal regimes in countries where the game is played. For Geras, such challenges arise no more clearly than in the land of his birth – Rhodesia then, Zimbabwe now. In the closing months of 2004, when Robert Mugabe had already driven his country far down the road to penury and despair, Geras denounced a scheduled England tour, demanding that officials look beyond the narrow confines of cricket to wider social duties. Here the concern for humanity that animates most of his work is explicit, and the extent to which cricket ultimately does matter is clearly stated.

Conclusion

Norman Geras's cricket writings are both a celebration of the best-loved game and a forceful defence of this exalted billing. In Test match cricket he finds a body of law and a set of shared understandings within which momentous human performance is possible. In those who participate in Test matches as either players or spectators, he seeks the decency, fair play, disciplined effort, and recognition of excellence that he values in other human pursuits. In leading cricketers of our day, he identifies greatness that will last for all days. Of cricket icon Shane Warne, he writes: 'Appreciate him: he was a long time coming, and he will be a long time gone.' Only Warney, the man with the golden arm, could elicit this most fulsome tribute. But in the injunction there is also a wider meaning.

For Geras, it is therefore nothing other than simple consistency to recoil from crude treatment meted out to the likes of Warne. 'In face of a skill and artistry so phenomenal . . . that.' One clear antidote to that, to sneering refusal to applaud what cricket at its best can offer, is Geras's own work, a stream of writing animated by passion and respect for Test match cricket, for those who grace its theatres, and for those who revel in and script its accomplishments.

Note

1 All cited material is by Norman Geras, and may be found in: N. Geras and I. Holliday, *Ashes '97: Two Views from the Boundary* (Tisbury: Baseline, 1997); N. Geras, *Men of Waugh: Ashes 2001* (Manchester: Geras, 2002); *normblog*, http://normblog.typepad.com/normblog.

18

Responses

Norman Geras

To be the subject of a volume of essays of this kind is at once a great honour and a source of some embarrassment. For the honour, and for the thought and work that have gone into the individual chapters, I express my warmest thanks at the start. I am most grateful to the two editors, my good friends Steve de Wijze and Eve Garrard, whose idea it was to produce a collection devoted to my work, and who then did what was necessary (including the application of a bit of gentle pressure on me) to bring it to completion. I am grateful, likewise, to all of the contributors for the trouble they have taken in thinking about themes and problems which have interested me at one time or another, or persistently, over the course of more than forty years.

This is where the embarrassment comes in. To see so many of one's thoughts – reasoned out (or at any rate arrived at) during such a long period – returning in the same place to be discussed by considerably more people than the mere one that I am is enough to give anybody pause. Did I think that then? Do I still? And whatever the answer to either question, can I make coherent sense of all the things which these chapters offer evidence of my having written over the period? Readers of the volume will see for themselves the generosity of spirit that has animated the contributors in engaging with my work. Yet, generous as they may be, they have raised between them critical questions that would take another book again to respond to adequately. I shall not be able to do their chapters justice. The best I can aim for is to deal with a small selection of the issues they address.

I shall begin with David McLellan's chapter: in part because his central focus is on my writings about Marx and Marxism, the area which was my major interest during twenty-five years of teaching and writing; but principally because it is not possible to think about one's own work, covering a span of four decades, without reflecting on the issue of intellectual continuity and discontinuity – and that is an issue with which David's chapter is very much concerned. It may, indeed, appear churlish on my part to first pick up two of the minor points of disagreement I have with him, given that on this overarching question of intellectual trajectory our views are in broad harmony. But I shall do so briefly in any case.

I do not see it as problematic that in interpreting Marx's thought I have a different approach to the fact/value distinction than Marx did. Naturally, this could lead someone astray who attempted to foist his own assumptions on to the thinker whose meaning he was trying to explain. But where it is a matter, not of exegesis, but of defending the soundness (as he sees it) of one or another proposition ascribed to the thinker in question – in this case, Marx's view that there is a trans-historical human nature – it seems to me unobjectionable for that defence to rely on arguments the thinker himself would not have chosen. I see no problem, either, in holding that human beings are 'absolutely continuous with the rest of the natural world' while drawing attention at the same time to specific capabilities which enable them to transform their natural environment as no other earthly species can. To speak of continuity in this context is just to claim that we are – are completely – natural beings, a part of nature; it is not to deny the existence of differences within the natural world, including between humanity and the rest of that world.

On the larger question, however, the question of intellectual development, it is gratifying to find my own understanding of where I have come from, so to say, or how I got from there to where I am now, confirmed by someone else, someone for whom this process was not lived from the inside but seen with the distance natural to an external observer. McLellan finds an 'underlying intellectual thread' in my work, 'striking continuities and consistencies'; and so (perhaps predictably) do I. There is more to be said about this – in qualification of it – and I shall be saying some of that in what follows. But the perception is a welcome one that can see past the combination, scandalous to some, of my earlier Marxist writing with the recent political positions I have taken, to the consistencies of thought behind it.

McLellan identifies not only the commitment to a universalist concept of human nature that runs between 1983 and 1994 and beyond, but also the defence within my Marxological work of a trans-historical notion of justice and rights, and the concern there for the distinctively liberal principles that must inform any genuinely democratic socialism. This is a concern I learned from Rosa Luxemburg among other people, as well as from John Stuart Mill. Its accents are clearly present in the essay I wrote on 'Classical Marxism and Proletarian Representation' as far back as 1980 (Geras, 1981). The work on the Holocaust that I did in the 1990s, and the work on the concept of crimes against humanity which I began in 2002 and have just completed, only served to reinforce the same liberal dispositions. It is all the more puzzling to me that anyone should regard my recent political standpoints, including that favouring the overthrow of a murderous tyrant in Iraq, as surprising. Though they may well look surprising in the light of the large number of others calling themselves Marxists who chose to align themselves differently, against the background of the consistencies just sketched they look entirely logical to me.

The chapters by David Aaronovitch, Nick Cohen, and Damian Counsell enable me to say something more on the issue of intellectual continuity and discontinuity. Making the elementary point that the support of progressives for the spread of democracy does not have to be equivalent to drop-of-the-hat military interventionism, the other David of this collection – Aaronovitch – insists nonetheless that 'progressives should always find themselves on the side of democracy first'. His negative reference points in saying so are the relativizing, instrumental, and ambivalent impulses of a section of the left with respect to political democracy. These impulses have been amply expressed in the years since 9/11, and that has had the effect of altering my relationship to Marxism – as a political constituency if not as a constellation of ideas.

The weaknesses of the Marxist tradition so far as democracy is concerned will not be news to anyone at this late date. Those weaknesses have been apparent for a long time, and critics of Marxism are not short of examples they can cite against it from the history of the twentieth century – the example, above all, of Stalinism. Until recently, however, my own view, put on record in an interview from 2002 which was published by the magazine *Imprints* (Geras, 2002–03), was that these were not terminal or permanently disabling weaknesses; they could be remedied. It was open to us, through fresh thinking, through drawing on the intellectual resources of other traditions, especially liberalism, to make good the gaps and deficiencies bequeathed to Marxism by its canonical thinkers, and to produce thereby a democratically committed body of ideas for the new century. I continue to think the same thing. It is one reason, along with the strengths I still perceive Marxism to possess, why I go on calling myself a Marxist.

Something, though, has changed for me, and what changed it was the realization that a new generation of Marxists (as well as of others loosely influenced by Marxism), schooled though many of them were in the critique and rejection of Stalinism and in the affirmation of Marxism's more democratic tropes, remained so wedded to a would-be anti-imperialism as to be willing to indulge in the old, familiar apologetics and evasions when it came to the patently anti-democratic and human-rights-violating practices of tyrannical regimes, terrorist organizations or nationalist movements aligned rhetorically and ideologically against the West. Why, I asked myself, this persisting moral failure on the part of a significant section of the left?

A full answer to that question would doubtless require more space than I have here, but one part of the answer, I have come to think, is this. The failure has its source in a group of temptations regularly displayed by a section of the Western left when confronted by (a) the undemocratic practices of supposedly socialist or anti-imperialist or (in some assumed sense) 'progressive' states, and (b) the claims made for the democracies of the wealthier capitalist countries.

There are three elements in this thematic grouping. There is (i) a temptation to look for considerations mitigating the lack of democracy in the countries just referred to under (a) above: considerations such as blockade, encirclement, underdevelopment, the legacy of colonialism, and so on. There is, then, (ii) an attempt to point to features compensating for that lack of democracy: principally social and economic achievements of one kind and another. Finally, there are (iii) arguments to the effect that the democracies of advanced capitalist societies are themselves either flawed and limited as democracies or not really democracies at all but disguised forms of dictatorship.

Now, it is not that there is nothing at all to be said in support of these themes. In turn: (i) a country mired in poverty has fewer democratic resources than a wealthy one; (ii) where there are achievements to note, there is nothing wrong with noting them; (iii) the democracies of the capitalist world are indeed flawed in certain ways – differently, and some more than others, but invariably failing to offer all their citizens an equality of influence and rights.

Nonetheless, there is a central piece of bad faith in the way that, for a section of the left, these three themes typically combine to enable their partisans to evade a single inescapable fact: namely that, flawed as they may be, the capitalist democracies are democracies, whereas none of the would-be anti-capitalist countries, anywhere, has managed to sustain comparably good or better democratic institutions over any length of time. I do not say that this means it could never happen. I do not believe that. What I do think, though, is that the democratic institutions we are familiar with have yet to be improved upon in any of those places that some leftists are given to casting an indulgent eye upon even while they seek to distance themselves critically from the political institutions of their own countries, institutions from which they benefit and which are superior. Unwilling to profess a clear allegiance towards what is democratically better, a certain type of leftist is always ready to make allowances for what is democratically worse.

This thematic configuration, it should be added, has not been exclusive to people or organizations calling themselves Marxist. All the same, the influence of a Marxist discourse familiar from the Stalinist apologetics of the last century is clearly recognizable within it. It is not a configuration I want to associate myself with; and, for that reason, while I continue to regard myself as a Marxist, the label still accounting accurately for an important part of how I think, I no longer regard myself as part of the Marxist left – anomalous though this pairing may sound.

I have no wish to identify myself, or to be identified with, the sort of consensus evoked in Nick Cohen's chapter: 'unwillingness to support the victims of psychopathic regimes and movements if their suffering cannot be blamed on the West ... failure to hold onto the old leftish virtue of solidarity with those who share your principles when they are suffering at the hands of ultra-reactionary forces ... a relativist willingness to tolerate abuses in other cultures you would never tolerate in your own'. Nick labels this consensus 'liberal', and I know why he does – because it has lately come to stretch well beyond the far left, with its Marxist attachments, into the opinion and letters pages of the liberal press. But what he says applies, in any case, to the issue I am addressing. He describes a standpoint that since 11 September 2001 has alienated me from the Marxist and Marxist-influenced political constituency to which I used to consider

I belonged. It is a standpoint more interested in its own anti-capitalism than it is in the struggle against political tyranny or in the opposition (obligatory for any principled socialism) to terrorist murder. Some, no doubt, will be upset by such a characterization of the evaluative priorities of that left from which I have come to take my distance, for it is not a ranking openly avowed as a rule. Yet, *practically*, in terms of the dominant polemical rhetoric coming from the relevant quarter, this is how it too often goes: the democracies of the West flawed, at fault, hypocritical, aggressors, and so forth, while quite appallingly anti-democratic movements and regimes are made apology for, and bathed in the mitigation of a shallow root-causes sociology, root causes for which some proximate 'we' are always said to bear the ultimate responsibility.

Though, consequently, I still believe in the substantial truth of Marxian historical materialism and the continued pertinence of the programme of social justice that Marxian socialism envisaged – educated and improved now, however, by the norms and constraints of liberalism – I have no wish to be connected with the ambiguities, and worse than ambiguities, that congregate under the banner of a section of the left still locked into a style of apologetics from yesteryear, and which were already discredited back then. Whether these explanations adequately dispose of the question implicitly raised by Damian Counsell I leave for readers to decide for themselves: where Damian sees Marxism as irredeemably rotten politically, productive, inevitably, of moral enormities, my own judgement, just sketched, is that Marxism's follies were indeed due in part to weaknesses original to the tradition, but that they are also remediable, since nothing prevents the integration of liberal and human-rights norms within Marxism's socio-economic explanatory framework and its vision of a just society for all.

The chapters by Cohen and Counsell, it may be added, focus on a branch of my writing that has cost me much time in recent years – my blogging. I am grateful to both for their warm commendations of *normblog*. The same goes for what Ophelia Benson says about it. The three of them, in fact, provide a most useful introduction to the specificities of blogging as a mode of writing, and they have made me more aware of what I have been involved with by my writing for *normblog* than I was before I read their contributions to the present volume. As much time as I have spent on that since July 2003 (and, believe me, it is a lot), I have never much thought about it as a part of my 'work' – in the way that I *have* always thought of my academic writing. Perhaps it was because at the start I so much enjoyed writing for the blog; and this remains true even now when blogging can no longer be described as a fresh enthusiasm of mine. In any event, I have done it without giving other than passing attention to the place of this new form of communication in the wider public life of democratic societies. The three chapters here are a good place to start in thinking about that: Counsell mapping some of the optimal requirements of the blog form; Cohen speaking of the way the blogosphere created a fresh intellectual space for challenging some of the standard conformities of the left-leaning media; and Benson, for her part, exploring the liberatory potential of the public diary form that is the blog. Her chapter reinforces, in addition, some of the points about intellectual continuity that I drew from the discussion of David McLellan's. In speaking of the human-rights content of much of the material on *normblog*, a blog she also highlights for its liberalism in an expansive sense of that word, Ophelia helps to bring out the linkages between my blog-writings since the summer of 2003 and my academic work both before and since the inauguration of *normblog*.

The chapter by Philip Spencer is of special interest to me in tracing a line between intellectual concerns that span some twenty years – running from my first book, on Rosa Luxemburg, published in 1976, to *The Contract of Mutual Indifference*, which appeared in 1998. Philip has taken Luxemburg's use of the socialism-or-barbarism formula – a subject of close analysis in the earlier book – and applied it to features of the Holocaust, the event that has been at the centre of my thinking about what human beings do and do not owe each other when some of them are faced with calamity. His attempt to show from this exercise why the Marxian aim of working-class self-emancipation must give way to projects of international rescue when genocide is in progress represents just the sort of fresh thinking that I have said, above, is needed within Marxism: to generate from its own internal resources conclusions that may be new to it, but are called for nonetheless in view of terrible realities not anticipated by earlier generations of socialists. Barbarism in the shape of modern genocide, along with the traditions of internationalist solidarity familiar within Marxist thought, surely suffices to support the principle of humanitarian intervention in certain emergency circumstances. As Spencer himself says, there are worse states of affairs than capitalism.

Yet it should be noted, at the same time, that while this conclusion is drawn from themes indigenous within early Marxism – socialism-or-barbarism, internationalist solidarity – they involve a law and enforcement perspective alien to the classical Marxist canon. The law in this case is international law; but that does not alter the fact that potent and tragic historical experiences since Marx's time have shown why historical progress cannot only be emancipatory – liberating people from oppressive constraints. It must also be protective and regulatory – saving them, if they need to be saved, from the criminal violence of states and other political organizations; upholding an international rule of law.

This is in tune with a conclusion I argued for in a paper from 2004 entitled 'How Free?' (Geras, 2004). My argument there is that a utopia such as was broadly anticipated in the Marxist vision could not, even were it feasible in other respects, feasibly be a stateless one. It would still require a framework of law, and some degree of compulsion to back that law. In formulating this argument I committed myself to the proposition that the denizens of such a utopia are bound to be less free than they were envisaged to be in the traditional Marxian picture. Being restricted by coercive law, they would not all be entirely self-willed. Without necessarily meaning to do so, Hillel Steiner takes issue with this proposition in his contribution to the volume. Or to put things more accurately, perhaps, my proposition that people would be less free in a Marxian utopia than traditionally envisaged by Marxists bumps up against Hillel's 'Law of Conservation of Liberty'. As he himself sums up the import of this law: 'the magnitude of each person's overall freedom is inversely related to that of others. And I take this to imply that negative liberty is such that it makes no sense to speak of it as being aggregately increased or diminished'.

I think any disagreement there is between us here is only a matter of different meanings of the terms 'liberty' and 'freedom', as used by the two of us. For though the concept I operate with in that paper is also, broadly, a concept of negative liberty, it is not the same strict negative concept that has been central to Steiner's work. I refer, rather, to 'freedom' in the rough and ready sense that would be understood by most people in day-to-day discussions about some countries being more free than others. On Steiner's strict definition, if we as citizens lose some of our freedoms to act, because of tyrannical laws, then there are others possessing certain freedoms for themselves at our expense. We may be less free than we were, but those who prevent us from what we could otherwise do, and previously did do, exercise freedoms of their own in blocking us. Overall, there is no more and less about it; aggregate freedom is now just differently distributed. I have no particular quarrel with thinking about things in this way for certain purposes. However, on another familiar understanding of freedom, a people living under the rule of more severe legal restrictions, and more punitive sanctions for disregarding these, is less free than a people that enjoys fewer such restrictions and less harsh penalties. The perspective of this common-or-garden meaning of negative liberty is the perspective of those who are living under, who are subjected to, the legal regime; and their aggregate freedoms are not computed together with those freedoms enjoyed by the law-imposing class in the freedom-restricting activities they exercise against others.

My disagreement with Gideon Calder's chapter is more substantial. Gideon pays me the compliment of acknowledging the influence of my book on Marx and human nature in helping to persuade him of the centrality of general human needs and capacities – of a common human nature, in fact – in determining the conditions for human flourishing. But he takes his distance from the idea, which has indeed become part of my thinking about catastrophes like the Holocaust and the incidence of other crimes against humanity, that human nature might encompass not only universal needs and abilities but also impulses of a negative kind – along, it goes without saying, with more benign ones. He has misgivings about the idea of (as he himself calls this) the *flawedness* of human nature. I am puzzled by his misgivings. I shall first offer a general reason for my puzzlement and then go on to point to what I think is a fallacy of argument in the way Gideon presents his opposition to the idea of human-natural flawedness.

If there is a common human nature, as is agreed between the two of us, and negative impulses – tendencies to aggression or cruelty, indifference to suffering, extreme selfishness, malice, and so on – are not a part of it, then we must assume that all inborn human impulses are benign or neutral, or a combination of these two. But why, on the evidence available to us, should we assume any such thing? This is not only a matter of observing what happens when the killers and the torturers are unleashed. Just look around you, at everyday life. The mixture of good, bad, and in-between or neutral is pervasive there.

The denial that there are *any* common natural impulses, though it is preposterous and so not worth taking seriously, at least has a kind of logic to it. Human beings, so it will be said, are not naturally cruel; but neither are they naturally kind. They are just empty vessels to be educated and socialized as may be. Once the absurdity of this way of thinking about a species with a material biology is recognized, however, to understand humankind as having no problematic impulses would seem to me to entail a view of its nature either as altogether indeterminate morally or as morally benign. The whole burden of understanding its considerable troubles then falls on 'bad' social structures and relations, an explanatory move based not on evidence but on faith. One might just as well turn things round and assume that everything good in human behaviour is due to society and everything bad in it due to human nature – an assumption that people on the left never make and that I am confident Calder would resist.

Turning now to the fallacy in the way he argues against the thesis of flawedness, this consists in setting up a polarity between explanation that draws on the human capacity for malign action, on one side, and explanation in terms of social structure and historical circumstance, on the other. 'If the point about radical evil is granted,' he writes, 'then the rest of the account ... in fact becomes peripheral'. Well, it *may* become peripheral, but there is nothing to say that it must do, and an insistence to the contrary merely seeks to dictate what it cannot show. If I explain the failure of George to do any work in the week running up to his final examinations by reference to his slothful tendencies (for which we have much prior evidence) and to his love of hard liquor (ditto), must I overlook the fact – the *social* circumstance – that throughout that week he was subject to the influence of loose-living friends who had no exams themselves at the time? I *might* overlook this context, but I do not have to. Again, Calder writes: 'But self-interest, or indeed aggression – or indeed any other such isolated psychological trait – simply does not seem in itself to account for acts of collective moral calamity'. It does not account for such things 'in itself' but only because it accounts for them (when it does) *in part*. By misconstruing claims that are not meant as total explanations as if they were, Calder finds them wanting. But it is a deficient argumentative technique. That the rainfall speeded the growth of the crops can be true even if their growth also required a collective effort of agricultural labour.

I will add, in passing, that when Calder takes my condemnation of the 'yes but' apologetics widespread after 9/11 to imply that one should not try to understand terrible events, because 'to understand their context is to forgive', he ascribes to me a view I do not hold and have taken care to distance myself from whenever it was relevant to do so. In the very interview to which he makes reference, as containing the material that gets him 'nervous' in this regard, I say 'To explain is not *necessarily* to excuse or justify. Yet it can be precisely that. It depends on the quality and substance of the purported explanation' (Geras, 2002–03: 207). His criticism on this score is at one with his reservations about the thesis of the flawedness of human nature. Both criticisms suggest that I discount or make light of the place and importance of historical explanation. But I do not.

Shalom Lappin's contribution to the volume is addressed to the history of anti-Semitism in Britain, and anti-Semitism – more generally racism and other ethnic hatreds – is one of the best illustrations you could want of what I have just been saying about human-natural flaws. Of course, to understand the contours and the principal features of any particular racism, one will have to be attentive to the historical forces, the structural and cultural factors, that have shaped it. But given the weight of these kinds of hatred in history, there must be some human propensity that inclines human beings to belittle or malign other human beings, *if only in certain circumstances* (and not in others). Imagine a species that had no such propensities. Unimaginable? But why? If humans have transformative capacities to a degree that other known species do not, why might they not be more disposed towards developing aggressive hatreds than are some other species, whether actual or conceivable? When an event like the Holocaust – or the Armenian genocide, or the Rwandan genocide, or a pogrom, or a massacre of civilians in war – takes place, to aver that natural impulses of one kind and another have no explanatory role or weight just makes no sense; unless as a species we have no natural impulses at all, a proposition that is impossible to defend with any persuasive force.

Shalom looks at the particularities of anti-Semitism in Britain and his survey supplies a corrective to certain earlier assumptions of my own on the future of anti-Jewish prejudice in this country and elsewhere. These assumptions were of a rather more generalizing kind, and may therefore be legitimately subject to a charge of not having been historically enough informed. For a long time I had believed that the relatively low levels of anti-Semitism in this country, as suggested to me by my own personal experience during some forty years, were due to a combination of historical shock and cultural shame as the full import of what had befallen the Jews of Europe sank in. So much so that, other than as a phenomenon of the political sewers, anti-Semitism as a serious feature of the life of democratic societies was over. This judgement, it has turned out, was both too optimistic and, within a broad historical perspective, too quick. The poison is back. It is on the streets, in all the media of communication including those boasting liberal credentials, and within the groves of academe (to their shame). The resurgence of anti-Semitism is in many ways international in scope. But Lappin's chapter has enabled me better to appreciate its local lineage, and thereby to recognize the naivety of my previous optimism. Nothing as rooted as anti-Semitism is after two millennia simply goes away and leaves no residue, no sources for a subsequent revival. To that extent Calder's argument for a historically informed framing of such issues is vindicated. And yet still – historical causation is not the only kind, and racial or ethnic hatreds like anti-Semitism are a potent proof of this.

Laurence Thomas's chapter sets itself the task of asking how we may most effectively put up barriers against the possibility of evil. It is his contention that forms of education and socialization which have the effect of affirming people when they live by good values, behave well towards others, are more important in creating barriers against evil than is the cultivation of autonomy, of rational judgement. As he puts it: 'What is more likely to deliver [moral] excellence: the right upbringing or rational reflection as such? History and the arguments of this essay ... would suggest that the former is much more likely to do so.' Further: 'Nothing makes justice more secure than a world in which, in the first place, the desire to do what is evil does not obtain a purchase upon our lives.'

I will not, for my part, gainsay the importance of an education in good moral values of the sort Laurence has in mind – such that the beneficiaries of that education are inclined to feel affirmed when they are seen to apply those values practically in life, to feel affirmed by others who subscribe to the same values. Yet, though he sees connections between this central thesis of his and aspects of my own work, the thesis strikes me as problematic. For social affirmation has a 'wild card' character to it. It is true that the emotional support that being affirmed by others provides, the sense of not being on one's own, plays a crucial role in most people's lives. But we know from crisis situations in history – the very ones in which there are temptations to do grave wrong, to get carried away, to walk hand in hand with the violation of other persons, other lives – that social affirmation can switch registers; it can change sides. Suddenly something that people have long thought was wrong has a wave of support behind it. What is socially affirmed and what is not socially affirmed now carry different contents. Autonomy in such contexts is a precious resource. For the resistance to great wrong, we also know from historical experience, almost invariably requires some individuals, whether key leaders or so-called ordinary people, to understand that in certain circumstances social affirmation for what has to be done is not to be easily had. It may well be that one of the reasons these same people grasp what has to be done is that they have learned the relevant values from others: parents, teachers, friends, other role models. But one thing they also need to have learned, and to have the courage to sustain, is that sometimes you may have to stand on your own or with a very small number of others. Being affirmed is desirable, but not if those doing the affirming have crossed the line. I think, consequently, that the opposition Thomas sets up between affirmation and autonomy does not work.

A writer who pondered these same issues as deeply as anyone was Primo Levi. Not a moral or political philosopher by training, Levi generated from his experiences at Auschwitz – and from his gifts as a writer and a personal wisdom that was the product of who knows what – a body of writing without equal. He is, to this day, not only incomparable as a witness, but also the greatest thinker to have responded to the catastrophe of the Nazi genocide. It is the merit of Alan Johnson's chapter to have set out clearly the overall shape of Levi's moral and political thought and some of its component elements. Levi's is a philosophy of hope in the shadow of catastrophe: one which insists that the struggle against injustice is never-ending because we as human beings contain, at once, potentialities for virtue and the capacity for wrongdoing, including the commission of vast evils, evils that are irredeemable. It is a philosophy which locates a responsibility in every person to 'diminish as much as he can the tremendous bulk of this substance which contaminates every life – pain in all its forms'. As Alan (who draws attention to this passage) writes for his own part: 'To view humanity in the perspective of Auschwitz ... is to cultivate a tragic sensibility that views human beings as "ill-constituted", civilization as fragile, and evil as real.' Earlier remarks of mine will explain my general concurrence with these sentiments. A responsible political philosophy today is burdened with the duty of not forgetting. It is no longer possible to entertain the illusion of perfection or hope in a flawless utopia.

Johnson's chapter also registers the way in which participation in, and appreciation of, some of the simple, everyday pleasures of life formed part of Levi's anti-perfectionist outlook; and I take this as giving me licence here to introduce a break in proceedings, as it were, in order to turn from questions connected with the commission of evil to ... cricket. As I write this, the first Test match of the latest Ashes series of 2010–11 is being contested by Australia and England in Brisbane. More or less whenever these two antagonists are on the field of play, my friend Ian Holliday and I are either in regular communication about it or else thinking about one another's likely reactions to the state of the game and of the series. For I have been supporting Australia against England at cricket since the age of eleven, while Ian is of the opposite persuasion. He bears a major responsibility, too, for the fact that I ever came to try my hand at writing about cricket. In 1997 he suggested that we follow the Ashes series of that summer – all of it – together, and our doing so led to the book we co-wrote, *Ashes '97: Two Views from the Boundary*. Had anyone said to me any time before then that one day I would be writing at length on this subject I would not have believed them. That my cricket writing might one day come to be the subject of analysis in a volume of essays devoted to my work would have seemed even more implausible. In any case, by his contribution to this book, Ian has now done me the further favour of undertaking just such an analysis, and I am in his debt once more. By his treatment of my cricket writing in an organized and analytical way he has drawn my attention to themes and unities there that I was either not aware of before or aware of only dimly.

A passion for Test cricket, as for other sports, is what it is, no more and no less: it is devotion to a game – though with that goes a whole tradition stretching back over more than a century, so that the game provides much more material for reflection and debate than those who have no interest in it can easily fathom. In the scale of what matters morally and politically the interest is relatively unimportant.

All the same, I get impatient with the tendency of some intellectuals, politically minded people prominent amongst them, to belittle the close attention to sport that so many – numbering in their millions globally – give. This tendency is a kind of snobbery and a kind of philistinism. It not only turns its face away from the activity, as is the right of anyone (since we cannot all be interested in everything); it also insists on denying, about a sphere it scarcely knows, the beauties and the virtues within it, the moments that are absorbing and the moments that are thrilling, and the validity of the enjoyments to be had from all of that. If perfect utopias are to be treated with suspicion because humankind is not capable of perfection, there is nonetheless much to be said for not neglecting or belittling the components of ordinary human happiness when they do no harm, those small intimations of a more limited utopia, present within common experience. How far my cricket writing has succeeded in putting any of this across I cannot say. But Holliday's contribution to the volume succeeds in conveying it eloquently.

I return now, after that interlude, to a darker human terrain – the terrain, in fact, of *in*humanity. Should we forgive the perpetrators of great evil? The question is asked by Eve Garrard, and her response to it is both careful and clear, with the reasons on both sides of the issue delineated with great precision. Forgiveness is not a topic I have ever worked on, and I am unfamiliar with the literature about it. My philosophical instincts, however, incline me against the view for which Eve argues, and the admirable clarity of her chapter has enabled me to confirm for myself why. I will give significant space, in responding to her chapter, to only two of the many issues she covers. One of these relates to a formal feature of her argument, the other to the substantive matter – human solidarity – that has been pivotal in persuading me against what she says. A preliminary point before taking these two issues in turn: the case is made by Eve in a general way vis-à-vis perpetrators of evil; however, I shall focus on those involved in committing genocide, individuals responsible for mass murder *and* who show no remorse for what they have done, as testing her case. For her argument to be convincing overall, it needs to persuade us about people falling into this category. In the interests of economy, I concentrate on them.

First, then, the formal point. It is an interesting feature of Garrard's argument in support of forgiveness for the perpetrators of great evil that, while it puts forward reasons in favour, it does not claim that these reasons are conclusive, that they defeat the reasons against. This feature of her case may not make it unique, but neither is it typical in moral advocacy. Often when we put forward reasons for a course of action, or disposition or what have you, we do precisely contend that these reasons are clinching, though we will likely allow that there are opposing reasons too. We see one set of reasons as outweighing the other. Unless I have misunderstood her, Garrard's case for forgiveness (involving, on her definition of it, 'the adoption of a stance of at least minimal good-will towards the perpetrator') does not work like this. She thinks that 'we have reason to forgive perpetrators'; but not only does she also cite reasons *against* forgiving them – she deals with seven – she accepts that these might appear to others as weighty enough to vindicate an unforgiving stance. Forgiveness, then, is morally permissible but not morally obligatory: 'it can't be demanded of the victim'; and 'there is nothing blameworthy in choosing to withhold it'. Put differently, while it is 'possible that a legitimate reason for resentment [and so non-forgiveness] may ... be legitimately outweighed', Garrard nowhere says that the reasons for non-forgiveness are *necessarily* outweighed.

Her case is that forgiveness is morally allowable; it is not that forgiveness is so morally compelling as to constitute a duty. Those therefore, like me, who do not feel that unrepentant mass murderers should be forgiven (and Garrard is explicit in including the unrepentant in the argument for forgiveness she makes) do not have a case to answer. There is no persuasive pressure on us from the case in favour of forgiveness. We can acknowledge the right, for others who are so minded, to forgive, but withhold forgiveness ourselves from those who we think are inappropriate objects of it. We have no need to confute Garrard's reasons, since she herself sees them only as reasons amongst other countervailing ones, and without any possibility of a decisive adjudication between the two sets.

More substantively, now, here is what is decisive for me in wanting to withhold forgiveness from unrepentant mass murderers and their ilk. It is the consideration of solidarity. Garrard gives human solidarity a central place in her argument. We are all frail and fallible and must consider the possibility that in certain circumstances we might have been perpetrators of great evil ourselves. In forgiving those who have become perpetrators, we acknowledge a common humanity. I have my reservations about the thesis that we all could do what such perpetrators do, since we know from the evidence that some people do *not*, not even in the most pressingly terrible circumstances. But let this pass: to sustain Garrard's point the thought will possibly suffice that many, at least, would do what the perpetrators do, and so you or I might be amongst them.

Still, overriding the impulse towards solidarity with the perpetrators is, for me, solidarity with the victims. It is crucial to this contention that there is a lack of repentance on the part of the perpetrator(s) in question. Consider the implications of the fact that a given perpetrator shows no remorse. In terms of his mental attitudes, this means that the situation is not relevantly different from when he is still in the process of committing the crimes for which forgiveness is being contemplated. If, on grounds of moral frailty, human solidarity and suchlike, we can forgive the perpetrator of past crimes, it is not clear why we should not similarly forgive him *even while* he is committing his crimes, even while he is engaged in terrible cruelties. That is a solidarity too far. Solidarity is a fine sentiment, and principle, and mode of activity. But it divides humankind as well as uniting it. When some people are hacking others to death, or driving them into gas chambers with whips and dogs, or torturing or working the life out of them, our human solidarity is owed to these others and not to their killers and tormentors. After the event, if the tormentors remain unrepentant, solidarity is still due to the memory of those they have destroyed, and to others who are bereft or permanently scarred by the destruction of people close to them. For the fact that the perpetrators have stopped committing their crimes is neither here nor there in this context if they continue to display attitudes of affirmation towards those crimes, a lack of all remorse. These attitudes suggest they would simply resume the crimes should the 'right' circumstances arise. To see forgiveness as appropriate to such people, on grounds of the unity of humankind and its common weaknesses, opens the way to forgiving those who oppress and torment others even while they are doing so. It is a misdirection of moral solidarity, diverting it from the victims to those responsible for their plight.

It may be said in defence of Garrard's position that solidarity does not have to be rationed; it can be extended to all. But given how much need there is for solidarity and other similar help in the world as it is, it remains to be shown that a solidarity of this very lavish kind, taking in unrepentant mass murderers *and* the innocent, could be of value to the latter.

Early in her chapter Garrard writes as if she might believe that unwillingness to forgive those responsible for genocide amounts to a desire to exclude them from the community of humankind. She says: 'One possible response is to banish them [those who have committed moral atrocities] perpetually from the moral community, to exclude them from our communal concern; another, contrasting, response is to forgive them.' Whatever she does believe on this score, the two alternatives she presents are not exhaustive. Someone, for example, declines to forgive a grave personal injustice they have suffered at another's hands without thereby wanting to exclude the person concerned from the normal rights, freedoms, and other benefits due to any member of society. In the same way, we can decline to forgive an unrepentant perpetrator of genocide while insisting that he retain his basic rights as a human being (other than those forfeited by him in acting so as to incur legitimate punishment). Even unforgiven, he should not be subjected to cruel or unusual punishments and should be treated with the elementary dignities we extend to all human beings. That is what we owe to other people just in virtue of their humanity, as members of our moral community. But the 'stance of at least minimal good-will' involved, on Garrard's definition, in forgiveness – this seems in no way appropriate for those who have not only committed terrible violations against others but still refuse to acknowledge any wrongdoing.

Otherwise the case for forgiveness here risks being a case for unconditional forgiveness of everyone for everything. If a person responsible for the deaths of thousands of people in the cruellest of ways may be forgiven on account of her human frailty even when she has not thought better of what she has done, does this not say to all and sundry in advance, *everything* is forgivable? For if anything – anything at all – can be forgiven after the event, that forgiveness can be anticipated before the event too. To obtain it nothing is required of any of us: not only the avoidance of adding, wantonly, vastly, to the continent of human pain; in addition, not even coming to see the evil in having done so. The perpetrator can indeed *rejoice* in the evil he has committed and still be forgiven. As Cynthia Ozick once wrote in a related connection, 'Sooner the fly to God than he' (Ozick, 1976: 190).

Michael Walzer's chapter returns us to some of the issues I discussed earlier, in connection with David Aaronovitch's. Michael, too, laments the failure of a section of the left to find itself on the side of democracy first: its willingness to engage in what he calls an 'internationalism with gritted teeth', internationalism in the company of brutal anti-democratic movements and regimes, and on account of a misguided anti-Americanism. In considering what a healthy left internationalism should look like, he calls for a more morally informed type of solidarity, one which chooses its comrades on the basis of what they genuinely stand for and work for politically, rather than on the basis of interests they putatively represent, or the status they may claim as speaking for the oppressed. This claim can be bogus and so, equally, can the assumed representation of the oppressed be manipulative and self-serving. 'Our comrades', Walzer therefore writes, 'are the ones with whom we share a politics and a morality.'

There is an interesting parallel between this argument, as he goes on to elaborate it, and the one I have just been making against extending forgiveness to people who have committed terrible atrocities and remain unrepentant about it. The parallel comes out in the following passage:

> Totalitarian movements, terrorist organizations, and parties with Maximal Leaders all claim to serve the interests of oppressed men and women, and all of them should be met with scepticism and hostility – scepticism because they almost certainly don't serve those interests, and hostility because they are, however they describe themselves, the enemies of freedom, democracy, and equality. Our comrades, by contrast, are the men and women who resist oppression and struggle to cope with their troubles in the name of socialist or social-democratic values. Left internationalism reflects a wide-ranging sympathy, but it is, it should be, a solidarity of leftists.

Not merely scepticism but hostility, then, towards totalitarian movements, terrorist organizations and parties with Maximal Leaders. On the other hand, for those who resist oppression and espouse socialist or social-democratic values, sympathy and solidarity. True, this is the political solidarity of left internationalism and not, as before, a component attitude of forgiveness. But the parallel is there, all the same. For it is a solidarity that *divides* socialists and democrats from 'the enemies of freedom, democracy, and equality', rather than simply uniting all of humankind in a community of common frailty. It sees hostility towards these enemies as the complement of solidarity with those whom they oppress and who resist them. It thereby contrasts with a solidarity of universal forgiveness. Walzer's argument draws an important line in specifying the contours of internationalist solidarity. As he puts it: 'there are moral limits: our comrades are not Maximal Leaders, or terrorists, or oligarchs. They must practise a politics of democratic solidarity with their own people before we can join them in a solidarity of left internationalists.'

The question which Stephen de Wijze tries to answer in his chapter occupies a terrain, as it happens, on which we are all in Michael Walzer's debt. The problem from which he – Steve – begins was addressed in passing by me in an essay written in 1988 on the subject of the ethics of revolution, and that essay was much influenced by Walzer's classic book *Just and Unjust Wars*. My contention there was that the effort of socialist revolutionary change, wherever it was just in conception and had a genuinely democratic mandate, must respect the same moral constraints as apply in war, the constraints, as they are called, of *jus in bello*. This entailed that the rights of the innocent, the rights of non-combatants – against being targeted, against being violated – must be respected. A just struggle for democratic revolutionary change was bound by moral constraints, just as war between states is so bound.

De Wijze quotes my saying in this connection that the rights of non-combatants or their political equivalents are *all but absolute* (Geras, 1989: 204), and then sets himself to enquiring what norms should apply to those exceptional situations that are implied by the difference in meaning between 'all but absolute' and 'absolute' *tout court*. He proposes three ways of limiting such exceptional ('dirty hands') violations of rights, when political leaders have concluded that they must permit these: proportionality; a reasonable prospect of success; and moral motivation (and no other). I shall not assess the adequacy of these moral constraints on 'dirty hands' political action, but merely express a worry I have about the very effort of codification in this area. I admire the impulse behind it, which I take to be to help bring light into a dark area. But my worry is that codifying, systematizing, the rules that must be followed in exceptional – 'dirty hands' – operations risks making them less exceptional than they ought to be. It risks lowering the bar. De Wijze writes, for example, that 'it is not clear how we should regard the cost of non-combatants' lives compared with those of soldiers', and he continues: 'Could we justify the death of two civilians if this would save the lives of one hundred soldiers, or vice versa?' It is only an example offered in passing, and the question is left without an answer; so I will not attach too much weight to it. But my own understanding of the 'all but absolute' restriction – influenced by Walzer's book and an article by Thomas Nagel – was much more stringent than one possible answer to this question implies. For what I wrote in explaining the restriction was this:

> That is to say that they [the rights of the innocent] may be overridden if and only if doing so is the sole means of averting imminent and certain disaster. I repeat: the sole means; and disaster which is otherwise imminent and certain. This is a proviso of impending moral catastrophe. (Geras, 1989: 204)

I do not know how to give, so to say, *codified* force to the height of the moral barrier these words are intended to point towards; I will simply leave it there by saying that the exceptions have to be exceedingly rare.

Like De Wijze's chapter, Jon Pike's is concerned with moral limits, in the context of considering the means and ends of political change. Before turning to Jon's main line of argument about this, I should like to acknowledge my agreement with what he says in introducing the topic: namely, that 'his [i.e., my, Geras's] later political development, including his support for and advocacy of humanitarian interventionism, is perhaps only fully explicable in relation to his thinking about socialist morality in the 1970s and 1980s.' That judgement returns us once more to the issue I discussed at the start of these responses, in connection with David McLellan's chapter; and Jon, to put it colloquially, hits the nail on the head. As I understand my own intellectual development at any rate, a clear line connects my thinking about Marxism and ethics to my subsequent work on the Holocaust and crimes against humanity, as well as to my recent political positions; and a key point on that line is occupied by the article on revolutionary ethics written in 1988.

Pike's chapter goes on to make something – and something substantial – of an idea to which I merely allowed room as a vague possibility when criticizing the notion of prefigurative revolutionary means. I said: '[O]ne may concede a value to some such rough idea. If we can exemplify, can display, our good ends in the good ways and means we use to achieve them, so much the better' (Geras, 1989: 188). However, I said this in rejecting prefiguration as the principal way of setting constraints on transformative political action, and the reason I rejected it was that I took it as an inadequate way of trying to be something *else*: a substitute for rights-type constraints. Pike shows, persuasively to my mind, that the idea of prefigurative constraints does not have to be thought of as an inferior way of stating the moral limits embodied in the concept of rights; it may be taken as a free-standing and separate constraint, making up, with rights norms and consequentialist considerations of effectiveness, a threefold division of the values political action for radical change needs to satisfy.

I have just one lingering doubt about his schema. It concerns the specificity of meaning of the idea of prefigurative political action. In the essay 'Our Morals' I expressed the doubt in an analogy, asking: 'what does a quantity of timber prefigure: a scaffold or a barn?' (Geras, 1989: 188). Pike sets my question aside on the grounds that, not being an act or possessing moral properties, a quantity of timber is in the wrong category for consideration as an act of prefiguration. But he overlooks the point of my question in failing to see past the analogical character of the example. Acts do not always (if indeed they ever) bear a single meaning, and this is arguably crucial to how we come to assess their prefigurative value. In a popular uprising against tyranny in which, let us say, sections of the people take up arms to fight against the military enforcers of tyranny – a professional elite, this could be, of highly armed men trained in the most ruthless methods of suppression – is fighting against these men, shooting some of them, prefigurative of the goals of the democratic revolution or not? The answer can surely swing both ways. In so far as shooting at others, with the possibility of killing them, is an act of violence even when (as here) it is justified violence, and one central aim of the revolution is a democracy of peaceful deliberation and peaceful conflict-resolution among political equals, shooting at the men of this S Brigade is not prefigurative. However, in so far as the same action, fighting against a human instrument of tyranny, is an assertion of the dignity of the insurgents and of their unwillingness to live any longer at the mere whim of others, it *is* prefigurative – of a hoped-for future of civic and human dignity for all. It would not be difficult to multiply examples of this kind.

Finally, I am grateful to Shane O'Neill for what I see as an ingenious way of 'narrowing the gap' between my own critique of Richard Rorty's anti-foundationalism and the perspective of discourse ethics, as represented most powerfully by the work of Jurgen Habermas. I remain sceptical of the discourse-ethics claim to dispense with every universalist, and in particular human-natural, foundation, in underwriting instead (in Shane's words) 'an inclusive and uncoerced dialogue where all human beings who may be affected by the outcome will have a chance to engage as effective participants'. The basis for my scepticism is that there are at least two universalist assumptions grounding the idea of such dialogue, and they are just as good candidates for being a foundation as anything else in this line. The two assumptions are, first, that we have a 'fundamental capacity as human beings' (Shane again), embodied in our ability to communicate discursively with others; and, second, that the kind of uncoerced discourse which is called for in discourse ethics is, precisely, an inclusive one, whereby no other human being with a stake in the outcome is to be forcibly left out. This presupposes a moral norm of inclusiveness that is not itself the outcome of the uncoerced dialogue but rests on some universalist moral notion logically preceding it (see Geras, 1999).

O'Neill narrows the aforementioned gap here by, on the one hand, accepting that there must be some such pre-dialogic universalist theoretical base to the discourse perspective, albeit only a thin one; and, on the other, by pointing – correctly – to my fallibilist views about philosophical and other argument. He writes that I accept that 'all substantive claims that might be made through philosophical argument stand in need of justification, and that all are corrigible'. If this brings me closer to Habermas, and the thin theoretical foundation brings Habermas closer to me, I am entirely happy about it; I cannot fault the way the closer union is achieved.

I have one small quibble about what O'Neill concedes to Rorty's view on the marginal (or is it non-existent?) role of philosophy in contributing to the improvement – moral, political, social – of the world. That is not a view for which I have any sympathy. Here, it is not a matter of claiming too much for philosophy and philosophers, vis-à-vis other types of activity and categories of person, with regard to inspiring people to engage in practices that make the world a better place. However, this ambition – in one way of talking about it, human emancipation – is not so easy of realization that we can afford to do without any potential contribution to helping it along. Philosophy – the search for clarity, for truth, for justification – is one part of a grand alliance in the emancipatory endeavour. Without attempting to define its exact weight, we should not do anything to discourage philosophy's reforming and emancipatory impulses.

Let me say in concluding that I am all too well aware of how much I have left unsaid in these responses, of how much more I could have written about so excellent a collection of essays, of the many questions raised by them which I might have tackled but have not. I could easily go through all of them again and compile a second set of responses. The editors, however, have forbidden this. I hope no one will take it as a sign of lack of gratitude on my part that I obey their injunction. My most sincere appreciation goes out to everyone involved.

Bibliography

Introduction

N. Geras, *The Legacy of Rosa Luxemburg* (London: New Left Books, 1976).

N. Geras, *Marx and Human Nature: Refutation of a Legend* (London: New Left Books/Verso, 1983).

N. Geras, 'The Controversy About Marx and Justice', *New Left Review*, 150, March/April (1985): 47–85.

N. Geras, 'Our Morals', in *Discourses of Extremity: Radical Ethics & Post-Marxist Extravagances* (London: Verso, 1990): 21–58.

N. Geras, 'Bringing Marx to Justice: An Addendum and Rejoinder', *New Left Review*, 195, September/October (1992): 37–69.

N. Geras, *Solidarity in the Conversation of Humankind: The Ungroundable Liberalism of Richard Rorty* (London: Verso, 1995).

N. Geras, 'Socialist Hope in the Shadow of Catastrophe', in L. Panitch (ed.), *Are There Alternatives? Socialist Register 1996* (London: 1996): 239–63.

N. Geras, *The Contract of Mutual Indifference: Political Philosophy after the Holocaust* (London: Verso, 1998).

N. Geras 'How Free?' *The European Legacy*, 9:5 October (2004): 619–27.

N. Geras and I. Holliday, *Ashes '97: Two Views from the Boundary* (Tisbury: Baseline, 1997).

S. Hampshire, *Innocence and Experience* (Cambridge, MA: Harvard University Press, 1989).

P. Levi, *The Drowned and the Saved* (London: Abacus, 1988).

B. Russell, *The Autobiography of Bertrand Russell*, vol. 1 (London: George Allen and Unwin, 1967).

1 Walzer

B. Brecht, *Poems 1913–1956*, J. Willett and R. Mannheim (London: Methuen, 1976).

N. Geras, *The Contract of Mutual Indifference: Political Philosophy After the Holocaust* (London: Verso, 1998).

G. Orwell, *The Road to Wigan Pier* (London: V. Gollancz Ltd, 1937).

L. Trotsky, 'The Stalinist Bureacracy and the Kirov Assassination', in *Writings of Leon Trotsky [1934–35]* (New York: Pathfinder Press, 1974); also at www.marxists.org/archive/trotsky/1934/12/kirov.htm.

2 McLellan

L. Althusser, *For Marx*, trans. B. Brewster (London: Allen Lane and Penguin Press, 1969).

L. Althusser and E. Balibar, *Reading Capital*, trans. B. Brewster (New York: Pantheon, 1970).

N. Geras, 'Essence and Appearance: Aspects of Fetishism in Marx's *Capital*', *New Left Review*, 65, January/February (1971): 69–85.

N. Geras, 'Althusser's Marxism: An Account and Assessment', *New Left Review*, 71, January/February (1972): 57–86.

N. Geras, 'Marxism and Proletarian Self-Emancipation', *Radical Philosophy*, 6, Winter (1973): 20–2.

N. Geras, *The Legacy of Rosa Luxemburg* (London: New Left Books, 1976. Paperback edition, Verso, 1983; second printing, 1985).

N. Geras, *Marx and Human Nature: Refutation of a Legend* (London: New Left Books/Verso, 1983; reprinted 1985, 1994).

N. Geras, 'The Controversy About Marx and Justice', *New Left Review*, 150, March/April (1985): 47–85.

N. Geras, *Literature of Revolution: Essays on Marxism* (London: Verso, 1986).

N. Geras, 'Our Morals: The Ethics of Revolution', in R. Miliband, L. Panitch, and J. Saville (eds), *Revolution Today: Socialist Register 1989* (London: Merlin Press, 1989): 185–211.

N. Geras, 'Seven Types of Obloquy: Travesties of Marxism', in R. Miliband and L. Panitch (eds), *The Retreat of the Intellectuals: Socialist Register 1990* (London: Merlin Press, 1990a): 1–34.

N. Geras, *Discourses of Extremity: Radical Ethics and Post-Marxist extravagances* (London: Verso, 1990b).

N. Geras, 'Bringing Marx to Justice: An Addendum and Rejoinder', *New Left Review*, 195, September/October (1992): 37–69.

N. Geras, 'Democracy and the Ends of Marxism', *New Left Review*, 203, January/February (1994a): 92–106.

N. Geras, 'Richard Rorty and the Righteous Among the Nations', in

R. Miliband and L. Panitch (eds), *Between Globalism and Nationalism: Socialist Register 1994* (London: Merlin Press, 1994b): 32–59.

N. Geras, *Solidarity in the Conversation of Humankind: The Ungroundable Liberalism of Richard Rorty* (London: Verso, 1995a).

N. Geras, 'Human Nature and Progress', *New Left Review*, 213, September/October (1995b): 151–60.

N. Geras, 'Socialist Hope in the Shadow of Catastrophe', in L. Panitch (ed.), *Are There Alternatives? Socialist Register 1996* (London: Merlin Press, 1996): 239–63.

N. Geras, *The Contract of Mutual Indifference: Political Philosophy after the Holocaust* (London: Verso, 1998).

N. Geras, 'Marxism, the Holocaust and September 11th: An Interview with Norman Geras', *Imprints*, 6:3 (2002).

N. Geras, 'How Free?', *The European Legacy*, 9:5, October (2004): 619–27.

R. Luxemburg, *The Accumulation of Capital*, trans. A. Schwarzchild (New York: Modern Paperbacks, 1968).

K. Marx, *Economic and Philosophical Manuscripts of 1844*, trans. M. Milligan (New York: Prometheus Books, 1988).

K. Marx, *Capital Vol. 1* (Harmondsworth: Penguin, 1976).

K. Marx and F. Engels, *The German Ideology* (New York: Prometheus Books, 1998).

3 Cohen

W.H. Auden, Collected Shorter Poems 1927–1957 (London: Faber and Faber Ltd, 1966).

4 Spencer

M.T. Allen, *The Business of Genocide: The SS, Slave Labor and the Concentration Camp* (Chapel Hill, NC: University of North Carolina Press, 2002).

H. Arendt, 'Rosa Luxemburg, 1871–1919', in *Men in Dark Times* (New York: Harcourt, Brace and World, 1968): 33–45.

H. Arendt, 'Reply to Eric Voegelin', in *Essays in Understanding* (New York: Harcourt Brace, 1994).

D. Bankier, 'German Social Democrats and the Jewish Question' in D. Bankier (ed.), *Probing the Depths of German Anti-Semitism:*

German Society and the Persecution of the Jews 1933–1941 (Oxford: Berghahn, 2000).

O. Bartov, 'The Missing Years: German Workers, German Soldiers', in D. Crew (ed.), *Nazism and German Society, 1933–1945* (London: Routledge, 1994).

O. Bartov, *Mirrors of Destruction: War, Genocide and Modern Identity* (Oxford: Oxford University Press, 2000).

Y. Bauer, *Rethinking the Holocaust* (New Haven, CT: Yale University Press, 2003).

Z. Bauman, *Modernity and The Holocaust* (Oxford: Blackwell, 1989).

A. Berger, 'The Holocaust: The Ultimate and Archetypal Genocide', in I. Charny (ed.), Genocide: A Critical Bibliography (London: Mansell, 1998).

C. Browning, *Ordinary Men: Reserve Police Battalion 101 and the Final Solution in Poland* (New York: Harper Collins, 1992).

J. Diehl, *Paramilitary Politics in Weimar Germany* (Bloomington, IN: Indiana University Press, 1977).

G. Eley, 'What are the Contexts for German Anti-Semitism?' in J. Frankel (ed.), *The Fate of the European Jews, 1939–45: Continuity or Contingency? Studies in Contemporary Jewry*, vol. 13 (Oxford: Oxford University Press, 1997).

F. Engels, 'The Origin of the Family, Private Property and the State', in K. Marx and F. Engels, *Selected Works*, vol 3. (Moscow: Progress Publishers, 1970).

S. Friedländer, 'The "Final Solution": On the Unease in Historical Interpretation', in *Memory, History and the Extermination of the Jews of Europe* (Bloomington, IN: Indiana University Press, 1993).

R. Gellately, *Backing Hitler: Consent and Coercion in Nazi Germany* (Oxford: Oxford University Press, 2001).

N. Geras, *The Legacy of Rosa Luxemburg* (London: New Left Books, 1976).

N. Geras, 'The Controversy About Marx and Justice', *New Left Review*, 150 (1985).

N. Geras, *The Contract of Mutual Indifference* (London: Verso, 1998).

H. Glaser, *The Cultural Roots of National Socialism* (London: Croom Helm, 1978).

D.J. Goldhagen, *Hitler's Willing Executioners: Ordinary Germans and the Final Solution* (London: Abacus, 1997).

J. Herf, 'German Communism, the Discourse of "anti-Fascist" Resistance and the Jewish Catastrophe', in M. Geyer and J. Boyer (eds), *Resistance Against the Third Reich* (Chicago, IL: Chicago University Press, 1994).

J. Herf, *Divided Memory: Nazi Past in the Two Germanys* (Cambridge, MA: Harvard University Press, 1999).

B. Lang, 'The Knowledge of Evil and Good', in *Act and Idea in the Nazi Genocide* (New York: Syracuse University Press, 2003).

H. Langerbein, *Hitler's Death Squads: The Logic of Mass Murder* (College Station, TX: Texas A & M University Press, 2004).

A. Lüdtke, 'German Workers and the Limits of Resistance', in C. Leitz (ed.), *The Third Reich: The Essential Readings* (Oxford: Blackwell, 1999).

R. Luxemburg, 'The Junius Pamphlet: The Crisis in German Social Democracy', in M. Waters (ed.), *Rosa Luxemburg Speaks* (New York: Pathfinder, 1970a).

R. Luxemburg, The Russian Revolution', in M. Waters (ed.), *Rosa Luxemburg Speaks* (New York: Pathfinder, 1970b).

L. McGowan, 'The Extreme Right', in Panikos Panayi (ed.), *Weimar and Nazi Germany: Continuities and Discontinuities* (London: Pearson, 2001).

K. Marx, 'Wages', in Karl Marx and Friedrich Engels, *Collected Works*, vol. 6 (London: Lawrence and Wishart, 1976a).

K. Marx and F. Engels, 'The Communist Manifesto', in *Collected Works*, vol, 6 (London: Lawrence and Wishart, 1976b).

J. Matthäus, 'Historiography and the Perpetrators of the Holocaust' in D. Stone (ed.), *Holocaust Historiography* (London: Routledge, 2005).

M. Mazower, 'Violence and the State in the Twentieth Century', *American Historical Review*, 107:4 (2002): 1158–78.

A. Merson, *Communist Resistance in Nazi Germany* (London: Lawrence and Wishart, 1985).

A. Milchman and A. Rosenberg, 'Two Kinds of Uniqueness: The Universal Aspects of the Holocaust', in R.L. Milklen (ed.), *New Perspectives on the Holocaust* (New York: New York University Press, 1996).

M. Morgan (ed.), *A Holocaust Reader: Responses to the Nazi Extermination* (Oxford: Oxford University Press, 2001).

D. Niewyk, *Socialist, Anti-Semite and Jew: German Social Democracy Confronts the Problem of Anti-Semitism, 1918–1933* (Baton Rouge, LA: Louisiana State University Press, 1971).

D. Peukert, 'Working-Class Resistance: Problems and Options', in

D.C. Large (ed.), *Contending with Hitler: Varieties of German Resistance in the Third Reich* (Cambridge: Cambridge University Press, 1991).

R. Pol-Droit, *Généalogie des Barbares* (Paris: Odile Jacob, 2007).

C. Rittner, J.K. Roth, and J.M. Smith (eds), *Will Genocide Ever End?* (St Paul, MN: Paragon House, 2002).

R. Rummel, *Death by Government* (New York: Transaction Publishers, 1994).

M.B. Salter, *Barbarians and Civilisation in International Relations* (Sterling, VA: Pluto Press, 2002).

P. Spencer, 'Marxism and the Shoah: Behind and Beyond Silence', in R. Lentin (ed.), *Re-presenting the Shoah for the 21st Century* (Oxford: Berghahn, 2004).

E. Traverso, *Understanding the Nazi Genocide: Marxism after Auschwitz* (London: Pluto, 1999).

E. Traverso, *The Origins of Nazi Violence* (New York: The New Press, 2003).

5 Benson

A. Damasio, *Descartes' Error: Emotion, Reason, and the Human Brain* (London: Picador, 1995).

M. Haddon, *The Curious Incident of the Dog in the Night-time* (London: Jonathan Cape, 2003).

J. Haidt, *The Happiness Hypothesis: Finding Modern Truth in Ancient Wisdom* (New York: Basic Books, 2006).

D. Hume, *A Treatise of Human Nature* (London: Penguin Classics, 1969, 2004).

M. Nussbaum, *Cultivating Humanity: A Classical Defense of Reform in Liberal Education* (Cambridge, MA: Harvard University Press, 1997).

F. de Waal, *Our Inner Ape: The Best and Worst of Human Nature* (London: Granta Books, 2005).

6 Johnson

C. Angier, *The Double Bond: Primo Levi, A Biography* (London: Penguin, 2003).

M. Anissimov, *Primo Levi: Tragedy of an Optimist* (London: Aurum Press, 1998).

BBC, *Primo Levi: The Memory of the Offence* (1992; available at You Tube: www.youtube.com/watch?v=T82HhWHgkmA).

M. Belpoliti and R.S.C. Gordon (eds), *The Voice of Memory: Primo Levi, Interviews 1961–87* (London: Polity, 2001).

M. Belpoliti and R.S.C. Gordon, 'Primo Levi's Holocaust Vocabularies', in R.S.C. Gordon (ed.), *The Cambridge Companion to Primo Levi* (Cambridge: Cambridge University Press, 2007).

P. Berman, *Terror and Liberalism* (New York: W.W. Norton, 2003).

F. Camon, *Conversations with Primo Levi* (Marlboro, VT: The Marlboro Press, 1989).

A. Camus, *The Plague* (Harmondsworth: Penguin, 1960).

B. Cheyette, 'The Ethical Uncertainty of Primo Levi', in B.Cheyette and L. Marcus (eds), *Modernity, Culture and 'The Jew'* (Cambridge: Polity, 1998), 268–81.

B. Cheyette, 'Appropriating Primo Levi', in R.S.C. Gordon (ed.), *The Cambridge Companion to Primo Levi* (Cambridge: Cambridge University Press, 2007).

M.S. Christofferson, *French Intellectuals Against The Left: The Antitotalitarian Moment of the 1970s* (New York: Berghahn Books, 2004).

M. Cicioni, *Primo Levi: Bridges of Knowledge* (Oxford: Berg, 1995).

M. Cicioni, 'Primo Levi's Humour', in R.S.C. Gordon (ed.), *The Cambridge Companion to Primo Levi* (Cambridge: Cambridge University Press, 2007).

Dante Alighieri, *The Divine Comedy* (Web edition, translated James Finn Cotter, 2006), www.italianstudies.org/comedy/index.htm (accessed on 10 January 2010).

R. Fine, 'The Concept of Totalitarianism: Three Comments on Claude Lefort', *Democratiya* 9 (2007): 187–91. At: http://dissentmagazine.org/democratiya/article_pdfs/d9Fine.pdf (accessed on 11 November 2009). (First published in *Papers in Social Theory* 2 (1988).)

N. Geras, *The Contract of Mutual Indifference: Political Philosophy After the Holocaust* (London: Verso, 1998).

N. Geras, 'Primo Levi: From the Depths', at *A Fistful of Euros*, http://fistfulofeuros.net/afoe/culture/primo-levi-from-the-depths (2004); also at normblog, http://normblog.typepad.com/normblog/2008/01/primo-levi-from.html (accessed on 11 November 2009).

M. Giuliani, *A Centaur in Auschwitz: Reflections on Primo Levi's*

Thinking (New York: Lexington Books, 2003).

R.S.C. Gordon, *Primo Levi's Ordinary Virtues: From Testimony to Ethics* (Oxford: Oxford University Press, 2001a).

R.S.C. Gordon, 'How much Home Does a Person Need: Primo Levi and the Ethics of Home', *Annali d'Italianistica*, 19 (2001b): 215–34.

R.S.C. Gordon (ed.), *The Cambridge Companion to Primo Levi* (Cambridge: Cambridge University Press, 2007).

F.D. Homer, *Primo Levi and the Politics of Survival* (Columbia: University of Missouri Press, 2001).

C. James, *Cultural Amnesia: Notes in the Margin of My Time* (London: Picador, 2007).

T. Judt, 'The Elementary Truths of Primo Levi', in T. Judt, *Reappraisals: Reflections on the Forgotten Twentieth Century* (New York: Penguin, 2008), 44–62.

L. Langer, 'Legacy in Gray: The Ordeal of Primo Levi', in L. Langer, *Preempting the Holocaust* (New Haven, CT: Yale University Press, 1998), 23–42.

P. Levi, *The Periodic Table* (New York: Shocken Books, 1984).

P. Levi, *If This is a Man / The Truce* (London: Abacus, 1987a).

P. Levi, *Moments of Reprieve* (London: Abacus, 1987b).

P. Levi, *The Drowned and the Saved* (London: Abacus, 1988a).

P. Levi, *Collected Poems* (London: Faber and Faber, 1988b).

P. Levi, *The Mirror Maker* (London: Minerva, 1990).

P. Levi, *Other People's Trades* (London: Abacus, 1991).

P. Levi, 'The Art of Fiction', *The Paris Review*, 134 (1995): 201–20.

P. Levi, *The Black Hole of Auschwitz* (London: Polity, 2005).

P. Levi, *A Tranquil Star: Unpublished Stories* (London: Penguin Classics, 2007).

R.J. Lifton, *The Nazi Doctors: Medical Killing and the Psychology of Genocide* (New York: Basic Books, 2000).

K. Makiya, *The Republic of Fear: Inside Saddam's Iraq* (written as Samir al-Khalil) (Berkeley: University of California Press, 1989).

A. Rabinbach, 'Totalitarianism Revisited', *Dissent*, 53:3 (2006): 77–84.

P. Rosanvallon, *Democracy Past and Future* (New York: Columbia University Press, 2006).

M. Sandel, *Democracy's Discontent: America in Search of a Public Philosophy* (Cambridge: Belknap Press, 1996).

J. Shklar, 'Putting Cruelty First', *Democratiya* 4 (2006): 81–94. At http://dissentmagazine.org/democratiya/article_pdfs/d4Shklar.pdf (accessed on 11 November 2009). (First published in *Daedalus* 111:3 (1982): 17–28.)

I. Thompson, *Primo Levi* (London: Vintage, 2003).

D. Ward, 'Primo Levi's Turin', in R.S.C. Gordon (ed.) *The Cambridge Companion to Primo Levi* (Cambridge: Cambridge University Press, 2007).

J. Woolf, 'From If This is a Man to The Drowned and the Saved', in R.S.C. Gordon (ed.), *The Cambridge Companion to Primo Levi* (Cambridge: Cambridge University Press, 2007).

7 Thomas

J. Deigh, 'Empathy and Universalizability', in *The Sources of Moral Agency* (New York: Cambridge University Press, 1996).

A.-M. Delcambre, *La Schizophreénie de l'Islam* (Paris: Desclé de Brower, 2006).

G. Dworkin, 'The Nature of Autonomy', in *The Theory and Practice of Autonomy* (New York: Cambridge University Press, 1988).

N. Geras, 'Our Morals: The Ethics of Revolution', *Socialist Register* (1989).

N. Geras, 'Language, Truth and Justice', *New Left Review* 1:209 (1995a).

N. Geras, 'Human Nature and Progress', *New Left Review* (1995b).

N. Geras, 'Minimum Utopia: Ten Theses', *Socialist Register* (2000).

I. Goffman, *The Presentation of Self in Everyday Life* (Garden City, NY: Doubleday, 1959).

P. Hallie, *Lest Innocent Blood Be Shed: The Story of Le Chambon and How Goodness Happened There* (New York: Harper & Row, 1979).

H.L.A. Hart, *The Concept of Law* (Oxford: Clarendon Press, 1961).

N. Henley, *Body Politics* (Englewood Cliffs, NJ: Prentice-Hall, 1977).

T. Hill, Jr, 'The Importance of Autonomy', in *Autonomy and Self-Respect* (New York: Cambridge University Press, 1991).

A. Hitler, *Mein Kampf*, ed. John Chamberlain, Sidney Fay et al. (New York: Reynal & Hitchcock, 1941).

J. Michel, *Le Lynchage aux États-Unis* (Paris: La Table Ronde, 2008).

J.S. Mill, *On Liberty* (London: J.W. Parker and Son, 1859)

H. Nuwer, *Wrongs of Passage: Fraternities, Sororities, and Hazing and Binge Drinking* (Bloomington, IN: Indiana University Press, 1999).

P. Paganon, *Femmes remarquables dans le monde antique* (Paris: Librarie Vuibert, 2009).

Pièces et Main d'Œuvre, *Le Téléphone portable: gadget de destruction massive* (Paris: Éditions Échappé, 2008).

Plato, *The Republic*, trans. and ed. I.A.Richards (Cambridge: Cambridge University Press, 1966).

R. Poznanski, *Les Juifs en France pendant la Seconde Guerre Mondiale* (Paris: Édition Hachette, 1997).

J. Rawls, *A Theory of Justice* (Cambridge, MA: Harvard University Press, 1971).

E. Robocanachi, *Le Saint-Siège et les Juifs: le ghetto à Rome* (Paris: Librairie de Firmin-Didot, 1891).

M. Terestchenko, *Un si fragile vernis d'humanité* (Paris: La Découverte, 2006).

L. Thomas, *Vessels of Evil: American Slavery and the Holocaust* (Philadelphia, PA: Temple University Press, 1993).

L.Thomas, 'Moral Equality and Natural Inferiority', *Social Theory and Practice*, 31:3 (2005).

P. Zimbardo, *The Lucifer Effect: Understanding How Good People Turn Evil* (New York: Random House, 2007).

8 Garrard

J. Amery, *At the Mind's Limits* (Bloomington: Indiana University Press, 1980).

T. Brudholm, *Resentment's Virtue: Jean Amery and the Refusal to Forgive* (Philadelphia, PA: Temple University Press, 2008).

S. Darwall, 'Two Kinds of Respect', *Ethics*, 88 (1977): 36–49.

E. Garrard, 'Forgiveness and the Holocaust', *Ethical Theory and Moral Practice*, 5:2 (2002): 147–65.

E. Garrard and D. McNaughton, 'In Defence of Unconditional Forgiveness', *Proceedings of the Aristotelian Society* (2002): 39–60.

C. Griswold, *Forgiveness: A Philosophical Exploration* (Cambridge: Cambridge University Press, 2007).

J. Murphy, *Getting Even: Forgiveness and Its Limits* (Oxford: Oxford University Press, 2003).

10 Pike

Aristotle, *Nicomachean Ethics* (Oxford: Oxford University Press, 1931).

M. Bookchin, *Post-Scarcity Anarchism* (Oakland, CA: AK Press, 2004).

C.A.J. Coady, 'Politics and the Problem of Dirty Hands', in P. Singer (ed.), *A Companion to Ethics* (Oxford: Blackwell, 1993).

G.A. Cohen, *If You're an Egalitarian, How Come You're So Rich?* (Cambridge, MA: Harvard University Press, 2000).

N. Geras, *The Legacy of Rosa Luxemburg* (London: New Left Books/Verso, 1976).

N. Geras, *Marx and Human Nature: Refutation of a Legend* (London: Verso, 1983).

N. Geras, *Literature of Revolution* (London: Verso, 1986).

N. Geras, 'Our Morals: The Ethics of Revolution', *Socialist Register* (1989), 185–211.

L. Trotsky, 'Their Morals and Ours', *The New International*, 4:6 (1938), 163–73.

J. Waldron, *Liberal Rights* (Cambridge: Cambridge University Press, 1993).

M. Walzer, 'Political Action: The Problem of Dirty Hands', *Philosophy and Public Affairs*, 2 (1973): 160–80.

M. Walzer, *Just and Unjust Wars* (New York: Basic Books, 1977).

B. Williams, *Ethics and the Limits of Philosophy* (London: Fontana, 1985).

J. Wolff, 'Fairness, Respect, and the Egalitarian Ethos', *Philosophy and Public Affairs*, 27:2 (1998): 97–122.

11 de Wijze

H. Arendt, *On Revolution* (London: Penguin Books, 1990).

G.J. Bass, 'Jus Post Bellum', *Philosophy & Public Affairs*, 32:4 (2004): 384–412.

R. Brandt, 'The Science of Man and Wide Reflective Equilibrium', *Ethics*, 100 (1990): 259–78.

B. Brecht, 'The Measures Taken', in *The Measures Taken and Other Lehrstücke*, ed. J. Willet and R. Manheim (New York: Arcade Publishing, 2001), 9–34.

A. Camus, 'The Just', in *Caligula and Other Plays* (Penguin Books:

London, 1984), 163–228.

C.A.J. Coady, 'Terrorism and Innocence', *The Journal of Ethics*, 8:1 (2004): 37–58.

N. Daniels, 'Wide Reflective Equilibrium and Theory Acceptance in Ethics', *Journal of Philosophy*, 76 (1979): 256–82.

S. Darwall (ed.), *Virtue Ethics* (Oxford: Blackwell Publishing, 2003).

S. de Wijze, 'Tragic-Remorse: The Anguish of Dirty Hands', *Ethical Theory and Moral Practice*, 7:5 (2005): 453–71.

S. de Wijze, 'Dirty Hands: Doing Wrong to Do Right', in Igor Primoratz (ed.) *Politics and Morality* (New York: Palgrave Macmillan, 2007), 3–19.

S. de Wijze and T. Goodwin, 'Bellamy on Dirty Hands and Lesser Evils: A Response', *The British Journal of Politics & International Relations*, 11:3 (August 2009): 529–40.

J.B. Elshtain (ed.), *Just War Theory* (New York: Basil Blackwell, 1992).

B. Ganor, 'Defining Terrorism: Is One Man's Terrorist Another Man's Freedom Fighter?', *International Institute for Counter-Terrorism* (2008), at www.ict.org.il/ResearchPublications/tabid/64/Articlsid/432/Default.aspx (accessed 7 October 2009).

N. Geras, 'Our Morals', in *Discourses of Extremity: Radical Ethics & Post-Marxist Extravagances* (London: Verso, 1990), 21–58.

N. Geras, 'Marxism, the Holocaust and September 11: An Interview with Norman Geras', *Imprints: A Journal of Analytic Socialism*, 6:3 (2002). Online content at http://eis.bris.ac.uk/~plcdib /imprints/normangerasinterview.html (accessed 20 November 2009)

J. Goldman, *The Lion in Winter: A Play* (London: Samuel French Ltd, 1964).

S. Hampshire, *Innocence and Experience* (London: Allen Lane, 1989).

R.M. Hare, 'Rawls' Theory of Justice', *Philosophical Quarterly*, 23 (1973): 241–51.

T. Hurka, 'Proportionality in the Morality of War', *Philosophy & Public Affairs*, 33:1 (2005): 34–66.

M. Ignatieff, *The Lesser Evil: Political Ethics in an Age of Terror* (Edinburgh: Edinburgh University Press, 2004).

F. Leverick, *Killing in Self-Defence* (Oxford: Oxford University Press, 2006).

S. Lukes, 'Marxism and Dirty Hands', in *Moral Conflict and Politics* (Oxford: Clarendon Press, 1991).

N. Machiavelli, *The Prince* (London: Penguin Books, 1981).

A. McIntyre, 'Doctrine of Double Effect', in *Stanford Encyclopedia of Philosophy* (2009) at http://plato.stanford.edu/entries/double-effect (accessed 23 November 2009).

T. Meisels, 'Defining Terrorism: A Typology', *Critical Review of International Social and Political Philosophy*, 12:3 (2009): 331–51.

H.J. Morgenthau, *Politics Among Nations: The Struggle for Power and Peace*, fifth edition, revised (New York: Alfred A. Knopf, 1978).

T. Nagel, 'The Problem of Global Justice', *Philosophy & Public Affairs*, 33:2 (2005): 113–47.

K. Nielsen, 'Philosophy as Wide Reflective Equilibrium', *Iyyun*, 43 (1994): 3–42.

B. Orend, 'Justice after War', *Ethics and International Affairs*, 16:1 (2002): 43–56.

B. Orend, 'War', in *Stanford Encyclopedia of Philosophy* (2005) at http://plato.stanford.edu/entries/war (accessed 23 November 2009).

B. Orend, *The Morality of War* (London: Broadview, 2006).

J. Rawls, *A Theory of Justice* (Cambridge, MA: Harvard University Press, 1971).

J.P. Sartre, *Les Mains Sales* (Paris: Éditions Gallimard, 1948).

T.M. Scanlon, 'Rawls on Justification', in S. Freeman (ed.), *The Cambridge Companion to Rawls* (Cambridge: Cambridge University Press, 2002).

K. Soper, 'Marxism and Morality', *New Left Review*, 163 (May/June 1987): 101–13.

M. Stocker, *Plural and Conflicting Values* (Oxford: Clarendon Press, 1990).

L. Trotsky, 'Terrorism and Communism' (1920), chapter 4 at www.marxists.org/archive/trotsky/1920/terrcomm/index.htm (accessed 14 November 2009).

Waldron, J. (2004) 'Terrorism and the Uses of Terror', *The Journal of Ethics*, 8:1 (2004): 5–35.

M. Walzer, 'Political Action: The Problem of Dirty Hands', *Philosophy & Public Affairs*, 2:2 (winter 1973): 160–80.

M. Walzer, *Just and Unjust Wars*, third edition (New York: Basic Books, 2000).

M. Walzer, 'Emergency Ethics', in *Arguing About War* (New Haven, CT and London: Yale University Press, 2004).

M. Weber, 'Politics as a Vocation', in *From Max Weber: Essays in*

Sociology, trans. and ed. H.H. Gerth and C. Wright Mills (New York: Oxford University Press, 1958).

B. Williams, 'Politics and Moral Character', in *Moral Luck* (Cambridge: Cambridge University Press, 1981).

12 Aaronovitch

P. Anderson, *English Questions* (Brooklyn, NY: Verso books, 1992).

B. Barber, Speech to the CTC International Solidarity Conference (May 2009), www.tuc.org.uk/international/tuc-16398 -f0.cfm?theme=brendan.

C. Irby, 'Teen Spirit: Baba Dalawarzada, 14', *Guardian* (10 October 2009).

S. Jenkins, 'Western Export of the Ballot Box Elixir is Pure Hubris' *Guardian* (20 October 2009).

M. Simons, The Great Compromiser' *Socialist Review*, 228 (1999).

C. Sunstein, *Going to Extremes: How Like Minds Unite and Divide* (Oxford: Oxford University Press, 2009).

13 Calder

J. Arlott, *How to Watch Cricket* (London: Collins Willow, 1983).

Z. Bauman, *Modernity and the Holocaust* (Ithaca, NY: Cornell University Press, 1989).

P. Blackledge, 'Marxism and Ethics', *International Socialism* 120, www.isj.org.uk/index.php4?id=486&issue=120 (accessed on 16 November 2008).

G. Calder, 'Relationality and Evil: Judging Bystanders', in Margaret Breen (ed.), *Minding Evil: Explorations of Human Iniquity* (Amsterdam and New York: Rodopi, 2005a), 223–40.

G. Calder, 'Pragmatism, Postmodernism, and the Possibility of an Ethical Relation to the Past', *Theoria: A Journal of Social and Political Theory*, 107 (2005b): 82–101.

G. Calder, *Rorty's Politics of Redescription* (Cardiff: University of Wales Press, 2007).

G. Calder, 'Ethics and Social Ontology', *Analyse & Kritik*, 30:2 (2008a): 427–43.

G. Calder, 'How Can the Past be Wronged? The "Holocaust Industry" and Moral Capital', *Bulletin of Tomsk State University: Philosophy, Sociology, Political Science*, 26:2 (2008b): 38–51.

A. Carling, 'Analytical and Essential Marxism', *Political Studies*, 45:4 (1997): 768–83.

E. Ceva and G. Calder, 'Values, Diversity and the Justification of EU Institutions', *Political Studies*, 57:4 (2009): 828–45.

S. Cohen, *States of Denial: Knowing about Atrocities and Suffering* (Cambridge: Polity Press, 2001).

N. Geras, 'Marxism and Proletarian Self-Emancipation', *Radical Philosophy* 6 (1973): 20–2.

N. Geras, *The Legacy of Rosa Luxemburg* (London: New Left Books, 1976).

N. Geras, 'Althusser's Marxism: An Assessment', in New Left Review (eds), *Western Marxism: A Critical Reader* (London: New Left Books, 1977).

N. Geras, *Marx and Human Nature: Refutation of a Legend* (London: Verso, 1983).

N. Geras, 'The Controversy about Marx and Justice', in A Callinicos (ed.), *Marxist Theory* (Oxford: Oxford University Press, 1989), 211–68.

N. Geras, *Discourses of Extremity: Radical Ethics and Post-Marxist Extravagances* (London: Verso, 1990).

N. Geras, *Solidarity in the Conversation of Humankind: The Ungroundable Liberalism of Richard Rorty* (London: Verso, 1995).

N. Geras, *The Contract of Mutual Indifference: Political Philosophy after the Holocaust* (London: Verso, 1998).

N. Geras, 'Marxism, the Holocaust and September 11' (interview), *Imprints: A Journal of Analytical Socialism*, 6:3 (2002): 194–214.

N. Geras, 'Redemptive and Other Meanings: Roman Polanski's *The Pianist*', *Imprints: A Journal of Analytical Socialism*, 7:1 (2003): 54–63.

N. Geras, 'How is Socialism to be Justified?', paper presented at the Marx and Philosophy Society conference, 19 May 2007, http://normblog.typepad.com/normblog.2007/05/how_is_socialis .html (accessed on 24 November 2007).

N. Geras and I. Holliday, *Ashes 97: Two Views from the Boundary* (Tisbury: Baseline, 1997).

R. Geuss, *Philosophy and Real Politics* (Princeton: Princeton University Press, 2008).

J. Glover, *Humanity: A Moral History of the Twentieth Century* (London: Jonathan Cape, 1999).

K. Graham, *Practical Reasoning in a Social World* (Cambridge:

Cambridge University Press, 2002).

I. Kant, *Religion within the Limits of Reason Alone*, trans. T.M. Greene and H.H. Hudson (New York: Harper and Row, 1960).

R. Keat, *Cultural Goods and the Limits of the Market* (London: Macmillan, 2000).

A. MacIntyre, *Ethics and Politics: Selected Essays*, vol. 2 (Cambridge: Cambridge University Press, 2006).

R.W. Miller, 'Marx and Aristotle: A Kind of Consequentialism', in K. Nielsen and S.C. Patten (eds), *Marx and Morality, Canadian Journal of Philosophy*, supp. 8 (1981): 311–35.

J. O'Neill, *The Market: Ethics, Knowledge and Politics* (London and New York: Routledge, 1998).

J. O'Neill, *Markets, Deliberation and the Environment* (London and New York: Routledge, 2007).

A. Sayer, *The Moral Significance of Class* (Cambridge: Cambridge University Press, 2005).

K. Soper, *Humanism and Anti-Humanism* (London: Hutchinson, 1986).

W. Styron, *Sophie's Choice* (New York: Vintage, 1976).

E. Traverso, 'For an Ethical Refoundation of Socialism: Norman Geras and Political Philosophy after Auschwitz', *Historical Materialism* 8 (2001): 417–31.

14 O'Neill

Marquis de Condorcet, *Sketch for a Historical Picture of the Progress of the Human Mind* (London: Weidenfeld and Nicolson, 1955 [1795]).

M. Foucault, *Power/Knowledge*, ed. C. Gordon (New York: Pantheon, 1980).

N. Geras, *Marx and Human Nature: Refutation of a Legend* (London: Verso, 1983).

N. Geras, *Solidarity in the Conversation of Humankind* (London: Verso, 1995).

N. Geras, *The Contract of Mutual Indifference: Political Philosophy After the Holocaust* (London: Verso, 1999a).

N. Geras, 'The View from Everywhere', *Review of International Studies*, 25 (1999b), 157–63.

N. Geras, 'Progress without Foundations?', in M. Festenstein and S. Thompson (eds), *Richard Rorty: Critical Dialogues* (Cambridge:

Polity Press, 2001), pp. 158–70.

N. Geras and R. Wokler (eds), *Enlightenment and Modernity* (Basingstoke: Palgrave Macmillan, 2000).

J. Habermas, *The Theory of Communicative Action*, trans. T. McCarthy, 2 vols (Cambridge: Polity Press, 1984/87).

J. Habermas, *Moral Consciousness and Communicative Action*, trans. C. Lenhardt and S.W. Nicholson (Cambridge: Polity Press, 1990).

J. Habermas, 'Richard Rorty's Pragmatic Turn', in R. Brandom (ed.), *Rorty and his Critics* (Oxford: Blackwell, 2000), pp. 31–55.

R. Rorty, *Contingency, Irony and Solidarity* (Cambridge: Cambridge University Press, 1989).

R. Rorty, *Philosophy and Social Hope* (Harmondsworth: Penguin, 1999).

R. Rorty, 'Response to Habermas', in R. Brandom (ed.), *Rorty and his Critics* (Oxford: Blackwell, 2000), pp. 56–64.

R. Rorty, 'The Ambiguity of "Rationality"', in W. Rehg and J. Bohman (eds), *Pluralism and the Pragmatic Turn* (Cambridge, MA: The MIT Press, 2001a), pp. 41–52.

R. Rorty, 'Response to Geras', in M. Festenstein and S. Thompson (eds), *Richard Rorty: Critical Dialogues* (Cambridge: Polity Press, 2001b), pp. 171–5.

15 Steiner

R. Arneson, 'Freedom and Desire', *Canadian Journal of Philosophy*, 15 (1985): 425–48.

I. Berlin, *Four Essays on Liberty* (Oxford: Oxford University Press, 1969).

I. Carter, *A Measure of Freedom* (Oxford: Oxford University Press, 1999).

I. Carter, Matthew Kramer and Hillel Steiner (eds), *Freedom: A Philosophical Anthology* (Oxford and Cambridge, MA: Blackwell, 2007).

J. Feinberg, *Social Philosophy* (Englewood Cliffs, NJ: Prentice-Hall, 1978).

N. Geras, 'How Free?', *The European Legacy*, 9:5 October (2004): 619–27.

M.H. Kramer, *The Quality of Freedom* (Oxford: Oxford University Press, 2003).

A. Sen, 'Welfare, Freedom and Social Choice: A Reply', *Recherches*

Economiques de Louvain, 36 (1990): 451–85.

H. Steiner, 'Individual Liberty', *Aristotelian Society Proceedings*, 75 (1975): 35–50; reprinted in David Miller (ed.), *Liberty* (Oxford: Oxford University Press, 1991); revised edn published as *The Liberty Reader* (Boulder, CO: Paradigm Publishers, and Edinburgh: Edinburgh University Press, 2006).

H. Steiner, 'How Free? Computing Personal Liberty', in A. Phillips Griffiths (ed.), *Of Liberty*, Royal Institute of Philosophy Lectures (Cambridge: Cambridge University Press, 1983).

H. Steiner, *An Essay on Rights* (Oxford: Blackwell, 1994).

R.H. Tawney, *Equality* (London: George Allen & Unwin, 1931).

C. Taylor, 'What's Wrong with Negative Liberty', in Alan Ryan (ed.), *The Idea of Freedom* (Oxford: Oxford University Press, 1979).

16 Lappin

I. Abella and H. Troper, *None is too Many* (Toronto, ON: Lester and Orpen Dennys, 1983).

M. Borowicz, 'Polish–Jewish Relations, 1944–1947', in Chimen Abramsky, M. Jachimczyk, and Antonly Polonksy (eds), *The Jews in Poland* (Oxford: Blackwell, 1986), pp. 190–8.

J.M. Burr and R.O. Collins, *Alms for Jihad* (Cambridge: Cambridge University Press, 2006).

D. Cesarani, 'The Anti-Jewish Career of Sir William Joynson-Hicks, Cabinet Minister', *Journal of Contemporary History*, 24 (1989): 461–82.

D. Clark, 'Accusations of Anti-Semitic Chic are Poisonous Intellectual Thuggery', *Guardian* (6 March 2006).

S. Cohen, 'Anti-Semitism, Immigration Controls, and the Welfare State', *Critical Social Policy*, 5:13 (1985): 73–92.

R. Dawkins, *The God Delusion* (London: Bantam Press, 2006).

H. Defries, *Conservative Party Attitudes to the Jews: 1900–1950* (London: Frank Cass, 2002).

R. Donadio, 'Libel without Borders', *New York Times* (7 October 2007).

H. Enriques, 'The Jewish Emancipation Controversy in Nineteenth-Century Britain', *Past and Present*, 40 (1968): 226–46.

R. Evans, 'Britain Censored over Decision to Drop BAE Saudi Corruption Inquiry', The *Guardian* (19 January 2007).

A. Hessayon, 'From Expulsion (1290) to Readmission (1656): Jews and England', address to the Jewish Genealogical Society of Great Britain, Goldmith's College, London, 6 December 2006 (available at www.goldsmiths.ac.uk/history/350th-anniversary.pdf).

B. Josephs, 'TGWU Joins the Campaign', *Jewish Chronicle* (5 July 2007).

A. Julius, *Trials of the Diaspora: An Essay on English Anti-Semitisms* (Oxford: Oxford University Press, 2010).

D. Katz, *The Jews in the History of England* (Oxford: Oxford University Press, 1994).

T. Kushner, *The Holocaust and the Liberal Imagination* (Oxford: Blackwell, 1994).

S. Lappin, 'Israel and the New Anti-Semitism', *Dissent* (spring, 2003): 96–103.

S. Lappin, 'The Rise of a New Anti-Semitism in the UK', *Engage Journal* (January 2006).

D. Leigh and R. Evans (2007), '"National Interest" Halts Corruption Inquiry', *Guardian* (15 December 2007).

L. London, *Whitehall and the Jews, 1933–1948: British Immigration Policy, Jewish Refugees and the Holocaust* (Cambridge: Cambridge University Press, 2000).

E. MacAskill, 'Atheists Arise: Dawkins Spreads the A-word among America's Unbelievers', *Guardian* (1 October 2007).

J. Mearsheimer and S. Walt, 'The Israel Lobby', *London Review of Books* (23 March 2006).

J. Mearsheimer and S. Walt, *The Israel Lobby and US Foreign Policy* (New York: Farrar, Straus & Giroux, 2007).

R. Miller, 'A Most Uncivil War: The Jewish Fellowship and the Battle over Zionism in Anglo Jewry, 1944–1948', *The Jewish Journal of Sociology*, 42 (2000): 37–72.

C. Roth, *A History of the Jews in England*, 3rd edition (Oxford: Clarendon Press, 1964).

J. Sacks, 'Anglo-Jewry at 350', *The Jewish Telegraph* (7 July 2006).

E. Said, *Orientalism* (London: Routledge and Kegan Paul, 1978).

M. Townsend, 'Rise in Anti-Semitic Attacks "the Worst Recorded in Britain in Decades"', *Guardian* (8 February 2009).

A. Toynbee, *The Study of History*, vol. 7 (Oxford: Oxford University Press, 1961).

A. Toynbee, *Experiences* (Oxford: Oxford University Press, 1969).

T. Traubmann, 'US University Heads Slam UK Boycott of Israeli Academe', *Haaretz* (8 August 2007).

B. Wasserstein, *Britain and the Jews of Europe 1939–1945* (Oxford: Clarendon Press, 1979).

18 Geras

N. Geras, 'Classical Marxism and Proletarian Representation', *New Left Review*, 125 (1981): 75–89.

N. Geras, 'Our Morals: The Ethics of Revolution', *Socialist Register* (1989): 185–211.

N. Geras, 'The View From Everywhere', *Review of International Studies*, 25(1) (1999): 157–63.

N. Geras, 'Marxism, the Holocaust and September 11: An Interview with Norman Geras', *Imprints*, 6(3) (2002–03): 194–214.

N. Geras, 'How Free?', *The European Legacy*, 9(5) (2004): 619–27.

C. Ozick, 'Notes Towards a Meditation on "Forgiveness"', in S. Wiesenthal, *The Sunflower* (New York: Schocken, 1976): 184–90.

Index